The New Testament Challenge by Aaron Mitchell is the perfect way to experience the New Testament in one year. The one page per chapter guide is perfect in helping you to understand God's truths and how to apply them to your life. One day at a time, one chapter at a time, will change your life over time.

Tom Ziglar
CEO of Ziglar, Inc.

I have known Aaron Mitchell for several years. During this time, Aaron has always impressed me with not only his knowledge of scripture, but also his ability to apply scripture. You will benefit from both. Each day, he will challenge you to apply these New Testament lessons by answering questions in the "Today's Journal" section. If you follow his plan, you will be enlightened, educated, and encouraged.

Bryan Flanagan
CEO Flanagan Training Group

Aaron Mitchell has provided an easy to use tool for the daily practice of personal spiritual discipline and the challenge of learning what the Holy Spirit wants to make out of the follower of Jesus Christ. Not only does he direct us in how to spend time in the New Testament for ourselves, but actually encourages us to digest and apply what we have read so we can use it in our daily practice as faithful followers of Jesus. As Aaron points out in his introduction, Christian living has the complex requirement of demanding a public witness but never at the exclusion of our private integrity. The New Testament Challenge will assist the reader in keeping a healthy integrated soul as well as a congruent public witness under the wise direction of the Holy Spirit and the Word of God.

John Phillips
Retired Pastor, The First Church
of God New Bethlehem, PA

THE NEW TESTAMENT CHALLENGE

A ONE-YEAR JOURNEY TO DEEPEN
YOUR UNDERSTANDING OF THE
NEW TESTAMENT

AARON MITCHELL

Chaplapreneur Resources

Rockwall, TX

Chaplapreneur.com

"helping the entire world to see Jesus more clearly"

Copyright 2020 © A Mitchell Holdings LLC

All rights reserved. No part of this publication may be reproduced, distributed, or transmitted in any form or by any means, including photocopying, recording, or other electronic or mechanical methods, without the prior written permission of the publisher, except in the case of brief quotations embodied in critical reviews and certain other noncommercial uses permitted by copyright law. For permission requests go to chaplapreneur.com (contact us page). Write "Attention Permissions" in Subject line.

ISBN: 978-1-7354340-2-5 (Paperback)

ISBN: 978-1-7354340-3-2 (Electronic)

LCCN: 2020924198

Scripture quotations are from The Holy Bible, English Standard Version, copyright © 2001 by Crossway Bibles, a division of Good News Publishers. Used by permission. All rights reserved.

Front Cover and Layout Design by Damonza.com

A Mitchell Holdings LLC DBA Chaplapreneur Resources

Contact Chaplapreneur Resources for permission to reproduce at

Chaplapreneur.com

Contact Us Page

This book is dedicated to my wife, Heidi Mitchell.

You are the strongest woman I know. You struggled through the entire process of writing this book with me. You believed in this idea from the beginning. I had a very low moment after being rejected for a ministry position. You were there to utter the words, "Hey, weren't you writing a book! That was the best idea you ever had!"

Those words gave me the needed grit to finish and believe in this idea again. Thank you for believing in me. For the record, marrying you was an even better idea.

I love you and our life together.

INTRODUCTION

Several years ago, while serving as an Associate Pastor of The First Church of God in New Bethlehem, Pennsylvania I first felt the nudge to write this book. I had committed my life to Christ while I was a college student, around five years before starting at this church. As a Bethel Seminary student, and because I was personally driven to do so, during this time I immersed myself deeply in God's Word. I would sometimes spend an hour in my Bible devotionally before going to the office. I listened to all types of preachers with various backgrounds and styles. I went to the Bethel campus in St. Paul, MN four weeks out of the year for intensives and then studied from home the rest of the year.

I often had the opportunity to speak five or six times each week in various events, teaching settings, and breakfasts. People came to church three times a week. In Pennsylvania, students were offered what was called "release time," meaning they could be taken out of school for religious education. The opportunities to teach God's Word were plentiful.

During this time, I began to see things one-dimensionally. People would come to me with real problems and do you know what my response was? I told them they needed to read their Bible more. "Knowing God's Word better," was the solution I gave to any problem. This train of thought spilled into my preaching and teaching. I would often preach:

"How can we expect to hear from God in the Spirit if we don't know what He sounds like?" or "We know His voice from reading His Word."

At the height of my immersion in biblical education and teaching, I had an experience that changed me. I was reading the Old Testament; Ezekiel 1. I found myself absolutely flustered with the meaning of the text. I got out my commentaries to understand the context. I got my Hebrew Bible and started trying to understand the original language. I read the passage from other translations. I read more slowly. I read faster. I tried to understand the book as a whole. I tried understanding it in segment. I searched online. I poured my heart into just trying to get a starting point to decipher the meaning of the text.

After considerable time, and after calling the church office to tell them I would be coming in later, I gave up. I was no closer to understanding the passage than when I first began. I slammed a large commentary shut and spoke out loud to heaven, "I give up!"

In that moment, God spoke to me. He said, "Now you know what it is like coming to *you* for help."

A sobering question came to mind. "If you are trained in this and you are having trouble, what do you think it is like for the person hearing you tell them they just need to 'read the Bible more'?"

I realized that I was setting people up for failure.

Something must be done. People need a system to understand the Bible and they need to understand the original meaning; I needed to be part of that solution. I began to ask questions like, "Why don't we educate lay people better on how to study the Bible in context?" This is the most educated time in human history. We have all the resources at our fingertips. Are we, as leaders, afraid that people might actually learn what the Bible says? How messed up is that?

Something else happened as I reflected on these questions. In thinking about a system for study, I counted the chapters of the New Testament. I couldn't believe there were 260 chapters in the Protestant New Testament! Why is that such a big deal? Chapters and verses were added after the New Testament was written. They are merely reference points for us while studying scripture. I did some math. In our North American culture, most people adhere to a five-day work week or five-day school week. Multiplying 52 weeks in a year times five days a week, you get 260! That just happens to be the same number of chapters in the New Testament.

So, the idea for **The New Testament Challenge** was born. It would be many years before it was completed, but the realization of that dream is in your hands. I believe God showed me the above numbers for a purpose. I believe he prepared me to write a book that comes alongside people as they read the New Testament. Obviously, this is only a starting point, because the Old Testament is equally important. Let's start here. Let's not only "read your Bible," but allow me to shed some light on what you are reading through explanation, journaling guidance, key points, and prayer.

I doubt I am the first person who had the realization to link the chapters of the New Testament with the weeks in a year. As I began to write this, I realized there are reasons someone else hasn't written this yet:

1. It is hard to sit on the fence on doctrinal issues when you write something about every chapter in the New Testament.
2. You have to address passages that are a problem to your own personal doctrine.
3. It is time consuming.
4. You have to know something about every book in the New Testament.
5. You are forced to think outside of denominational boundaries and risk losing those supporters.

It is a risk to write a book like this, but the world needs it. Churches need it. My prayer is that it will help each person who takes The New Testament Challenge.

How do I use this book?

First, decide that you are going to take the challenge. Every year people declare their intent to "read through the Bible" and use various tools to do so. Some are overwhelmed before they even begin. We are reading through just the New Testament. It is manageable to digest and glean what God has to show you. Embarking on this goal with at least one other person will help keep you accountable.

You will need three tools.

1. Your Bible.
2. This book.
3. A journal and something to write with.

You begin by reading the assigned chapter for that day in your own Bible. The first day of the challenge, you will read John 1. I use the English Standard

Version (ESV), but if NIV, NASB, NKJV or one of the other translations works best for you, then go for it. After you read the chapter in your Bible, turn to the corresponding day in this book. Read the entry. There are many, many lessons to be learned from any one scripture passage. I expand on what God impressed upon me to share with you. Following the entry is a personal journaling question. Answer the question in your journal or notebook. If the daily entry has guided any further thoughts, write those down, too.

Following your journal time, there is a brief prayer for each day of the challenge. I know many of you pray more than one or two sentences a day. Use the prayer prompt as a starter in your conversation with God for that day. I always pray in Jesus' mighty name. Each day also has a point to ponder and a key scripture passage from what you've read.

If you embark on the challenge with a small group or partner, when you meet together you can share from what you read in the Bible, *The New Testament Challenge* entries, and your own personal journal. A group leader can choose to focus on one or several of the entries that were completed in the time between group meetings. Regardless of how it is done, you will actually have a group that is prepared to discuss and pray with each other. You will have all read the same thing, with devotional guidance, and insight into context and meaning.

Some cautions: I know for a fact that if you are a deep thinking person who is reading this book to grow and for all the right reasons, you will probably not agree with everything I say in this book. That is good! What we are doing is inviting people into the discussion. It was a step of faith for me to write a book that came alongside every chapter of the New Testament knowing there may be critics. Some may read this book and think, "I wish I would have written this book, I could have done it better than this." The Bible is God's living Word. He will show you things relevant to your life that may differ from what is immediately presented.

But, please don't throw it out because we have different ideas about women in ministry, or I don't align enough with your doctrines of Wesley, Luther, Calvin, or Arminius. The goal is to get people talking and understanding the Bible devotionally, while picking up insight about original context, meaning, audience, and author. If I am in error in an area of doctrine, then your group may need you. But, keep in mind they needed a tool like this book to get them started.

I pray that you find this to be a wonderful journey and a worthy challenge. I look forward to hearing what The Challenge did for you, whether you are a professional theologian, well-studied layperson, new believer, seeker, atheist, or someone coming from a completely different perspective.

With love I wrote this for God, then for you. Thank you for taking the challenge. Take it seriously. Hold each other accountable. Have a party or a banquet at the end of the year celebrating everyone who completed The Challenge and talk about what it did for you.

Aaron Mitchell

Book:	Days Covered:	Begins on Page:
John	Day 1 - Day 21	2
Matthew	Day 22 - Day 49	44
Mark	Day 50 - Day 65	100
Luke	Day 66 - Day 89	132
Acts	Day 90 - Day 117	180
Romans	Day 118 - Day 133	236
1 Corinthians	Day 134 - Day 149	268
2 Corinthians	Day 150 - Day 162	300
Galatians	Day 163 - Day 168	326
Ephesians	Day 169 - Day 174	338
Philippians	Day 175 - Day 178	350
Colossians	Day 179 - Day 182	358
1 Thessalonians	Day 183 - Day 187	366
2 Thessalonians	Day 188 - Day 190	376
1 Timothy	Day 191 - Day 196	382
2 Timothy	Day 197 - Day 200	394
Titus	Day 201 - Day 203	402
Philemon	Day 204	408
Hebrews	Day 205 - Day 217	410
James	Day 218 - Day 222	436
1 Peter	Day 223 - Day 227	446
2 Peter	Day 228 - Day 230	456
1 John	Day 231 - Day 235	462
2 John	Day 236	472
3 John	Day 237	474
Jude	Day 238	476
Revelation	Day 239 - Day 260	478

Day 1

John 1

Scribe to the Heart

"In the beginning was the Word, and the Word was with God, and the Word was God."

(John 1:1)

Point to Ponder

Jesus is the light. I am created for people to see the light.

Today's Journal

Do I allow the light of Jesus to shine through me? Will I commit to shining His light in any situation I face?

Prayer for the Day

Holy Spirit, Shine Your light through me into someone else's life today. As I embark on this journey, I pray to be used more and more by You. It is not my desire to use You; I want You to use me. I pray in the name of Jesus Christ. Amen.

JESUS IS THE LIGHT

WELCOME TO DAY one of your journey through the New Testament. I hope you were able to read John 1. Each entry is written under the assumption that you read the suggested chapter for the day. Whatever trials and tribulations you face in the upcoming year, you need to always remember the truth of this first chapter: Jesus is the Light. No matter what, Jesus is the only one that can save us from our darkness. The beginning of this chapter talks about John the Baptist. He was not the light. John was a witness to the light and his job was to prepare the way for the light. Jesus is willing to clean us up and help us to live His way daily. The minute we forget Jesus is the light, we may try to be the light. We may try to be someone else's Savior, or even the judge of others. It is our job to live a life of worship, so the light (Jesus) can shine through us.

In my early teenage years, my younger brother and I went to a friend's house one night to play hide and seek in the dark. My younger brother jumped off the porch. In the dark, he wasn't able to see the ground. He had seen the other kids jumping off the porch. The other kids were not only much older, but they knew the yard better. My brother jumped only one time and broke his ankle.

My brother had to live with the consequences of trusting in himself. Had he made the same jump during the day he probably would not have had any problems. The light would have revealed to him that the ground was not level. He would have seen all the bumps and holes.

My brother didn't sin in this story. However, when we trust in our own efforts and judgments, there is a price to pay. We are naturally born into darkness. For us to live and find the meaning of this life, we must trust in Jesus Christ. Jesus alone will save us from our sin and shine light onto our path. If we allow Jesus to be the light, nothing will surprise us. We will see clearly how we are to live. Those around us will also see God clearly through the light of Jesus shining through us. We will get to know God better. If we know Him better, we will love Him more. If we love Him more, more will know Him. It is not our job to be the light. It is our job to let the light shine through us.

John 2

Scribe to the Heart

"And he told those who sold the pigeons, 'Take these things away; do not make my Father's house a house of trade.'"

(John 2:16)

Point to Ponder

We are to build bridges to Jesus and not barriers through empty religion.

Today's Journal

How can I build less barriers of religion and more bridges to Jesus?

Prayer for the Day

Holy Spirit, Teach me to love You and follow You. Teach me about my religious ways. Teach me how to represent You in this world. Use me to be Your witness today. Amen.

BUILD BRIDGES TO JESUS

IT IS NOT surprising that in chapter 2 Jesus has already had an encounter with the Pharisees. The Pharisees were the gold standard of religion; they set the bar. Basically, as far as the people were concerned, the Pharisees made the rules. Inside the temple courts animals were provided for the purpose of sacrifice. Poorer families might not have any animals to spare, so some were available at the temple to purchase. At one point, I am sure there was probably some good intention in this practice, but as is often the case, when man gets his hands on something, it gets corrupted. It became nothing more than a business opportunity. Poor people needed animals for their sacrifices, and those who had them wanted to profit. It was business 101; supply and demand.

I am sure the average devout God-fearing worshipper would have overpaid for an animal to sacrifice. Besides, it is for God. If that is what it costs, then that is what it costs, right? Jesus had been observing the Pharisees. For the Jews to continue worshipping in their temple, they had to keep the Romans happy. There were probably many shady dealings between the two parties. God had taken a backseat to the business of the temple for many years. Jesus knew what was really going on in their hearts.

Stopping the exploitation of the poor is something Jesus cared deeply about. Abolishing empty religion is a theme He comes back to often throughout His teaching. The religion of the day was making poor people feel small. Something in the temple that day sent Jesus through the roof. What He saw made Him say, "Enough!"

The sacrifices in the temple were not to be about supply and demand. It was not to be a great day for fundraising. The sacrifices were supposed to enable people of all economic classes to draw closer to God. Jesus is not a salesman. He doesn't want us to create barriers for worship. He wants us to build bridges.

John 3

Scribe to the Heart

"Jesus answered him, 'Truly, truly, I say to you, unless one is born again he cannot see the kingdom of God.'"

(John 3:3)

Point to Ponder

You must be born again!

Today's Journal

Have I ever been born again? Why or why not?
Do I tell people about my experience? Why or why not?

Prayer for the Day

Jesus, I thank You for dying on the cross for all of my sins. I confess that I am a sinner and I am in need of You. My desire is to stop sinning and become more like You. I want to be born again. Teach me how to follow You. Make me into a mature Christian person.

ARE YOU BORN AGAIN?

IN THIS CHAPTER you read about a man named Nicodemus. Nicodemus was a Pharisee. The Pharisees were very distinguished. A devout Jewish believer in the days of Jesus followed the Law of Moses and the laws of the Pharisees to please God.

Nicodemus saw there was something missing and empty about his religion. He saw Jesus had something he did not have. Nicodemus was a spiritual leader who could not be seen learning from Jesus, so he went to Jesus at night when no one would see him. Jesus did not condemn Nicodemus for his actions, but He talked openly to Nicodemus about the kingdom of God. Jesus explained to him that he must be born again to be part of God's kingdom. Nicodemus did not understand how you could enter into your mother's womb a second time. Jesus then explained that first you are born of your mother and then you are born of the Spirit. We have all been born physically, but to reach the kingdom, you must be born again by the Spirit.

Jesus asked Nicodemus how he could be the religious leader that he was and not know this? Nicodemus needed to know that giving money, doing good deeds, or even praying using really big words was not going to get him into the kingdom of God. He also needed to understand that having Jewish heritage wouldn't get him there either. To be a part of God's kingdom on earth and to spend eternity with Him, you must be born again. You must confess your sins and ask Jesus Christ into your heart. Have you been born again? If not, you need to ask Jesus Christ into your life today. Pray today's prayer at the bottom of the page with a sincere heart. If you have been born again, give thanks. Ask for God's help to grow into a mature Christian. You need to ask Jesus into your heart. Every day open yourself to allow Him to change you. It is not the words of the prayer that make you born again, it is about a person coming to a place of repentance, and beginning to live a life that is God-directed. If you are not sure about being born again, continue to read this book and ask God to show you more on a daily basis.

John 4

Scribe to the Heart

"But the hour is coming, and is now here, when the true worshippers will worship the Father in spirit and truth, for the Father is seeking such people to worship him."

(John 4:23)

Point to Ponder

Jesus Christ will take you, mold you, and shape you.

Today's Journal

Do I really believe Jesus has forgiven me? Do I really believe He can and will use me?

Prayer for the Day

Father, Use me in amazing ways to do Your will. Thank You for forgiving me of my sins.

UNCLE SAM WANTS YOU

THERE WAS SO much happening in John 4. Notice what happened right away in verses 1-3. The Pharisees were getting annoyed because they were supposed to be the religious authorities and Jesus was the one baptizing many people. Jesus baptized more people than John the Baptist did. John baptized many in the desert while preparing for Jesus' coming.

While the Pharisees are mad that they are losing influence and power, Jesus was giving power out to others. He took a bunch of random, uneducated people—the disciples—and He gave them the authority to baptize. This would have been a disgrace to the Pharisees, who took pride in how educated and worthy they were as the religious leaders. Jesus was allowing people to baptize who could probably barely read. Jesus takes people where they are and carries them to higher places. It doesn't matter what we have done or where we have been. When we trust Jesus, we can start over fresh.

The chapter continues with the story of the Samaritan woman. It is often preached that she was a tramp because she was divorced five times. However, in that culture a woman could only be divorced by her husband. The woman was not allowed to leave the man. She had been rejected her whole life and now she was accepted by Christ. I am not minimizing the fact that she probably did make mistakes in her life. The amazing thing is that Jesus loved her no matter what.

This woman knew that Jesus loved her. She wanted to know Him better. This woman, who came to Jacob's well to get water in the middle of the day when no one would see her, now found purpose in her life. She was there at that time of day to avoid people and the shame she so often felt. She had an encounter with Jesus just one time and went and told the whole town.

There used to be a sign in front The U.S. Army offices. It had a picture of Uncle Sam pointing outward and the caption read: "Uncle Sam wants YOU." The army is willing to train you to be a great soldier. They will take you and make you into the person they want you to be. Jesus will also take you—no matter what you have done and no matter what your situation is. He will make you into the person He wants you to be.

John 5

Scribe to the Heart

"So Jesus said to them, 'Truly, truly, I say to you, the Son can do nothing of his own accord, but only what he sees the Father doing. For whatever the Father does, that the Son does likewise.'"

(John 5:19)

Point to Ponder

Sometimes we hinder ourselves from moving forward.

Today's Journal

What is stopping me from picking up my mat and walking?

Prayer for the Day

Father, Thank You for healing. Help me to pick up my mat and walk today. Amen.

BECOMING GOD'S HANDS

THE LIFE OF our Messiah continues to be action-packed in chapter 5. Take note of the man that was healed at the pool. This man sitting by the pool was an invalid for 38 years. There were other people around the pool who were lame, blind, and paralyzed. This man could not even get into the pool because someone would always jump in front of him. People would not help him. It doesn't sound like he lived a happy life.

Jesus asked the man a strange question: "Do you want to be healed?" Of course, the man wants to be healed! He has been waiting around for years to get healed. I believe Jesus identified something about the man—self-pity. Sometimes we can have something wrong with us, or even carry out sinful behavior, and we think that is just who we are. This man saw himself as the poor guy who couldn't get into the pool. He saw himself as the unfortunate man who couldn't walk. Jesus knew how to fix this. He looked at him and commanded him to take up the mat and walk. This man, who was lame for 38 years, got up and walked. This is amazing! This man had to have been jumping out of his skin! Sometimes, God needs to address something in us before we can take our mat and move on.

Jesus happened to do this on the Sabbath day. The Pharisees focused on that. They were not celebrating that the man could now walk. Their focus was on the rules. Jesus fulfilled a need. He later told the man to stop sinning so that something worse did not happen to him. The Pharisees were only interested in control. That is what the religious seek—control.

It is interesting what Jesus had to say about this religious bondage in verse 19. Jesus had one mission in mind: He explained why He healed people on the Sabbath. He said that He can only do what He sees the Father doing. The man needed help with his problem and he needed a connection with God. This was a moment where Jesus acted as the Spirit told Him. Many people try to work for God without ever praying and asking what He thinks. Before we can be God's hands, we need to be connected to His body, and especially to His heart.

John 6

Scribe to the Heart

"Whoever feeds on my flesh and drinks my blood abides in me, and I in him."

(John 6:56)

Point to Ponder

It is a hard command to eat Jesus.

Today's Journal

Has it been hard for me to follow Jesus fully? What can I do to consume more of Him?

Prayer for the Day

Lord, When things are hard, I pray that I will follow You anyway. Help me to serve You in a way like I never have before.

EATING JESUS IS NOT EASY

THROUGHOUT THE LAST five days, we saw Jesus calling people out of sin and religion and into a real relationship with Him. Often, we Americans want everything to be easy. Frequently, we organize our life into little compartments. In this chapter, we see Jesus feeding five thousand people. This story is one of the few stories found in all four gospels. These people were seeking to hear from Jesus. Jesus miraculously changed a little bit of food into a bountiful dinner that provided more than enough for five thousand men, plus women and children.

Then, we see Jesus again operating in the miraculous by walking on water. These stories are no small matter. Take some time to think about them today. Jesus told the people who were following Him that they were not there because they saw miracles, but because He provided food for them. Jesus told them that if they wanted to eat so they could live forever, they needed to eat His flesh and drink His blood.

It was nice that Jesus was able to do this great miracle, but the real miracle is that people who are sinners can become acceptable to God. Many of the people following Jesus left at this point. It was a hard teaching for them to understand. They didn't just leave because this teaching was hard; they left because Jesus was calling them to something deeper. Jesus asked the disciples if they wanted to leave too, but they told Him they weren't going anywhere because Jesus was the one who had the keys to eternal life. They were ready to follow God.

What does it mean to "eat" Jesus' body? It doesn't mean that the wafer at church actually "becomes" Jesus. We don't eat Him physically. So, what does it mean? Did it mean that they were going to share in His broken body? Would they have to suffer for being His followers? Would they have to eat Jesus by remembering what He had to go through, and choose not to let sin into their lives? Would they be eating Jesus by praying and meditating on His words daily? I believe so. Following Jesus is hard to do. If you don't think so, ask yourself today if you are really following Him. It is a hard command to eat Jesus.

John 7

Scribe to the Heart

"The one who speaks on his own authority seeks his own glory, but the one who seeks the glory of him who sent him is true, and in him there is no falsehood."

(John 7:18)

Point to Ponder

Our job is not to look good. We are to make God look good.

Today's Journal

What ways do I live to make myself look good? In what ways do I strive to make God look good?

Prayer for the Day

Father, Reveal to me how I can make You look good. Help me to not try and make myself look good.

SEEKING TO HONOR GOD

THIS CHAPTER BEGINS with Jesus' brothers telling Him He needs to go to the Feast of Tabernacles. After all, if He was trying to be a public figure, He needed to be in the public. They were speaking from a place of disbelief and were looking at Him as more of a politician. Jesus told them that it was not His time to go. Jesus doesn't ever waver on what is right because He is tuned into the Father all the time. He knew that going at that time might not have been the safest thing for Him. He knew the right decisions to make at the right time. Jesus' focus on the Father is complete.

Jesus later went to the feast and made a fascinating statement. Many different people were there, including the Pharisees. Jesus said, *"The one who speaks on his own authority seeks his own glory, but the one who seeks the glory of him who sent him is true, and in him there is no falsehood"* (John 7:18).

As Christians, we always have to make sure we are doing things for the right reasons. The Pharisees did many good deeds, but why did they do them?

People do things to bring themselves honor every day. Today while you are at school, work, or wherever you are, count how many people act tough or try to show off. More importantly, look and see how many times a day you do things like this. How many people know the real you? Do you hide from people? Do you do things to make yourself look better? We are children of the light, which means we need to live in the light.

Many people even do things in church to look good. A person who preaches, teaches Sunday School, leads worship, ushers, sings specials, or does anything else without seeking to make God look good is doing things for the wrong reasons. Ask yourself, if no one but God saw me doing the ministry I do, would I still do it? Would I still go on mission trips, go to conventions, sing, teach, etc.? Is it about God, or is it about me?

Day 8

John 8

Scribe to the Heart

"To the Jews who had believed him, Jesus said, 'If you hold to my teaching, you are really my disciples.'"

(John 8:31)

Point to Ponder

You are God's child.

Today's Journal

What does it mean to be God's child? What things do I want Him to change in me?

Prayer for the Day

Jesus, Destroy the sins I put into my life. Thank You for dying so that I can be a child of God. I am so thankful to be a child of God today.

WHOSE CHILD ARE YOU?

THERE ARE MANY things to talk about in this chapter. We see the story of the woman caught in adultery, and Jesus doesn't condemn her. We also see Jesus speaking boldly with the Pharisees about who their father is. We have come to a place in the book of John where the religious people have a strong hate for Jesus. They want the Son of God dead! Jesus continues to have a strong commitment to the truth. He told them that they are children of the devil because if they were children of Abraham, they would obey His teachings. Jesus let them know the reason they wanted to kill Him was because they didn't have room for His word.

There are many well-meaning people in God's church who are weighed down with religion. We will talk more about this tomorrow, but I find it funny that Jesus explained to the Pharisees that they had no room for His word. Many people are so religious, they too have no room for His word. They worry about the style of music in a service, or how people dress at church, or even if things look good. This is a mess. God wants our hearts, and that is it.

Dead religion is of the devil. Relationship is of Jesus. The hard truth is that many are at one extreme or the other. If you have no room for the teachings of Jesus because of religious rules that you follow, you may be a child of the devil. At best you are an immature Christian. If you don't have room for the teachings of Jesus because you either want to live your own way or you don't have time for Him, you may be a child of the devil as well. When you are born again, God begins to change you. Some changes happen fast, while some change is slow, but if God doesn't change you at all, then you are not His child.

If you have been born again, you are God's child. There are things in your life that are undone. I know that because it is true for me and every other person. There is a guarantee that He is working to change those undone things. Begin by asking the Holy Spirit into those areas. You need to take authority over any sin you have in your life. Your sins began with the desire to do them, so ask Him to destroy your sinful desires daily. Walk as God's child today.

John 9

Scribe to the Heart

"Jesus heard that they had cast him out, and having found him he said, 'Do you believe in the Son of Man?'"

(John 9:35)

Point to Ponder

Religion is for the blind.
Jesus is for those who see clearly.

Today's Journal

In what areas am I spiritually blind? How much of my Christianity is filled with empty practices? How much is life-giving?

Prayer for the Day

Jesus, Open my eyes today. I want to see clearly so I look more like You.

RELIGION IS FOR THE BLIND

IN THIS CHAPTER, once again we see Jesus in conflict with the Pharisees. The Pharisees may have started their spiritual journey wanting to serve God. They wanted to keep the law and please Him. Over time, many of them fell in love with the authority they had. They liked being considered important people.

Jesus healed a man who had been blind all of his life. When the Pharisees drill the man with many questions, he tells them that all he knows is that once he was blind but now he could see. This was his story. The man's parents didn't share in the story because they hadn't had their spiritual eyes opened yet. They were still blind to spiritual things. His parents didn't want to be thrown out of the synagogue, so they declined comment. Those who are trying to please God with religion are blind spiritually. The Pharisees could only lead people who had spiritual blindness, so they threw the man out. This man's eyes were opened physically, and they were also opened spiritually.

You may be trying to please God by going to church, reading your Bible, or taking communion. Those things don't make you a Christian any more than going swimming makes you a fish. You need to ask for forgiveness of your sins, and ask to walk with God for the rest of your life.

A Christian can still have some areas of blindness. If you can't worship God unless you are singing hymns, you are spiritually blind in this area. The same is true if you can only worship God through fast-paced contemporary music. If you can't worship God when you don't "feel" Him, that is an area of spiritual blindness. If you are completely against God stirring your emotions, and believe that God only speaks through the Bible academically, you are also spiritually blind.

Christianity is about being connected with God. Christianity is about knowing God and knowing Him well. It is about loving Him with all of your heart, and loving your neighbors as you love yourself. It is about getting to know Him better alongside of other believers. Choose not to walk in blindness today. When his eyes were opened, the man saw Jesus. Seek to see and know Jesus today. Don't live religiously. Connect to God through Jesus Christ.

John 10

Scribe to the Heart

"I am the good shepherd. I know my own and my own know me, just as the Father knows me and I know the Father; and I lay my life down for the sheep."

(John 10:14-15)

Point to Ponder

Listen to God.

Today's Journal

What do I want God to speak to me about today? What decision do I need Him to guide me on? What do I want to learn from Him today?

Prayer for the Day

God, Speak to me about the desires of my heart and needs in my life today. I trust that You want to speak to me because I am Your child.

HEARING THE SHEPHERD'S VOICE

JESUS DECLARED HE is "The Good Shepherd." He knows His sheep and they know Him. They hear His voice. They know that He is willing to lay down His life for them. The important point I want to make from this chapter is: God speaks to people. If you are a child of God, He will speak to you. It doesn't always have to be through a pastor. It doesn't always have to be through the Bible. Those are ways He chooses often, but when you know God, you get to know His voice.

This type of thinking scares people. Sometimes liars stand up and say that God has spoken to them about this or that. God will deal with them, but you need to believe God loves to speak to people. If you know Him, He may speak to you often. He loves to talk back to you when you pray. He loves to let the words jump off of the pages at you when you are reading Scripture. God loves people enough that He sent Jesus to die for them, so it is ridiculous to think He won't speak to us too!

This passage refers to us as sheep. Sheep, by nature, are not smart animals. They need a Shepherd to lead them. We need to read the Word and we need to listen to teachers who instruct us from the Word, but God also wants you to hear directly from Him. He wants you to know that you are valuable to Him. You are so valuable to Jesus that He was willing to lay down His life for you. He wants to guide you in the decisions you have to make. The last time you had to make an important decision, did you pray about it? Did you ask God to guide you and expect that He would? God will speak to you in whatever ways He chooses. However, if you don't believe He speaks to people, or you are not listening, you might miss it.

John 11

Scribe to the Heart

"Jesus wept."

(John 11:35)

Point to Ponder

Jesus understands my pain.

Today's Journal

Do I believe God understands my pain? How does God feel my pain? What do I need Jesus to help me through today?

Prayer for the Day

Lord Jesus Christ, I pray for Your healing presence on the pain in my life. You are the great healer. I know that through my pain I will know You better.

HE FEELS MY PAIN

THE STORY OF Jesus raising Lazarus from the dead shows us both sides of Jesus. Human Jesus wept beside the tomb of Lazarus. Jesus was a close friend to Martha, Mary and Lazarus. He ate with them. He probably felt He could relax around them. Jesus the Christ came to raise Lazarus from the dead. It was part of His purpose.

"Jesus wept"

(John 11:35).

This is the shortest verse in the Bible. It is barely a sentence, but it says so much. Jesus went through real life situations and He really does feel our pain. He wasn't some robot on a mission.

He came as God, who decided to become human and go through every part of this life without sinning (Hebrews 4:15).

When you go through hard situations, do you remember that Jesus has been there? Do you remember that Jesus is there for you? Do you remember that He will not waste your pain? Do you remember that when you choose not to sin in your pain, you become stronger? As an athlete, I used to lift weights. The times I lifted the hardest were when I had someone pushing me to do one or two more reps. I completed the reps because my workout partners did them too. They went through the pain, so I knew I could.

Jesus never sinned. All of us have sinned, but we no longer have to. Jesus makes us all look like wimps. We have made excuses and taken the easy way out too many times. When Jesus was dying on the cross, He cried out for His persecutors to be forgiven. He felt my pain and He still does today. In this passage Jesus prays for Lazarus to be raised, so that others would believe. He loved Lazarus, but He raised Lazarus from the dead so that others would believe in God. He always thinks of others, even when He is feeling pain. He is there for you because He knows what you are going through. God loves you beyond what words can say.

The next time you think God doesn't understand you, or that He is not there to listen to you, remember that He felt your pain, and He feels your pain now. He felt the pain of loss, rejection, and the pain of the cross. Jesus Christ is there for you today and forever.

John 12

Scribe to the Heart

"Leave her alone, so that she may keep it for the day of my burial. The poor you always have with you, but you do not always have me."

(John 12:7-8)

Point to Ponder

God honors the motives of the heart.

Today's Journal

Do I serve God so others see me and I can be glorified in their eyes? Do I do it for God? If I knew I would be hated for doing the right thing would I do it? Why? Why not?

Prayer for the Day

Lord Jesus, Teach me to understand the motives of my heart. Teach me what things I do for the wrong reasons. Teach me how to love You more than I love myself.

GOD HONORS THE HEART

IN THIS CHAPTER we find Jesus in one of His favorite places. He was at the house of Lazarus, Mary and Martha. Martha prepared the meal, while Lazarus sat at the table. Yesterday, we read that Lazarus had died and Jesus raised him from the dead. Today, Lazarus is sitting at the table with Jesus, seemingly without a care in the world. The chief priests were making plans to kill Lazarus, yet, we find him relaxed at the table. This man already experienced death, and he wasn't afraid because his friend is also his Savior.

We also see Mary, who loved to sit at the feet of Jesus, wiping the feet of her master with expensive perfume intended for His burial. This may have been a little early. It may have been a waste of expensive perfume, but Jesus saw the heart of Mary and He knew that Mary loved Him. Judas, on the other hand, was the keeper of the money and sometimes stole money for himself. He began to talk about the poor and how many people could be fed if they sold the expensive perfume. Judas may have been right, but his concern wasn't with the poor. His concern wasn't about the best interests of Jesus, either. Judas may have had the most practical answer from a humanly perspective, but Jesus knew Judas' heart. Jesus knew that his intentions were bad, and He rebuked Judas.

He honored Mary and her heart to serve God. All of us have probably wondered if we please God or not. Most of us have wondered if God is in the plans we are carrying out. God honors those who want to honor Him. If we are not about honoring God, He doesn't want to be included in our plans, even if it is a good idea. That's a hard reality. He wants us to constantly be pointing to Him. When we sing, our voice may squeak; when we preach, we may stutter. We may spill food on a hungry person we are trying to feed, but God sees the motives of the heart. We must strive hard so that people are blessed and many are saved.

John 13

Scribe to the Heart

"Jesus answered him, 'What I am doing you do not understand now, but afterward you will understand.'"

(John 13:7)

Point to Ponder

To live like Jesus means to serve all people.

Today's Journal

Who is a hard person for me to serve? What can I do to serve him or her today?

Prayer for the Day

Jesus, Thank You for serving me. I commit to serve You today. Help me to serve others.

THE WORLD NEEDS FOOT WASHERS

ONE OF THE most basic teachings of Jesus is how to be a leader and a servant at the same time. This is called servant-leadership. The timing of this chapter is just before the famous last supper. You have seen the paintings where they are all sitting on the same side of the table. It probably didn't look like that.

In the Middle Eastern region of the world, most men wore sandals as they walked the roads during the day. They may have stepped in the camel droppings left on the path. Their feet were definitely dirty from the dusty road. Traditionally, some houses had foot washers. However, our Savior took the basin and washed the feet of His disciples. Does that seem weird or humiliating to you? The disciples were probably disturbed, to say the least.

People define ministry as serving for God's glory in areas where one is gifted or talented. That is exactly why the church isn't what it is supposed to be in our country. Jesus did something any common person could do. Jesus got right in there and scrubbed between the toes. He is the Savior of the world; He is not supposed to be the guy scrubbing the feet of these men. Yet He did it!

It seems like a degrading place to be, but this is how Jesus taught us to lead and we shouldn't dismiss it. So many people in the church only serve if they get something out of it. Some people can't serve unless they are "up front" all the time. Peter knew this was no place for a Savior, and He didn't want Jesus to wash his feet. Jesus explained to him that it was the only way. He could have said, "Peter, wash your own feet. Die for your own sins. Your feet smell, and you have lived a sinful life." But He didn't. Jesus loves us all that much.

Judas was also there. Within the next few hours, he would betray Jesus. The great test for us is to love our enemies. Jesus washed the feet of Judas, even though he knew Judas would betray Him. Jesus died for Judas' sins. Jesus died for people who crash planes into buildings. He died for people who reject Him. He died for a sinner like me. Praise God today for being a God who washed your nasty, sweaty, smelly feet. Allow Him to teach you to embody Christ-like love.

John 14

Scribe to the Heart

"If you love me, you will keep my command- ments. And I will ask the Father, and he will give you another Helper, to be with you forever,"

(John 14:15-16)

Point to Ponder

Spiritual weightlifters become strong in the Spirit through obedience to God.

Today's Journal

In what area of my life do I need God to help me to be obedient? What blessings am I missing when I am disobedient? How do I plan to become obedient in this area?

Prayer for the Day

Lord, Teach me to obey You and become spiritually stronger today.

SPIRITUAL WEIGHTLIFTING

JESUS WASHED THE feet of the disciples. He predicted Judas' betrayal and Peter's denial. Now Jesus comforts and assures them. He tells the disciples that in the Father's house are many rooms, and He will go and prepare a place for them. Jesus lets them know that He will be going away, and it is for their own good.

Many people miss some of the most exciting points in this passage. Look closely at what Jesus has to say in verses 15-17: *"If you love me, you will keep my commandments. And I will ask the Father, and he will give you another Helper, to be with you forever, even the Spirit of truth, whom the world cannot receive, because it neither sees him nor knows him. You know him, for he dwells with you and will be in you."*

First, if you are in love with Jesus, you will obey His command. The more you love God, the more you will naturally trust and obey Him. You will think and act more like Him every day. Verse 16 is critical. The result of obeying God is the gift of the Spirit. Jesus already assured them of salvation. The message here is if we obey God more, we will experience the Spirit more. He tells the disciples that they already have the Spirit with them, but now the Spirit will be in them. Before you can experience the Spirit, you need to obey the Spirit.

People love to talk about spiritual gifts. Can people speak in tongues? Do people still experience the prophetic? These things can happen in the church, but they are not the mark of spiritual maturity. Being a good musician, preacher, or administrator doesn't make you spiritually mature either. Obeying God is what makes a person spiritually mature.

The fruit of the Spirit is the sign of maturity, not the gifts of the Spirit. Obeying God is like spiritual weightlifting. Every time we obey God, we are allowing our Spirit to become stronger. Every time you say no to sin, your Spirit has the opportunity to grow. Sin makes us spiritually fat and lazy. We need to be strong enough to strive forward. If you truly want the Spirit in your life, you will choose to be an animal in the spiritual weight room. Pay the price with the right program of obedience, prayer, Bible reading, church attendance, and time with other believers.

Day 15

John 15

Scribe to the Heart

"This is my command- ment, that you love one another as I have loved you. Greater love has no one than this, that someone lays down his life for his friends."

(John 15:12-13)

Point to Ponder

A disciple of Jesus is a disciple all of the time.

Today's Journal

What situations distract me from following Jesus? How can I better trust Him in these areas of my life?

Prayer for the Day

Lord, Teach me how to be a true disciple. Teach me what that means in my life today.

ARE YOU HIS DISCIPLE?

CHAPTER 15 IS intricate. Jesus wanted the disciples to understand the cross. He instructed them that the Holy Spirit would come to help them. But how do you convey who the Holy Spirit is, if they haven't personally experienced Him yet? The apostles didn't understand much of what Jesus said until later. However, here we see Jesus' most important point. Times will be tough for the disciples (as they will be for us), but He will carry them through. He wants them to see that He will die, yet He will live again. He wants them to understand He is going to leave, yet He will still be here. These ideas are confusing and overwhelming.

To add to this difficult message Jesus told the disciples that those who hate Him, will hate them, too. He went so far as to say the world will hate them. It was going to be quite a time of testing. He tells them they will do great things for God if they continue to follow Him.

Jesus explained to them that they were to continue on in the work anyway. Look what He said: *"This is my commandment, that you love one another as I have loved you. Greater love has no one than this, that someone lays down his life for his friends"* (John 15:12-13). The disciples didn't fully understand. However, they experienced Jesus in very powerful ways over the previous 3½ years. Would they continue to follow Jesus when they don't get it? Would they continue to do what is right when it seemed like Jesus was not around? Would they trust God when the good old days were gone?

How about you? Are you going to get drunk when times get hard? Are you going to look elsewhere when your spouse doesn't treat you well? Are you going to return to your old ways, when Christianity is no longer new and the love you have for God gets stale? What are you going to do? Will you be prepared for the testing? Are you willing to read the words of Jesus, knowing that you will not fully understand some of them until you need them? Will you press forward?

John 16

Scribe to the Heart

"Nevertheless, I tell you the truth: it is to your advantage that I go away, for if I do not go away, the Helper will not come to you. But if I go, I will send him to you."

(John 16:7)

Point to Ponder

Jesus has something to say. He can't tell you until you are ready.

Today's Journal

How can I allow God to speak to me today?

Prayer for the Day

Lord Jesus, I want to be more obedient to You today. I want to hear from You. Help me to follow You with my life. Teach me what You want me to know.

PRESS PLAY

IN CHAPTER 16, Jesus continued to pour even more hard concepts into the disciples for them to process. Jesus told them He is going away. He assures them that it is to their advantage that He leaves, so that the Holy Spirit can come. He tells them their coming grief will turn to joy. He gave them deep truths and affirms that He overcame the world.

Jesus told them all of these things because they were essential truths for facing the obstacles that were ahead. Interestingly enough, He said, *"I still have many things to say to you, but you cannot bear them now. When the Spirit of truth comes, he will guide you into all the truth"* (John 16:12-13a). Jesus already told them a lot, but there was much more He wanted them to know.

There was a sense of urgency in Jesus' teaching in this passage. Jesus gave them as much as they could handle in the moment. Jesus wants to take them deeper in their relationship with God the Father. However, at that time, Jesus only focused on what was immediately needed for their survival.

When I think about this statement Jesus made, I have to wonder if there are things Jesus wants me to know that I am not ready for yet. Am I ready to go deeper with Him? Is there rebellion in my Spirit that I haven't dealt with? Are there sins in my life that keep me from knowing God better? Am I keeping myself from growing in ways that are important to my future?

God always has something to say to you. You may not actually hear Him mouth the words, but there is much more He wants to tell you. He withholds lessons when you are not ready to hear them. Many of our spiritual walks are a paused movie. We will not move forward in our spiritual walk until we are able to better to handle ourselves when under trial. God has something to say to you today. Are you willing to listen? Are you willing to obey? Are you willing to press play?

John 17

Scribe to the Heart

"I in them and you in me, that they may become perfectly one, so that the world may know that you sent me and loved them even as you loved me."

(John 17:23)

Point to Ponder

The Father loves me as much as He loves Jesus.

Today's Journal

How can I better realize God's amazing love for me each day?

Prayer for the Day

Lord Jesus, teach me about how much I am loved today, and help me to love You and others the same way.

LOVED LIKE JESUS?

IN THIS PASSAGE, Jesus turns His attention towards God the Father. Jesus begins to pray. There are so many things to learn about this prayer. Jesus prayed intensely for the believers' protection, and that they would be witnesses in this world. He prayed for those their ministry would touch. The most exciting concept is found in verse 23: *"I in them and you in me, that they may become perfectly one, so that the world may know that you sent me and loved them even as you loved me."*

Did you catch it? Jesus is talking to the Father. He prays that believers would be united, and the world would see there is something special about them. The world is to look on the unity of the church and see Jesus was sent for them, and He loves them with a holy intensity. How much are they loved by God? God the Father loves them with the same amount of love that He has for Jesus. Let me say it again. GOD THE FATHER LOVES YOU WITH THE SAME AMOUNT OF LOVE THAT HE HAS FOR JESUS THE CHRIST! It is right there in verse 23. Many of us haven't been taught the love of God very well. God thought you were worthy enough to lead His only Son to the cross for you.

You are only a Christian because you are loved. God loves sinners with this amazing love. He wants people everywhere to know Him. You have no idea how much God loves you. It is no secret Jesus is perfect and we are not. It isn't anything you do that makes God love you. He just does. You were valuable enough to save, and you are valuable enough to daily grow and become a better disciple.

People everywhere need to know God loves them. The world needs to see believers giving unconditional love. They need to see us working together. It is possible for the world to see this amazing love. However, first things first, do you believe God the Father loves you as much as He loves Jesus? Do you really believe God is in your corner? Do you really believe He loves you when you fall short? Do you really believe He loves you the same, no matter what you do for Him? You should only serve God because you love Him. Enjoy being His child today, and talk to Him as your perfect loving Father.

Day 18

John 18

Scribe to the Heart

"Jesus answered, 'You say that I am a king. For this purpose I was born and for this purpose I have come into the world—to bear witness to the truth. Everyone who is of the truth listens to my voice.' Pilate said to him, 'What is truth?'"

(John 18:37-38)

Point to Ponder

Truth is the way of Jesus.

Today's Journal

What is truth? Am I living according to Jesus' truth or someone else's opinion of truth?

Prayer for the Day

Lord Jesus, When I hear something that is not truth, allow me to recognize it quickly. Deepen my understanding of truth.

WHAT IS TRUTH?

OUR WORLD ASKS "What is truth?" every day. Many have decided that truth is whatever they want it to be. The sentiment is often echoed that one can believe whatever he or she wants, as long as one is sincere. This is ridiculous. Truth is absolute. Right is right, and wrong is wrong. Jesus is the only way to God; the only One who was willing to die for you. He is the only One who is always there for you. He is the only One who reaches out to you because you could never reach Him, no matter how hard you try.

In these next two chapters, we see Jesus standing before Pontius Pilate. Jesus is about to be sentenced to death by crucifixion. Pilate isn't comfortable with Jesus being punished, however he plays his role in the crucifixion because of pressure from the Jews.

The truth that Jesus brought was hard for the Jews. They were waiting for the Messiah, but He wasn't what they expected. What He brought was truth. No matter how religious people are or how righteous they act, we all need Jesus. This is a hard truth.

Jesus told Pilate that all who listen to truth listen to His voice. Pilate then asked, "What is truth?" and walked away. Pilate was a powerful man who decided if men were put to death or if they went free. He made laws and governed the people. He thought Jesus should have seen him as truth.

There was another truth at play. Pilate was not well-liked by the Jewish people. They threatened to involve Caesar and accused Jesus of being anti-Caesar. Setting Jesus free could result in death for Pilate. That was the truth Pilate saw.

Jesus brought truth. Many want to do to truth what they did to Jesus in John 18. They want to kill the truth; however, truth is eternal, like Jesus. It cannot be permanently destroyed. A statement is either true or false. Jesus only spoke truth. If you follow Jesus, you follow the way of truth.

John 19

Scribe to the Heart

"Jesus answered him, 'You would have no authority over me at all unless it had been given you from above. Therefore he who delivered me over to you has the greater sin.'"

(John 19:11)

Point to Ponder

Jesus is the truth.

Today's Journal

Do I live as if Jesus really is the truth?

Prayer for the Day

Lord Jesus, I declare that Your way is the truth. Continue to teach me truth and give me the strength to live that way.

WHO IS TRUTH?

YESTERDAY I ASKED, "What is truth?" Pilate felt he determined truth because of his power over the lives and freedom of the people he oversaw. He also knew of another truth, the pressure he felt from the Jews.

Today, we need to get more personal. The real question is, "Who is truth?" Jesus told us that He is the way, the truth and the life. (John 14:6) In John 1, we learned that He was there at the beginning of everything. (John 1:1-2) Jesus is ultimately who we are going to answer to. Jesus is the truth.

In chapter 18 Pilate didn't understand what Jesus was saying. Maybe the light is coming on because Pilate tries to set Jesus free. Jesus lets Pilate know there is no power over him that isn't given from above. Oddly, Pilate then tries harder to set Him free. Eventually, Pilate's loyalty to Caesar is challenged. Pilate then knew that he could lose his own life trying to protect Jesus. He gave in to the Jews.

I find it interesting that Pilate put a sign on the cross above Jesus that read "King of the Jews" in three languages. The chief priests challenged this but Pilate responded, "What I have written, I have written." In other words, "That is the way it is. Whether you like it or not, Jesus is your king."

You don't have to approve of Jesus or even believe for Him to be in authority over you. He is; whether you like it or not. You don't have to agree with Him to make His teachings right. They just are. Whatever problem you have with God, it is your problem and not His. He loves you and wants to guide you, but ultimately it is your problem. Jesus is the only truth and way to eternal life.

You can beat truth up. You can humiliate truth. You can nail truth to the cross. You can try to destroy truth. However, Jesus is the truth, and He defeated death. People have a problem with His truth, but He is more alive than ever. He rose from the dead. Truth is that Jesus died for each of us. If we are not living for Him, that is our problem.

John 20

"*Jesus said to her, 'Mary.' She turned and said to him in Aramaic, 'Rabboni!' (which means Teacher)*"

(John 20:16)

Jesus doesn't hold your past against you.

Today's Journal

Is there something that keeps me from believing God loves me? What is it?

Prayer for the Day

God, Teach me more about Your deep, unbelievable love today.

FORMER PROSTITUTE REPORTS SEEING JESUS ALIVE!

IF YOU HAVE ever stood at the checkout counter in a grocery store, you've seen the sensationalized headlines. Where do they come up with this stuff? Elvis and Princess Diana are always spotted somewhere. Justin Bieber and Oprah are really mother and son from another planet, sent here to take over the earth. Real news just isn't as interesting to many people as the tabloid stories.

Some people buy the magazines with the outrageous headlines for entertainment; but some believe them, without ever reading the article or verifying the facts.

The story in John 20 could have been one of those headlines. Mary Magdalene used to be a prostitute. In those days women were not as important as men. A woman who had been known to have a sexual history outside of marriage was considered very low in society. A prostitute (even a former one) was looked upon as worthless. However, Jesus decided that she had worth. Mary was worthy enough that He went to her before anyone else. Mary was no longer a prostitute. She was someone who used to live that way, but she was now a disciple of Christ.

Because of her past, people wouldn't believe that she had seen Jesus alive. In the minds of many in society, she should have been stoned to death long ago. The devout Jews would surely have not believed her, not even considering her story because of her past. As such, they missed out on knowing the risen Christ.

This story would have been on the cover of a magazine at the checkout counter in ancient Jerusalem. Many would roll their eyes. If Jesus really is the Messiah, surely He wouldn't come and talk to a former prostitute. There are many more important people that He would talk to first. Right? That is what we would think. How small is our faith? When Jesus spoke Mary's name, she knew exactly who it was. This man changed her life, and their friendship was deep and eternal. Jesus doesn't hold your past against you. Get to know Him today.

Day 21

John 21

Scribe to the Heart

"When they had finished eating, Jesus said to Simon Peter, 'Simon son of John, do you truly love me more than these?'"

(John 21:15)

Point to Ponder

God's will can be found when we love Jesus more than anything else.

Today's Journal

If I was standing in front of Jesus and He asked me, "Do you love me more than these?" how would I answer? Is there something or someone I love more than Jesus?

Prayer for the Day

Jesus, Show me if there are things I need to put in proper place. Help me to love You more than anything else.

DO YOU LOVE ME MORE THAN THESE?

THE DISCIPLES HAD been through a lot in the last three and a half years. They probably didn't even remember who they were. Their heads were still spinning from recent events. They knew Jesus rose from the dead. They just saw Him in the last chapter.

Think of all of the changing that went on in their lives. Peter, who used to be a fisherman, makes the statement, "I'm going fishing." Peter doesn't know what to do, so he returns to his roots. He was a fisherman when Jesus first found him. He was still Peter and he missed fishing. Other disciples went with him. They hadn't caught anything. Then Jesus appears and tells them to put the net on the other side of the boat. Instantly there were 153 fish.

Peter was excited to see Jesus. Peter jumped out of the boat to meet Jesus and found Him with more fish, and a nice warm fire. Jesus asked Peter, "Look at these fish, do you love me more than them?" Then Jesus told Peter three times to feed His sheep. Peter was hurt because Jesus was reminding Peter that he denied Him three times.

After Peter told Jesus three times that he does love Him, Jesus tells Peter, "Follow me!" Peter knew Jesus was talking about persecution, and maybe even death on a cross. Peter then looked to John and asked Jesus, "What about him?" Peter and John had a competitive thing going. In chapter 20 John wrote that he outran Peter. Now Peter says, "If I am going to die for you, what about him?" Jesus told Peter that what happens to John was none of his business. Peter needed to be willing to follow Jesus no matter what happened to him or the people around him. We have talked a lot in the book of John about how much God loves you. Before Peter could become the person God wanted him to be, or to do the things that were to come in his life, he needed to make the decision that he loved God more than anything else. Jesus asked Peter, "Do you love me more than anything?" In your life, are you in love with someone or something more than Jesus?

Matthew 1

Scribe to the Heart

"The book of genealogy of Jesus Christ, the son of David, the son of Abraham"

(Matt. 1:1)

Point to Ponder

The New Testament continues a story that is already thousands of years in progress.

Today's Journal

Can I better understand how to follow Jesus by reading the Old Testament? How?

Prayer for the Day

Lord Jesus, Help me to understand the importance of the whole story.

THE STORY CONTINUES

THE TERM "EPISODE IV" means something for *Star Wars* fans. It was the first *Star Wars* movie. Episodes one through three weren't released until long afterward. It was a brilliant ploy by writer/director George Lucas. You pick up the story halfway through. Many years later, you got to watch what happened earlier in the timeline. It made many things clear for the *Star Wars* fan.

Christians must understand the importance of the Old Testament. You don't need to be confused by it. The Old Testament sets the scene for the New. It has been said the Old Testament is the New Testament concealed, and the New Testament is the Old Testament revealed. Much of what happened in the Old Testament was foreshadowing what was to come later. It is a complete story. They are both parts of a larger whole.

Matthew begins with genealogy. This list of people stretches across hundreds, even thousands, of years and includes all types of people. Some served God well. Most struggled. Matthew was writing to the Jewish people, and the genealogy leading up to the Messiah was important to them. In the eastern hemisphere genealogy is considered to be of much greater importance than we consider it to be in the west.

These stories had been passed down for thousands of years. At the time Matthew wrote, many had lost track that Jesus' family was part of this lineage. However, establishing this case was vital for the purpose of outreach to the first century Jew who was still waiting for the Messiah. It is also to be noted that Jesus was from the lineage of King David, and didn't have children. This builds a stronger case for Jesus as the Christ. The genealogy ends with Him, and is fulfilled in Him, so long as He is the rightful successor.

You can't understand Christianity at its fullest without the Old Testament. The lesson we learn from *Star Wars* is that it is important to study the beginning of the story to fully understand the rest of the story.

Matthew 2

Scribe to the Heart

"Where is he who has been born king of the Jews? For we saw his star when it rose and have come to worship him."

(Matt. 2:2)

Point to Ponder

Satan wants to destroy you.
Only God gives you the ability to not be destroyed, but to succeed.

Today's Journal

In what ways have I allowed Satan to hurt my walk with Jesus? How can I better worship God?

Prayer for the Day

Lord Jesus, Thank You for winning the war. Help me not to listen to Satan's lies about my life.

THE TRAIN WRECK

HAVE YOU EVER met anyone who seemed to always have a problem? Do you know someone who is always in a bad situation? Sometimes bad things happen to people; however often we create them ourselves. When you are young the world tells you to have as much fun as you can. You need to drink, have sex, and do drugs. You need to have a great time because these are the best days of your life. You can get serious when you are older.

The problem is when people go down this road, many don't find their way off of it. Some people dig a hole so deep for themselves they will never be able to fully come back. People occasionally find God in these situations, and that is wonderful. However, temptation for the younger generation to sin is a major problem in our culture.

This worldly-focused message is a lie. Teenagers get the message that these are the best days of their lives. They hear that drinking and having sex is important now, because one day you are going to get married and life will be all downhill from there. That is a tragic message. Don't fall into that. What if the best days of their life are not now? What if life is a journey filled with all kinds of bumps in the road? Maybe it is an opportunity to know God better every single day?

Satan wants to eat our young before they can effectively stick up for themselves. King Herod was threatened by the birth of Jesus. He wanted to kill Jesus before He could defend Himself. Satan wanted to destroy Jesus, and He wants to destroy you. He gives us many promises, but they are all lies because that is what he does the best. Satan is the father of lies. His goal is to destroy you. You can only play with sin so long before you will be injured very badly. There is a war going on, and the only way to win is through knowing Jesus personally and battling in prayer every day.

Matthew 3

Scribe to the Heart

"Now John wore a garment of camel's hair and a leather belt around his waist, and his food was locusts and wild honey."

(Matt. 3:4)

Point to Ponder

Be willing to be a dirtball for God.

Today's Journal

In what ways am I resisting God in order to blend in with others? Am I willing to change? How?

Prayer for the Day

Jesus, Give me strength to follow You, no matter what it looks like to others.

DIRTBALL PREACHING

JOHN THE BAPTIST was a dirtball. This guy would likely be thrown out of today's churches. He certainly wouldn't be allowed inside to preach. John didn't preach where the Pharisees were. This man did his work out in the desert. His clothes were made of camel's hair. His belt was made of leather. He ate locusts and honey.

He didn't preach a feel-good gospel message. His message was that the Messiah was coming and you better get things right. You need to confess your sins and start following God with your life. Confession means you admit your sins, and you are going to begin to do right.

Again, he was dirty. His clothes were less than stylish, and he preached about people's sin. Why would anyone even come to hear him? They came because they saw that God was behind it, and they were hearing the truth. John the Baptist prepared the way for Jesus to come and preach His message. People knew the Messiah was coming because John the Baptist told them.

God used this dirtball because he was open to God's will. John didn't base his decisions on what people thought of him. If you aren't willing to serve God no matter what other people think of you, God can't use you to be a John the Baptist. If you aren't willing, you aren't usable at all!

Are you willing to be a dirtball preacher for God? Are you willing to tell your friends about Jesus, even if they laugh at you? Are you willing to serve your church in areas that are uncomfortable for you? Do all those around you know you walk with Jesus? God is looking for people who will serve Him; not to look good, but so He will look good. John was willing to be a dirtball. He was willing to tell the truth. He was willing to stand in the desert and tell people to repent. This dirtball got the privilege of baptizing Jesus. What are you willing to do for God?

Matthew 4

Scribe to the Heart

"But he answered, 'It is written, Man shall not live by bread alone, but by every word that comes from the mouth of God.'"

(Matt. 4:4)

Point to Ponder

God is our life source.

Today's Journal

Do I trust in God alone to satisfy me? Do I look to other sources for life? What are they?

Prayer for the Day

Lord, Give me life today through Your Spirit.

SOURCES OF LIFE

IN MATTHEW CHAPTER 2, Satan tried to destroy the little baby Jesus. He wasn't able to because God the Father protected Him. Even though we are only in chapter 4, Jesus is now much older. He is about thirty years old and He has just been baptized.

Satan still is working hard to get at our Messiah. He couldn't kill him as a baby, but now he is going to try to tempt Him to go off-course and sin. Something to notice in the last chapter is the conversation between Jesus and John the Baptist. Jesus decided to become one of us humans. John knew he wasn't worthy to baptize Jesus (Matthew 3:14). Jesus told John it was the right thing to do to fulfill all righteousness. At this, John went along with it by faith, while probably still not fully understanding.

John's baptism was about repenting. Jesus didn't need to repent, but He was going to pay for all of our sins when He got to the cross. He was going to take the sin responsibility off of humanity. Again, Jesus didn't sin, but decided to take the responsibility for it.

Jesus knew where His life source was—God the Father. First, Satan tried to get Him to transform stones into bread. Jesus lets him know that physical food isn't His only life source. The words that come from God are a life source.

Satan next puts Him on the Temple. Jesus told Satan that he wasn't to put the Lord to the test. Obedience is a source of life. If you aren't living in obedience to God, He will not allow you to live according to the fulfilling mission He has planned for you.

Finally, Satan makes the empty promise of giving Jesus this entire fallen world. In reality, Jesus came to take back the world. Satan, however, wanted Jesus to worship *him*. Jesus told Satan to get lost because another source of life is our worship to God. Knowing God's Word, living in obedience, and worshipping only Him are sources of life that defeat Satan, just as Jesus showed us.

Matthew 5

Scribe to the Heart

"You therefore must be perfect, as your heavenly Father is perfect."

(Matt. 5:48)

Point to Ponder

Following Jesus is extreme.

Today's Journal

Am I living the extreme life Jesus calls me to in this chapter? How? In what ways am I not?

Prayer for the Day

Holy Spirit, Give me the power to live my life to the extreme.

EXTREMES

"WHY DO I go to extremes?" Billy Joel asks that question in one of his old hits. Jesus started His earthly ministry with extremes right out of the gate. In chapter four, Jesus physically healed people. He also called some of the first disciples.

These next three chapters deal with what is called The Sermon on the Mount. If you study it, you will see it is an actual sermon. It has an introduction, a main point, several supporting points, and a close. Notice something: He didn't start out in a passive voice—Jesus went to extremes in His message right from the get-go. The problem people have with following Jesus is that He makes it clear that He wants total commitment.

No one goes to practice once a week and expects to be good at anything. To play a sport or an instrument you need to practice for hours. Olympic athletes train their whole lives, hoping for one shot at a medal. Why is it in Christianity that we think we can be good Christians when we don't pray much, read our Bibles, talk about the Lord with other people, or serve Him with our time? We want to win without going to practice.

Jesus' message here is extreme. He says not only should you not murder, but if you are even mad at someone you are in danger of the fires of hell. Not only, "don't commit adultery," but if you have lusted after another person you already have done so in your heart. If someone slaps you across the face it is better to give him the other cheek instead of fighting. Roman soldiers used to make the Jews carry their heavy armor for a mile. This took the load off of the soldier, even though it wasn't fair to the civilian Jew. Jesus told the Jews take the armor and walk with them for two miles.

The Sermon on the Mount lessons are extreme. If you strive to live according to the message in these three chapters, you are extreme. The world is your practice field. You are becoming a better Christian every single day. Jesus teaches you should pray for those who want to hurt you. Be perfect as your heavenly Father is perfect. These are hard things! The only way to accomplish them is through prayer and with Jesus' help. It is impossible for us to truly wish well for our enemies and be perfect. Only Jesus is perfect. We need to let Jesus in.

Matthew 6

Scribe to the Heart

"Beware of practicing your righteousness before other people in order to be seen by them, for then you will have no reward from your Father who is in heaven."

(Matt. 6:1)

Point to Ponder

God wants you to be real with Him.

Today's Journal

What do I need to say to God that is "real"? What have I been hiding from myself?

Prayer for the Day

Dear God, Show me the areas that I've been trying to hide. Help me to be real with You today.

LET'S GET REAL

IN MATTHEW 5 we talked about how Jesus asks us to go to extremes in The Sermon on the Mount. In chapter 6, Jesus is still telling us how to be extreme, but He is also telling us to get real. This chapter is about getting real with God. God sees everything we do and we can't hide anything from Him. However, many are good at hiding their own sins from themselves. We are usually quicker to see the sins of others before we see sin within ourselves. A Christian may have an ugly sin in his or her life because he/she doesn't recognize it as a sin. They continue doing it because other Christians condone it as OK. Sometimes certain sins even make us look more spiritual. Jesus warns against giving so that other people see you doing it. Some people do good deeds or serve in the church so that people will see them. If they were asked to do something where people didn't see them, they would not follow through with that act. People want their pastor to know they go to church; and they stay home when the pastor is on vacation. The things we want others to see are strange, and they can be sin.

Jesus tells us that when we fast, we are not to show it. We should go about our business. We should not seek pity. It is not about other people seeing how spiritual you are. It is an act of worship and obedience to God. When we worship God in ways like this, He tends to do miraculous things and gives us miraculous witnessing opportunities. We are not to show off how spiritual we are like a bunch of Pharisees. We are to follow the teachings of Jesus the Christ. We are to be real with God and the people around us. That is what God is looking for: someone who will get real with Him.

Matthew 7

Scribe to the Heart

"Ask, and it will be given to you; seek and you will find; knock, and it will be opened to you. For everyone who asks receives, and the one who seeks finds, and to the one who knocks it will be opened."

(Matt. 7:7-8)

Point to Ponder

Seek Jesus and you will find Jesus.

Today's Journal

What does seeking Jesus look like in my life? What do I need to change to truly seek Him in all things?

Prayer for the Day

Lord Jesus, I seek You today. Let me find You in every situation I face.

IF YOU SEEK, YOU WILL FIND

SOME OF YOU have Bibles where most of the text is red in color between Matthew 5:3–7:27. The words are all red because Jesus is speaking them. Some people believe The Sermon on the Mount was not truly a sermon, that Matthew just compiled a bunch of things Jesus said and put them all into one section. I don't believe that's true because this is very clearly a sermon from Jesus. This message has an introduction (5:3-12, a main point (5:13-14, the main body of the message that supports the main topic (5:17- 7:23), and an intense call to commitment in its conclusion (7:24- 27).

If you are ever seeking an answer and you don't know where to turn, turn to the manuscript of Jesus' sermon. It is riveting, life-changing, and different from any other sermon. That is why the people were amazed and recognized Him as a person of spiritual authority who was greater than their normal religious teachers. Throughout the message, Jesus lays out this impossible standard of righteousness. The conclusion of the message is a command to build your house on the Rock.

In the midst of all of this, I want you to notice an important promise Jesus gives us in today's verse. If you seek Jesus, you will find Him. I am not only talking about salvation. Jesus will touch your hurts. You'll find Him in your pain. Jesus is with you all the time because you are looking for Him.

There is one fundamental difference between a mature believer and a baby Christian. Mature believers look to Jesus. When money is tight, they seek God. When they are tempted by sin, they seek God. When they are angry, they seek God. When they need direction in their life, they seek God. When they are empty, they seek God. When they are successful and content, they still seek God. Jesus promised we would find Him if we sought Him. If you can't find Him, I would contend that you need to truly look.

Matthew 8

Scribe to the Heart

"And behold, a leper came to him and knelt before him, saying, 'Lord, if you will, you can make me clean.' And Jesus stretched out his hand and touched him, saying, 'I will; be clean.'"

(Matt. 8:2-3)

Point to Ponder

Jesus is willing to reach out and heal your unclean life.

Today's Journal

If I put myself in this story, how would I feel if I were the leper? One of the disciples? Jesus, Himself?

Prayer for the Day

Lord Jesus, Show me those in my midst who need healing. Heal me where I need healing.

IF YOU ARE WILLING

WHEN HIV AND the AIDS virus initially began to spread, people were not sure where it came from or how it was contracted. There is still no cure. We now know it can only be transmitted through blood contact, but originally people felt they could contract it much like a cold. Out of fear, people began to shun people with this disease and acted hateful, just to keep them away.

In ancient times, leprosy was the disease people feared. Only it truly was highly contagious. Lepers were shunned from society. They lived away from their families and had to find means of supporting themselves outside of the community. Sometimes they would team up together with other lepers. Just imagine for a second how lepers dreamed that someone could help them. The dream was ridiculous, since everyone was afraid to be around them.

Then a dreamer catches the glimpse of a man. This man is said to be the Christ, the Messiah, the very Son of God. He thinks about approaching Him, but is afraid. After all, *"This is the Son of God!"* But in faith and utter desperation he goes to meet Jesus. He asks to be healed and he is healed! He asks if Jesus is willing, because most people were not willing to pray for him. They didn't want to touch him. But Jesus Christ reaches out His hand. He then does only what the Son of God would do. It was a moment in which He could have declared publicly that He was God. He could have drawn more people to Himself. However, in wisdom, Jesus asks for the man to give testimony to the priests, and go to worship. Jesus did not want a big deal made about Him.

Jesus knew it would get around. He focused on the man who needed Him. Jesus is willing to reach out and touch your unclean life today.

Matthew 9

Scribe to the Heart

"As Jesus passed on from there, he saw a man called Matthew sitting at the tax booth, and he said to him, 'Follow Me.' And he rose and followed him."

(Matt. 9:9)

Point to Ponder

A Jesus encounter will change your life.

Today's Journal

How has my life been touched by Jesus?

Prayer for the Day

Jesus, Help me to feel and act today in a way that reflects Your goodness and Your grace.

TALES OF THE FAMOUS

EVERYONE HAS A story about someone famous they happened to meet, or whom they knew before that person became popular. It might be a minor celebrity. If you are in ministry, it could be a popular pastor. If you are an athlete, you may have been on a high school or college team with someone who hit it big and went professional. You may have gone to school with a famous musician. Some people will say they knew all along there was something special or different about the one that became famous. Other times it wasn't so obvious. But in all the stories I have heard, there is none quite like this.

Matthew had settled into the margins of society. He made a good living as a tax collector. He probably wasn't well-liked by others. After all, he made his money by adding on to the tax of the people, and chances are he did quite well. There is so much that could have been said about this story, yet Matthew reveals so little.

Matthew was sitting at the tax collector's booth, going about his business, and Jesus came to him. He didn't seem to be looking for Jesus. Actually, it doesn't appear that he was looking to find anything deeper in life. It was just another day at the office. Then Jesus came. There is no reason to believe Matthew needed anything else for his life to be better. But in that moment Matthew must have had some hidden needs we aren't privy to. Maybe he was lonely. Maybe he was rich, but weighed down with guilt. Maybe he was bored. Jesus came into his life and changed it for eternity. Meeting and knowing Jesus is different from our stories about coming in contact with someone famous. He called Matthew to commit to Him, and in that moment Matthew did. Celebrities and today's cultural influencers will have their time, but when it is done, it is done. The man Jesus Christ continues to change lives today. When Matthew encountered Jesus, he left his livelihood and followed Him.

Day 31

Matthew 10

Scribe to the Heart

"Heal the sick, raise the dead, cleanse lepers, cast out demons. You received without paying; give without pay."

(Matt. 10:8)

Point to Ponder

God's calling is strange and specific.

Today's Journal

What does it mean to "take God's word and make it into a sentence"? Have I ever done that?

Prayer for the Day

Lord, Give me strength to follow You according to how You call me and what You call me to do.

STRANGE YET SPECIFIC

JESUS GAVE STRANGE yet specific instructions. When Jesus gives specific instructions, it is important to follow them to the T, even if they seem odd to you. In this passage, Jesus gave the disciples a taste of what ministry was like. He told them to go out and preach, heal, raise the dead, and even touch people who had leprosy. They were given authority. Also, it is important to note Jesus didn't ask them to leave Israel. They were not supposed to come to us (the non-Israelites) yet. They were to go to the Jews first. They also were to depend on God and those to whom they were preaching for their provisions. They didn't have a place to stay, and they were not to take extra clothes or food. It was strange; downright weird.

I am sure it felt much different on the road without having Jesus with them. They were given a taste of what the future would hold. They were to freely give out as they had been freely given to. Sometimes we are given specific instructions. God may call us to do an activity or to reach out to a friend, coworker, or family member. The longer I walk with God, the more I realize that God says what He means and it is important to get it right.

What I mean by "get it right" is there have been times that I felt God calling me to a ministry or something specific. God gave me a word or a nudge in a clear direction. When God gives you a word, don't make it a sentence. I have done that. Sometimes we add to it. What if the disciples would have tried to preach to the gentiles prematurely? It would have been a disaster. They needed to be prepared to give up some customs to make themselves relevant. God may be calling you to something. If it is weird and non-specific at this point, be patient. Don't make a word into a sentence.

Matthew 11

Scribe to the Heart

"All things have been handed over to me by the Father, and no one knows the Son except the Father, and no one know the Father except the Son and anyone to whom the Son chooses to reveal him."

(Matt. 11:27)

Point to Ponder

Follow Jesus with a sure faith.

Today's Journal

Would I say I have a "sure faith" as I follow Jesus?

Prayer for the Day

Lord Jesus, I want to follow You with sureness. Show me how to do that.

FICKLE PEOPLE

PEOPLE ARE FASCINATING. We change our minds all the time. We go with the crowd. Listen to what people said about Jesus and John the Baptist. *"For John came neither eating nor drinking, and they say, 'He has a demon.' The Son of Man came eating and drinking, and they say, 'Look at him! A glutton and a drunkard, a friend of tax collectors and sinners!' Yet wisdom is justified by her deeds"* (Matthew 11:18-19).

It seems that great people are able to rise above what people think about them. I recently watched a documentary on Mike Ditka, the football coach of the great 1985 Chicago Bears. It was filled with stories about working hard and going against the grain. He didn't care what people thought of him, and was downright rude with the media. One of the major themes was "be your own person, because the media is fickle." Great people do this. They do it well because what makes someone great is they are different.

It was no different 2,000 years ago. People were as fickle then, as they are now. Listen to what was said about John the Baptist and Jesus: *John is demon-possessed. Jesus is not fasting, and is eating and drinking with sinners.* People usually find ways to bring others down. It is much easier than answering the call to greatness. Being a Christian is a special calling. It is a call to uniqueness. God asks us to do weird things. We are called to grow and go against the grain. Following Jesus takes commitment and an assurance that most do not have. That assurance is to be found and maintained through our connection to Jesus Christ.

Day 33

Matthew 12

Scribe to the Heart

"I tell you, something greater than the temple is here."

(Matt. 12:6)

Point to Ponder

Jesus is greater than religion.

Today's Journal

Do I ever let my religious thoughts interfere with Jesus?

Prayer for the Day

Jesus, Give me clear thinking in regards to following You and religious thinking.

JESUS > TEMPLE

IN ANCIENT TIMES, to be considered a good worshipper of Yahweh, you followed the Law that was given to Moses. This Law is found in the books Moses authored, which are the first five books of the Old Testament (Also called the Pentateuch.) The Pharisees reprimanded Jesus because the disciples did not follow a Sabbath Day law. The Pharisees decided you should only walk so many steps on the Sabbath Day. You were not to pick grain or do any work. These were in support of keeping the Sabbath Day holy.

Jesus had sent the apostles into the community to spread the good news. They were hungry, so they picked some grain. In response to the Pharisees, Jesus quotes an Old Testament story about the great King David and his men. It is interesting that the Pharisees were not concerned that the apostles were picking someone else's grain. Imagine their faces when Jesus tells them, "Something greater than the temple is here." They didn't feel anyone or anything was above the Law or the temple. Jesus wanted them to see that He was greater than the temple. He was the one they were trying to connect with. The kingdom the Pharisees were waiting for had come and the church was to be its vessel.

The Pharisees would follow the Old Testament law every day, hoping to win favor with God by how many steps they took on the Sabbath Day or by attending public worship. Jesus was simply saying, "I am the one for whom you are doing these things." Aren't you just trying to connect with God? Imagine going to church every week, doing good deeds, busying yourself with the business of the church just to win God's favor. In the end you find out Jesus only wanted a relationship and was willing to do the work for you. He died. He rose. He lives today. He is the reason for religion. Don't get hung up on rituals. We were given Jesus Himself. He's the one we worship. He is the one who loves us. He is the one who is greater than the temple; even the faith and the church itself. Jesus is greater than it all. He is the reason for it all!

Matthew 13

Scribe to the Heart

"And they took offense at him. But Jesus said to them, 'A prophet is not without honor except in his hometown and in his household.'"

(Matt. 13:57)

Point to Ponder

Sinners want an excuse to dismiss a hometown prophet.

Today's Journal

Am I blind to a me to a godly messenger, because I have known them most of my life?

Prayer for the Day

Lord Jesus, I want to proceed with pure motives and a clean heart. With Your strength I can do that. Help me, Lord.

HOMETOWN HERO

EVERY HOMETOWN HAS its heroes. If you grew up watching older heroes, you may have seen them in two different lights. As a youngster trying to follow in the hero's footsteps, you'd think they could walk on water. They could do nothing wrong. You would give anything to be just a little like them one day. As an adult you see them as they are. You still see the qualities you want to emulate, but you begin to notice their faults. Sometimes the faults may be many.

There is something about community that helps us to see each other for our victories and our defeats. We become known for both our strengths and our weaknesses. Sometimes a person may even get categorized unfairly. There is something about seeing someone grow up that makes you say, "I understand them. I know who they are. I have them all figured out."

You can see how the townies may have been confused about the prophets. A prophet in the biblical sense has a godly message that addresses sin. He has loving, godly motives, but the message is confrontational in nature. When Jesus preached in His hometown, people thought they had Him all figured out (verses 54-57). They knew the family. They knew Him. They were amazed by His miracles, but it was too easy for them to dismiss Jesus. They were people without faith. They were not impressed. Not because Jesus wasn't impressive. It was because it was easy to dismiss Him as the hometown boy. The fact is people are sinful. They want to keep on sinning. The people of Nazareth took the devil's bait that Jesus was just like them, a hometown boy from Nazareth that wasn't any better than they were. Most of the time this is a safe bet, but this time, as it pertained to Jesus, they were tragically wrong.

Day 35

Matthew 14

Scribe to the Heart

"Prompted by her mother, she said, 'Give me the head of John the Baptist here on a platter."

(Matt. 14:8)

Point to Ponder

Living for God is worth it!

Today's Journal

How does John the Baptist and how he lived apply to my life?

Prayer for the Day

Jesus, Allow me to prepare the way for You in the lives of others. Let me stand for You.

THE END OF JOHN?

IN THE SONG "Imagine" the Beatles sang, "Imagine there is no heaven." Think for a moment about martyrdom. It is an ugly concept, but, as a believer, we can think of it as beautiful. We know Jesus and will live with Him, in the fellowship of the saints, for all of eternity. But, imagine for a second there is no heaven. What a tragic end it would be! From the world's perspective, a person like John could not have been more insane. John the Baptist lived on a voluntary diet of bugs and honey. His clothes were rough and he was probably dirty. He was in the hot desert, shouting so he could prepare the way of the Lord. Some likely thought, "What a nut-job. Someone should tell him to come inside or to go home!" From the world's perspective, his activities would seem like a waste of time.

To make matters worse consider for a moment the way in which he died. He was imprisoned. Herod let a female dancer decide that it was time for John's head to be chopped off. One of the most influential preachers ever was killed because a provocative dancer wanted him dead. It is appalling! We know from the gospel of Luke, John was about six months older than his cousin Jesus. So, John died at about age 30, maybe 32. It's tragic. He was young. He had his whole life ahead of him.

The words from the writer of Hebrews were not penned yet, but John certainly had this idea etched in his heart: *"Now faith is the assurance of things hoped for, the conviction of things not seen"* (Hebrews 11:1). Jesus affirmed John as being greater than anyone who has ever lived (Matthew 11:11). Jesus saw the amazing faith of John. Praise God. He doesn't judge us as the world does. John went against the grain in every way, but he lived a life of conviction. A life of conviction sometimes ends in martyrdom. This martyr lives forever as a man of faith, a man who announced Jesus' coming. He lives as a man who pleased God.

Day 36

Matthew 15

Scribe to the Heart

"She said, 'Yes, Lord, yet even the dogs eat the crumbs that fall from their masters' table.'"

(Matt. 15:27)

Point to Ponder

Jesus responds to great humility and large faith.

Today's Journal

How would I have felt if I were the Canaanite woman, approaching this man of a different ethnicity who was doing amazing things?
Would the presence of His disciples intimidate me?

Prayer for the Day

Jesus, Teach me more about what it means to have great humility and large faith.

FOOD FOR DOGS

THE STORY IN this chapter found in verses 21-28 is so strange. There is no denying the fact that Jesus is compassionate. He is walking around healing and ministering to anyone who is placed in His path. Then a Canaanite woman comes to Him. He let her carry on, and didn't send her away when the disciples asked Him to, but when He comes face to face with the woman it initially seems cold. He basically tells her that the lost sheep of Israel are the ones He is here for, and not someone like her.

The casual observer's mind is racing at this point. How could He? How dare He? Was Jesus being racist? Was Jesus being selfish? He declared what His ministry was about. He came to minister to Israel. He obviously came to save the whole world—or else this blondy from Texas wouldn't be writing about Him. However, Jesus needed to come to Israel first. The ministry would later reach the gentiles through His apostles.

Jesus declared His vision for ministry, but then still heals and has compassion on the woman. He tells her that she has great faith. She asks just to be a dog begging at the master's table. For the witnesses present this must have been confusing. Jesus had compassion on a persistent gentile. She had great faith for seeking and begging. At this point does a Jewish observer still feel entitled because of his or her heritage? Jesus calls at least some of them lost sheep. One of the most interesting ways Jesus deals with people is to give them a truth and then let the message stew. Unlike many of us ministry types who like to give away the answer, Jesus gave them lot to think about. The woman asked to be treated like a dog. He responded by calling this great faith.

Matthew 16

Scribe to the Heart

"'An evil and adulterous generation seeks for a sign, but no sign will be given to it except the sign of Jonah.' So, he left them and departed."

(Matt. 16:4)

Point to Ponder

Jesus is God. We can't make Him into our image, we are to be more like Him.

Today's Journal

Do I ever try and make God into my image? How can I break that habit?

Prayer for the Day

God, Mold me into the image of Your Son. Reveal where I am trying to mold You into my image.

TYPES OF CHRIST

THEOLOGIANS OFTEN TALK about types of Christ in the Old Testament. First, a type of Christ is typically a person found in Scripture who points us to Christ, by emulating Him in some way. They are never perfect. Joseph was a type of Christ, even though at the very beginning of his story, he appears a little boastful with his brothers.

Jonah is another type of Christ. Not because of the things we see him do in Scripture; Jonah's best examples of obedience and faith are probably not recorded in his story. Jonah was a prophet to Israel. In the Old Testament book of Jonah, we see Jonah running away from preaching to the people of Nineveh. I believe he fled, not out of fear, but out of racism. He knew God could save Nineveh, but he didn't want Him to. He didn't like the Ninevites.

When the Pharisees ask Jesus for a sign, He refers them to the sign of Jonah. Let's set the scene. The Pharisees and Sadducees are sitting around stewing over how much they don't like Jesus. They continue to try to make Him into their image. They demand a sign from Him. In their minds He owed them that. Jesus tells them there will not be a sign for a wicked generation except for the sign of Jonah.

Jonah spent three days in the belly of a large fish. He was as good as dead, but then God did a miracle. When Jesus later died on the cross, He was in the tomb for three days. Jesus was dead! Then God did a miracle. This was the sign of Jonah. The Pharisees wanted a sign on their terms, but didn't see there were signs all around them. They just needed to pay attention. The sign of Jonah was on its way!

Matthew 17

Scribe to the Heart

"He was still speaking when, behold, a bright cloud overshadowed them, and a voice from the cloud said, 'This is my beloved Son, with whom I am well pleased: listen to him.'"

(Matt. 17:5)

Point to Ponder

Jesus is Holy, yet He interacts with us.

Today's Journal

If I was the fourth disciple in that inner circle, what would I have done when I saw the transfigured Christ?

Prayer for the Day

Lord, Give me a glimpse into the beauty of Your holiness today.

THE GAP

HAVE YOU EVER noticed when someone dies everyone is suddenly affected by them? Memories of the person become magnified—for the good and the bad. Some remember the person in such a beautiful light that the deceased is almost deified, nearly sainted in their minds. To another person, the deceased might be demonized; they remember only the awful. Either way, there is an obvious gap between those who remain on earth and those who have passed on.

The word "transfigure" means to be changed into something more beautiful. Jesus' transfiguration happens on a mountain with Peter, James, and John in attendance. These three men were floored when Jesus began to shine. Then, seeing two prophets of God who had been dead for years (Moses and Elijah) shakes them up too.

The vocal message from God the Father was, "This is my Son! Listen to Him!"

Jesus is greater than the other two. Moses and Elijah, great prophets, may have had "saint status" in the minds of the apostles. They immediately wanted to build shelters for them all, but suddenly only Jesus remained. Jesus instructed that they were not to speak of what happened until after the resurrection. Something tells me this was an object lesson in the authority Jesus carried. They probably listened; afraid to say anything. It wasn't like some of the other times when Jesus raised someone to life and told the onlookers not to tell. What they had experienced shook their flesh. These men would have never forgotten it. Jesus is God. We need not add anything to His greatness.

Matthew 18

Scribe to the Heart

"Again, I say to you, if two of you agree on earth about anything they ask, it will be done for them by my Father in heaven. For where two or three are gathered in my name, there am I among them."

(Matt. 18:19-20)

Point to Ponder

The power of God is unlocked through agreement in community under Christ.

Today's Journal

Who am I in conflict with? Who do I need to reach out to?

Prayer for the Day

Lord, Give me wisdom to handle conflict as You instruct. Give me love to gently restore relationships when needed.

THE GOAL IS AGREEMENT

I ONCE HEARD a youth pastor read the passage from verses 15-20 as he taught on how to handle conflict. When he got to the part about dealing with the person who is not in agreement with the church, and treating them like a tax collector, the conclusion the youth pastor made was "do not have anything to do with them." Maybe you think this way too. I'd like to challenge that thought. Consider the fact that this book was written by a man who was sitting at the tax collector booth when Jesus found him. Jesus said, "Follow Me," and he did. His life was forever changed. Matthew then invited his friends (sinners and tax-collectors to eat with Jesus).

So, when Matthew goes through the process of conflict resolution in the church, I doubt he would want to consider himself, or any of his friends, to ever be shunned by the church.

This passage gives the way we should handle a conflict among believers and in our churches. First, go to a person one on one. Then take someone else who is more of an authority, godly or diplomatic for the purpose of talking through things and not ganging up on the person. If need be, then go to the elders and the church. If there still isn't resolution and repentance of sinful behavior the treatment changes. I think when he refers to Jesus' instructions, "treat him like a tax collector or gentile," that means, "this person is unrepentant and doesn't understand the way of God, so you must treat him as if he were outside the church." How do we treat those outside the church? We reach out to them. Seek to bring them into agreement. The goal is always reconciliation. There is no reason to believe Jesus would suggest you ignore someone. He is suggesting that they need to be evangelized to. Don't put them in a position of Christian authority, because they are acting outside of how Christ would act. Maybe this inconsistency has entered into your personal theology. Please, for Jesus' sake, stop it!

The method becomes more about how to love the person. The goal is agreement with Jesus—not with you or with church doctrine. This is what we should all be looking for.

Matthew 19

Scribe to the Heart

"Jesus said, 'Let the little children come to me and do not hinder them, for to such belongs the kingdom of heaven.'"

(Matt. 19:14)

Point to Ponder

Be like the children who depend on Jesus, not like the ruler who depends on himself.

Today's Journal

How can I approach Jesus more like the children and less like the rich young ruler?

Prayer for the Day

Jesus, Show me how to approach You as I should. If I am hanging on to anything, show me what I need to release.

GOOD VS. GODLY

TO GAIN PROPER context for any passage of Scripture, it is good practice to read what is before and after the story to get the full picture. In this chapter, before the story of the rich young ruler (verses 16-24) you see a brief incident in which children were being hindered from Jesus' presence and Jesus declares to let the little children come to Him.

Children are dependent. They have fun and don't typically get stressed out or worked up. Children know how to play. They don't hold grudges for long. Most of all they do not divide people up into social categories like adults do. This wicked sin is called entitlement.

To have an indication if someone has this sin in their life, watch how they approach a cashier or a waiter/waitress. How do they talk to children? Or, how do they treat people they are in authority over? The fact is, it is an adult sin and we all can be guilty of it in some way.

The rich young ruler had power. He had money and he had youth. He most likely hadn't seen anything he couldn't buy. Society had little to no hold on him. There is no reason (in his mind) he can't approach Jesus the same way. It is no different than when Herod looks for a sign and intensely questions Jesus in Luke 23. In Herod's thinking, Jesus owed it to him. Herod was a legend in his own mind, but Jesus didn't flatter him. The rich young ruler declared he had kept the commandments since his youth. He truly had everything going for him. But, like many who are self-made from a worldly standpoint, when Jesus called to him for commitment, he couldn't do it. He went away sad instead of giving up any of his money, social standing, time, or talent. He would have been happy going to the synagogue once a week and throwing some money in the plate. It wasn't supposed to truly cost everything.

Matthew 20

Scribe to the Heart

*"Jesus answered, 'You do not know what you are asking.
Are you able to drink the cup that I am to drink?'
They said to Him, 'We are able.'"*

(Matt. 20:22)

Point to Ponder

*Humble yourself before the Lord and He will
promote you when you are ready.*

Today's Journal

How can I better go through my day with a focus on promoting Jesus and not on promoting myself?

Prayer for the Day

Lord Jesus, I want to promote You; not me. Strengthen me to promote You.

PROMOTE ME, JESUS

OUR WORLD IS extremely fast-paced. Things can be vicious and cut-throat; especially in matters of business. Our economic situation has pushed people to reevaluate and some are not doing it very well. Some have become mean, and don't play fair. Some have gotten shadier in how they conduct business deals. Companies don't treat employees well. Loyalty is out the window.

During Jesus' day times were also tough. People went without food. Widows had no source of income. There was a type of desperation the Jews had under Roman rule. People tried to show how they were different from other workers, just as they do today. They wanted their employers to keep them around. They wanted to be valued and ultimately climb the internal ladder of success.

Jesus had just finished talking about His approaching time of death (verses 17-19) and then James and John's mother shows up (verse 21). I would have liked to have seen the original conversation, because Mark talks of James and John asking Jesus directly for the most prominent places in the kingdom, but Matthew brings their mother into the mix. Either way, this conversation was involved. It made some of the others upset. The timing appears to be awful. It often is when we try to promote ourselves.

Jesus looks at them and lets them know such things come at a price. He wants to know if they can drink from the cup He would drink. This must have been so irritating to Jesus; while He is telling them about His own death, they are lobbying for position.

We live in two separate worlds. The promote me/notice me world and the kingdom of God, which is built on humbling yourself so you can be exalted in due time (1 Peter 5:5-7). God notices your little acts of obedience. He cares about your heart. When you care for your heart, He cares for you.

Matthew 21

Scribe to the Heart

"So they answered Jesus, 'We do not know.' And he said to them, 'Neither will I tell you by what authority I do these things.'"

(Matt. 21:27)

Point to Ponder

There is a major difference between religious control and godly obedience.

Today's Journal

In what ways does my religious thinking interfere with my relationship with God and with others?

Prayer for the Day

God, Break me of my religious thinking. Extinguish it so I can grow my relationship with You. Amen.

DIDN'T WE PUT CONTROLS IN PLACE?

IN THIS CHAPTER Jesus is welcomed into Jerusalem. People are beginning to catch on and understand. He is riding on a colt, just like Isaiah promised over 700 years prior. The people are praising Him. In only five short days He will go to the cross. There will be some women, one of His apostles, and some others there for Him. The masses will have chanted for His death. Most of His apostles will have run and hid.

In Mark 11 we will focus more on Jesus' clearing of the temple (also found in this chapter). The shady exploitation of the poor provoked Jesus. The parables Jesus chooses to tell are aimed strongly at the Pharisees in this chapter. Jesus knows they are taking Him to the cross soon and the need to teach the people about the current religious system, and to address the Pharisees, is intense. His time is short.

The Pharisees try to trap Jesus. They may have had Him arrested too early if He had answered wrong, but our perfect Savior answered perfectly. They asked Him where His authority to do the things He was doing came from? Jesus, knowing what they were doing, put it back on them and asked about John the Baptist. The people loved John. If the Pharisees answered positively about John, they were acknowledging someone as a prophet who they didn't want to honor. Had they talked badly about John they would have angered the crowd. The brilliant Pharisees come up with the answer, "We don't know." Jesus tells them that He is not to tell them by what authority He does these things.

The religious are frustrated more than anything with their inability to control people. They needed to get rid of Jesus because He was a threat to them. They were thinking, "Didn't we have controls put in place? How did this guy work his way in here?"

Jesus opens things up and shows us truth. He reveals our wickedness so we can have a true relationship with God. He wants us to rid ourselves of strong religious bondage that holds us hostage. Some religious thinking is so strong that if Jesus Himself stood in front of a person they wouldn't see their error. It is our responsibility to humbly seek God daily.

Matthew 22

Scribe to the Heart

"But Jesus answered them, 'You are wrong, because you know neither the Scriptures nor the power of God.'"

(Matt. 22:29)

Point to Ponder

Relationships in heaven will be beyond our wildest dreams and the barriers of earth.

Today's Journal

Are there areas where my lack of knowledge of Scripture keep me from having pure Christian relationships? What can I do?

Prayer for the Day

Lord, Give me a pure heart to love others.

HOW GREAT IS THE LOVE OF GOD?

I REMEMBER HOW radiant and beautiful Heidi looked walking down the aisle on our wedding day. In the perfect dress, she was so happy to see me there. She smiled. She believed it was right and wanted to start her life with me. Since then we have been through many things together. She is my best friend on earth.

Many romantics curse at the story we are looking at today, because talking about marriage and the kingdom of God together makes for a hard passage (verses 1-14). The Sadducees, who didn't believe in a resurrection at all, tried to trip up Jesus on His afterlife doctrine (verses 23-33). They basically wanted to know who is married to whom in the kingdom if a woman outlives seven husbands. Here on earth this kind of situation gets tense, and they try and make it seem even more so for heaven.

Jesus gives them an interesting answer. He tells them they do not know the Scriptures or the power of God. This would have been very insulting for them because they were people who read Scripture and tried to follow their religion closely. It was then stated people will be like the angels. This means not married and possibly not even gendered. People will be with the God of the living.

The teaching doesn't stop there. The teaching continues with the Great Commandment. We are to love God with everything and our neighbors as ourselves. If we do this perfectly, we are doing everything right.

I believe the Bible teaches our relationships matter here and it is reasonable to believe that a husband and wife will still have a special bond in heaven. However, be careful. Don't insert your feelings into the text. Part of reading the Bible is reading the Bible and not the Bible reading you. Take into account Jesus' main point here, and realize our continuing relationships do not seem to be a part of this text. The point Jesus is making is we don't even begin to understand what our relationships can be like without all of the games we play. We can have pure relationships with God and others in heaven. It is beyond the love we know on earth. It is not to make us sad, but to give wonder, amazement, and a marvelous hope.

Matthew 23

Scribe to the Heart

"O Jerusalem, Jerusalem, the city that kills prophets and stones those who are sent to it! How often would I have gathered your children together as a hen gathers her brood under her wings, and you would not!"

(Matt. 23:37)

Point to Ponder

*Be careful of the system.
Follow Jesus and be led only by those who also follow Jesus.*

Today's Journal

What does the Bible say is God's intention for the church? What can I learn from Jesus' rebuke to the Pharisees?

Prayer for the Day

Holy Spirit, show me the difference between man-made religion and true godliness.

O JERUSALEM, JERUSALEM

JESUS' TIME IS drawing near. The Passover is on the way. Very soon the Pharisees will complete their conspiracy and end the earthly life of Jesus. Jesus ups the intensity.

In my Bible the added subtitle for verses 1-36 reads: "Seven Woes to the Scribes and Pharisees." Jesus says, "Woe" out of deep rebuke. We need to read these verses slowly to truly understand what He is saying. He talks to them about what a mess they are on the inside, even though they try to look so good on the outside. They are like extremely clean graves. He talks about their ability to find converts but then make them twice the sons of hell as they are. He talks about their greed; how they make it harder for people to see the kingdom of God. These words were not taken lightly I am sure.

He then speaks of them as murders of prophets. Even though they say they would never have killed God's prophets, Jesus knows differently. He tells them that they would have done just that. There is no doubt that Jesus is challenging the Pharisees with a strong rebuke.

Here is the most surprising part. People were making their way to Jerusalem for the feast as He spoke. Many were already there. Jesus was standing in Jerusalem slamming the practices of the city. He moves on from the Pharisees and talks about Jerusalem as a city that kills prophets. The inhabitants of Jerusalem were unwilling to be drawn by Jesus.

The religious center of the world for the Jews was and still is Jerusalem. Yet Jesus says He is departing and they will not see Him until they say, "Blessed is He who comes in the name of the Lord." It looks like a reference to His return. Jerusalem is going to be in the dark for thousands of years. The entire religious establishment was corrupt. As He provokes them, they help Him complete His mission. They put Him on a cross. He was the sinless Lamb of God who placed Himself on the cross to atone for the sin of the world.

Matthew 24

Scribe to the Heart

"But concerning that day and hour no one knows, not even the angels of heaven, nor the Son, but the Father only. As were the days of Noah, so will be the coming of the Son of Man."

(Matt. 24:36-37)

Point to Ponder

Look at each passage as though seeing it for the first time.

Today's Journal

What presuppositions that I hold interfere with my understanding of Scripture?

Prayer for the Day

Holy Spirit, When I look into the Word of God, reveal new things to me. Allow me to be open to seeing them.

ADVENTURES IN THEOLOGY

IF YOU WANT an adventure in theology this chapter is where things get fun. If you are set in your ways as to what your "end of days" theology (eschatology) is, then you might not like this entry so much. In this chapter Jesus instructs the disciples both on events they will be around to see and some they will not. In yesterday's entry Jesus rebuked the Pharisees before finally bringing it all home to Jerusalem. Jesus presented Jerusalem as a city that killed prophets and was not as pleasing to God as some might think.

Jesus then goes right into the temple. The temple in Jerusalem was the center of the Jewish faith. The temple that took forty years to build would eventually be destroyed. Jesus told them every stone would be thrown down. This type of event would have been catastrophic to a Jewish believer. With killing involved it would be considered a worse attack than 9/11 was to our modern world. They would have seen it as an attack on heritage, nationality, religion, and security. People associated the temple as the home of God. The event Jesus prophesied happened in A.D. 70.

Then Jesus begins to speak about several things. He gives the disciples instructions for the persecution they will face. He also refers to His return; which we know is a future event.

I find verses 36-37 to be the most fascinating verses in this text. There is a real movement among some groups to map out exactly what the end of the world will be like. There are very popular systems that use date references to walk us through exact timelines as to when the Son of Man will return.

I do not knock their contribution, nor do I want to alienate them. I want to challenge this thinking. I encourage you to dig deep. We have all of the tools available to help us understand exactly what the original audience would have heard, and how they would have heard it. We have other believers and leaders to walk with us. My exhortation today is to dig deeper. Jesus didn't give us maps and graphs. He gave us specific instructions mixed with mystery for a reason.

Matthew 25

Scribe to the Heart

"Before Him will be gathered all the nations, and He will separate people one from another as a shepherd separates the sheep from the goats."

(Matt. 25:32)

Point to Ponder

Sheep follow the shepherd. Goats depend on themselves.

Today's Journal

Do I hear the voice of the Shepherd when He speaks to me? What can I do today to put myself in a better position to hear from Him?

Prayer for the Day

Lord Jesus, Thank You for being the Good Shepherd. Guide me and protect me from my enemies. Allow me to better hear Your voice.

HERE SHEEP, SHEEP, SHEEP...

IN THIS CHAPTER, Jesus continues to talk about events concerning the end and continues to prepare the disciples for events they would see in their lifetime. The apostles probably didn't understand the difference. Jesus doesn't seem to want to make a distinction to them either. He has very specific points to make. In typical Jesus fashion, He teaches them using parables.

He includes a seemingly odd parable about sheep and goats. I have only personally known of a few people who have had goats as pets. Heidi and I know someone named Jaimie who has spoken often of Odie the Goaty. Jaimie spoke positively of her favorite "Goaty" as a pet. However, overall, goats are not affectionate animals. They like to be alone, they do their own thing, and they do not listen to a shepherd's voice.

Sheep are not smart. They are not particularly advantaged in the wild. On their resume they have no special skills and, oh, did I mention they have a reputation for being not smart? I want that to be clear: sheep are dumb! However, it seems that Jesus calls us (His followers) sheep. He wants us to listen to His voice and not depend on ourselves. Ultimately, we answer to Him.

A shepherd would sort goats and sheep according to which animals would listen to his voice. A goat is likely to go its own way and a sheep will listen to the master. From a distance they look the same. They might even look similar up close, there is no fooling the master. He knows the sheep.

Matthew 26

Scribe to the Heart

"You know that after two days the Passover is coming, and the Son of Man will be delivered up to be crucified."

(Matt. 26:2)

Point to Ponder

Live a life that sees God, and not your position on the Ferris wheel.

Today's Journal

Do I ride the emotional Ferris wheel? How can I have peace, no matter what storm I face?

Prayer for the Day

Holy Spirit, When storms come upon me, give me peace. Strengthen me, just as Jesus was strengthened in connection to the Father.

GET OFF OF THE FERRIS WHEEL

FROM TODAY'S READING I want you to see that in life, you must fight not to get caught up in your position on the Ferris wheel. The Ferris wheel at an amusement park usually has a long line. Some parks are known for having one of significant height. It may be advertised as the highest in the world, or in a certain area of the country. At the top, you can see the entire park and beyond. The moment you reach the very top you begin to go back down. At the very bottom you begin to go back up again. I'd like you to picture this as the wheel of life.

It has been said, "We are either in a storm right now or about to be in one." That is life! Bad things happen. Life is hard. But God is good. The wheel will begin to go back up again. But, your perspective, obedience to God, and emotional stability do not have to be subject to the wheel. You can have peace regardless of your circumstances. You can choose to live in obedience and prayerful connection with God no matter what. Life should not be dictated by the wheel. The Christian life finds God working all things out for those who are His (Romans 8:28). This life is free.

Jesus is quite aware of this. I imagine the disciples were having an emotionally great moment in this chapter. Jesus just really socked it to the Pharisees and the entire religious system. He spoke of the temple coming down. He did a great teaching. The disciples would have been awestruck. Not to mention Jesus just had received a hero's welcome into town. Their thought must have been, "The Messiah has finally come to make things right."

But, in the near future Jesus would endure much pain. The last supper would have been a powerful spiritual moment. In it, we see the prediction and the fulfillment of Jesus' betrayal from Judas. Then, Jesus has this ultra-lonely moment praying at Gethsemane. Worst of all, we see it all begin. Jesus is condemned and tortured. But, His connection to the Father kept Him from being a "Ferris wheel" believer. The storm was strong but He had a job to do. Jesus was prepared and we can be, too. Live a life that is full of peace. Live a life that sees God and not your position on the Ferris wheel.

Matthew 27

Scribe to the Heart

"And about the ninth hour Jesus cried out with a loud voice, saying 'Eli, Eli, lema sabachthani?' that is, 'My God, my God, why have you forsaken me?'"

(Matt. 27:46)

Point to Ponder

Connection to the Father is the only way to get through hard times.

Today's Journal

Why did Jesus need to connect with God? What do I learn from His last moments on earth?

Prayer for the Day

Father, Thank You that I can connect with You. Keep me close. Keep my perspective true.

TWO DEATHS

THERE ARE SO many important things to look at in a chapter dealing with Jesus being delivered, tortured, and ultimately dying on a cross. However, I would like to consider the contrast between two deaths that we read about in chapter 27.

Judas is left without excuse. He betrayed the Christ. To paraphrase, it is said, "it would have been better for him to have never been born" (Mark 14:21). Judas walked daily with the Son of God for three and a half years and then betrayed him. Oddly, enough Judas was dead before Jesus was. Judas was a Ferris wheel type of guy. Imagine, the Son of God was right in front of Him. He could have connected with Him all the time. But his emotions and behavior went up and down to extremes.

Jesus went through much pain in this chapter. He was publicly humiliated and tortured. Through it all, His connection to the Father was vital. It was a source of strength for Him to endure what He faced. He prayed so hard in Gethsemane that His sweat became thick like drops of blood (Luke 22:44). The pressure was immense. He was taking on the sin of humanity. He would defeat the devil and redeem the world. It would be painful and hard. There's no room for Ferris wheel thinking on this mission.

On the cross, Jesus cried out some interesting words (Matt 27:46). Many critics of the faith have used them to try to tear down Christianity. Jesus was actually quoting from a psalm that was written by King David during a time of his own great duress, but, as is the case with many Old Testament references, the wording is prophetic to our Christ. It gets its final fulfillment in Jesus' crucifixion, even though it was written hundreds of years prior. Jesus didn't feel strong physically, but He drew from the strength He had through God the Father. He drew from the scriptures that were in His heart.

In summary, Jesus stayed connected to the Father. He fought for His spiritual well-being and ours in these vital hours. Judas gave in to temptation due to his perspective from the Ferris wheel of life. He caved for so little. Jesus' connection to the Father was proven untouchable.

Matthew 28

Scribe to the Heart

"Go therefore and make disciples of all nations, baptizing them in the name of the Father and of the Son and of the Holy Spirit, teaching them to observe all that I have commanded you."

(Matt. 28:19-20)

Point to Ponder

Follow God's plan! His plan is the Great Commission!

Today's Journal

What is my calling? How does God want me to fulfill the Great Commission?

Prayer for the Day

Father, Use the Holy Spirit to reveal to me the calling You have on my life.

GOOD INTENTIONS

IT HAS BEEN said there is a certain type of asphalt on the road to hell. It is a pavement of good intentions. I don't know that I fully agree with that saying, however, I have experienced something that causes deep reflection. At the end of this chapter we find the famous verses known as The Great Commission. Matthew 28:18-20 is the full statement and reads: *"And Jesus came and said to them, 'All authority in heaven and on earth has been given to Me. Go therefore and make disciples of all nations, baptizing them in the name of the Father and of the Son and of the Holy Spirit, teaching them to observe all that I have commanded you. And behold, I am with you always, to the end of the age.'"*

We are to go into the world and give Jesus to people. Making disciples means we are to make them followers, not just dependent people in a church pew, but vibrant, life-giving people who make this world better. They are to represent Jesus on earth. Our own conversions stem from the obedience of these original apostles and many disciples after. Now it is our turn.

Notice Jesus declares the authority after the Resurrection was given to Him. Therefore, the apostles and disciples of Jesus from then on are commissioned to go. Our connection to Jesus is vital. We are to go where He tells us. We do not get to decide which battles we fight. Tragic things happen to people when they decide for themselves where God is leading them.

In light of the last two chapter entries I'd like you to spend time in reflection on this. I am speaking from experience: Going off on your own idea and walking in God's will can look very much the same at first glance. Unfortunately, the outcome is very different. So, what is it God is calling you to do? In what way does He want you to fulfill the Great Commission? There is no feeling like when you are doing exactly what God wants you to be doing and He blesses you in the moment beyond what you could ever ask, think, or imagine. (Ephesians 3:20) There is no feeling like it because God has granted you the ability to help shape eternity. Don't be timid or scared. Pray through it. It takes a great amount of connection, reflection, and self-awareness. You may find it initially hard to put into words but I know you will find it.

Mark 1

Scribe to the Heart

"John appeared, baptizing in the wilderness and proclaiming a baptism of repentance for the forgiveness of sins."

(Mark 1:4)

Point to Ponder

Each gospel was written with a specific audience in mind.

Today's Journal

Mark's gospel gives the bottom line for what we need to know. Do I see the value of understanding the gospel from a bottom-line standpoint?

Prayer for the Day

Lord Jesus, When I talk to people about You, give me an awareness of how to speak so it is relevant and specific to whom I am speaking.

IMMEDIATELY!

A MAN NAMED John Mark recorded what we know as the book of Mark. Evidence seems to indicate it was the first gospel written. It is dated shortly after the destruction of the Jewish temple in Jerusalem in 70 A.D. Mark wrote the gospel as if he were writing to a Roman audience. The Romans' mindset was much like that of shrewd American businessmen today: *Tell me the bottom line, or the main idea. Don't give me details I don't need.* Mark is a very easy gospel for us to relate to because of our culture.

Matthew and Mark contain much of the same information. Mark is just a shorter version of it. 90% of what you'll see in Mark you can also see in the book of Matthew. Mark is more to the point. Matthew was writing for the Jews and he explains more in regards to Jewish tradition. As such, Matthew's gospel also includes more Old Testament references than you will find in Mark's.

The most common adverb in the book of Mark is "immediately." There is a fast-paced feel to his writing. Mark's gospel starts with the appearance of John the Baptist on the Jewish scene. John is preparing the way. It doesn't start with Jesus' genealogy and birth, as Matthew did. Jesus is already an adult at the beginning of Mark's gospel, and we see right away the situation is urgent.

Although he does not quote a lot of Old Testament references, in this first chapter he does quote from the prophet Isaiah. This would have been 700 years, give or take, after it was originally written. He quotes Isaiah to give context for who John the Baptist was. John's mission was to prepare the way for the Lord. Get ready! You are about to get an extremely quick glance at the life and ministry of Jesus through the book of Mark.

Mark 2

"I say to you, rise, pick up your bed and go home."

(Mark 2:11)

Point to Ponder

Wow moments show you the difference between dead religion and a life-giving God who loves you.

Today's Journal

The last wow moment I remember from God was...

Prayer for the Day

Jesus, I pray for You to show me the wow moments in my midst. Do not let me be distracted and miss them. Amen.

WOW!

I WENT TO church while I was growing up. There were days that I felt like I learned something. I enjoyed it. People seemed to care about me. It was an atmosphere where I could be myself. I was accepted. I learned how to pray, and what it meant to pray. I even had God moments in my childhood in which I know I truly experienced God.

When I got older, I committed my life to Jesus Christ (you don't have to wait until you are older, that is just how it happened for me). Leading up to this event and after, the wow moments began! I remember when I first really became burdened for evangelism. I sensed a deep urgency for family, friends, teammates, and strangers to know Jesus. It was overwhelming, yet very fulfilling, to know I was called to this and that part of my purpose is following God in this way.

I was also extremely humbled when, following my speaking, students and adults would weep and desire to follow a God who loved them. I am thankful for each wow moment.

In this passage, the crowds watched Jesus preach, saw Him declare forgiveness of sins, and heal people. A man actually was lowered through the roof where Jesus was speaking! Jesus forgave and healed him. Then the man got up and walked away. If that isn't a wow moment, I don't know what is! The people stated they'd never seen anything like it. They were in wonderment. They saw true God moments through Jesus. When God gives you a wow moment, you see up close the difference between dead religion and a life-giving God who loves you. Embrace and remember those.

Mark 3

"Whenever the evil spirits saw Him, they fell down before Him and cried out, 'You are the Son of God.' But He gave them strict orders not to tell who He was."

(Mark 3:11-12)

Point to Ponder

Jesus is concerned with touching every human life you encounter.

Today's Journal

In my life, how can I touch other lives in a meaningful way and keep it under the radar?

Prayer for the Day

Lord, Help me touch the lives of the people You put in my path. Show me how to do this while keeping the focus on You.

DON'T TELL ANYONE

THE LATE GREAT Reggie White is a hero of mine. As a church-going youngster who had not yet committed my life to Jesus Christ I cheered for a Reggie White-led defense every week. The Philadelphia Eagles from those years are often discussed as one of the all-time great defenses. The fact that they are in the conversation without any Super Bowl experience during those seasons is spectacular. Reggie White was known as the Minister of Defense. He was a leader on and off the field. He averaged over a sack a game while playing for the Eagles, and was vocal and active about a love for Jesus Christ. Those who played with him said he didn't judge or Bible-beat people. He lovingly remained strong and unshakable in his walk.

Every Tuesday Reggie would go into the poorer neighborhoods of Philadelphia. He brought food, hung out with kids, and talked to them about Jesus. A sports columnist once asked if he could go with him. Reggie White told him, "I will let you go on one condition, if you *don't* write about it." I believe Reggie never wanted the focus of his activity to change. He wanted Jesus to be lifted up. I also believe he wanted kids and others to be reached. He even wanted the writer to be touched as well. He obviously wanted to do things for the right reasons.

It is hard to speculate why Jesus was healing and displaying power and would not want people to say anything about it. Demons declared who He was. There were signs and wonders. It truly was something to talk about. I think more than anything He remained focused on touching the people in front of Him. When we do great things for God, others see it. We can have a great influence on others by living for Jesus, and acting on Jesus' behalf in front of them.

Day 53

Mark 4

Scribe to the Heart

"He also said, 'This is what the kingdom of God is like. A man scatters seed on the ground. Night and day, whether he sleeps or gets up, the seed sprouts and grows, though he does not know how."

(Mark 4:26-27)

Point to Ponder

God's will can be found when we love Jesus more than anything else.

Today's Journal

Do I spread the seed (the word of God) often and without worry?

Prayer for the Day

Lord Jesus, Make me fearless as I scatter the seed. Let me trust You to make the sprouts grow.

WHAT MAKES US DIFFERENT?

AS WE WORK through the book of Mark at rocket-speed, we will see more chapters like this one that contain several stories that deserve to be talked about. Mark 4 includes the famous discussions about the Mustard Seed and the Parable of the Sower. Jesus also teaches we are to be a lamp on display, and not in a hidden place. Jesus even calms a deadly storm in this passage.

Sometimes passages get overlooked just because of personal preference. The most overlooked parable in this chapter is in verses 26-29. It is possibly Jesus' most encouraging words for me in regards to ministering to the world around us. It is what makes us different.

Preachers, teachers, and parents do their best to teach others about Jesus. We write lessons and labor over the Bible. You may stay up late into the night trying to think of new ways to present Jesus' messages. Sometimes, especially when dealing with children and youth, you may think you are not getting through. But then you have the moment! The moment when the one you were trying to teach quotes you, and you think, "How did they get it? They were distracting the others. They were not listening." Our job is to be like the man and throw the seed. Don't stay up all night and worry about it. Throw a lot of seed. God makes the seed grow, not us. The word of God, when it goes out of our mouths, is doing its work whether we stay awake or go to sleep (Isaiah 55:11). We don't know how it works, but we can trust that it does.

Mark 5

Scribe to the Heart

"So the man went away and began to tell in the Decapolis how much Jesus had done for Him. And all the people were amazed."

(Mark 5:20)

Point to Ponder

We can reach thousands by just allowing God to change us in front of others.

Today's Journal

Do people see a difference in me because I have been touched by Jesus?

Prayer for the Day

Jesus, I want my friends and family to see a change in me because I have been touched by You. Allow me to have a good witness.

AN UNLIKELY EVANGELIST

OUTSIDERS TO THE church are quick to notice when religious people do not want to get their hands dirty. We are good at inviting people to come to us. However, when someone does what we are actually called by God to do, to go out into the world and serve, it can seem surprising. It is an oddity to see people out on the streets feeding the hungry, clothing the poor, or taking the gospel message to the public. Jesus went into the gentile region of the Gerasenes. He comes across a man who was demon-possessed (unclean), dirty (unclean), and was located at a place where pigs (unclean animals) were being raised. Jesus encounters this man who no one can contain (dangerous). Upon Jesus' demand, the demons declare who they are, and He casts the demons into the pigs. The probable embankment where this encounter took place can be seen today, and one of the features is its steep slope. Once a pig began to run down the hill it wouldn't be able to stop. It says the demons were cast into a group of pigs which numbered 2,000.

Once healed, this man asked to go with Jesus and the other disciples. He was truly touched by God. No one had wanted to be around him before. Now he was clothed, in his right mind, and wanted to be with Jesus. Jesus commanded him to go and tell others, his family and friends in particular, that he was healed.

When there is a life-change right before our eyes, we cannot deny God's power. I heard the fallen minister Ted Haggard explain his calling. He feels God called him to minister right in front of the people who saw him crumble. God didn't let him run away. His family stayed in Colorado Springs and started a new church. To paraphrase his words, "The crucifixion happened in Jerusalem. Therefore, the resurrection needed to happen in Jerusalem too. Jesus was faultless. I was crucified for my own faults, but the power of the resurrection needs to be lived out in front of the people who saw the death." I've paraphrased this, but I want you to see that when God touches us in front of the people who once saw us in our sin, great things happen. The demon-possessed man was changed and people were now listening to him.

Day 55

Mark 6

Scribe to the Heart

"When He went ashore He saw a great crowd, and He had compassion on them, because they were like sheep without a shepherd. And He began to teach them many things."

(Mark 6:34)

Point to Ponder

Jesus provides for us as we follow Him and put our faith in Him.

Today's Journal

Do I trust Jesus with my time and attention when I am tempted to go and be somewhere else?

Prayer for the Day

Lord Jesus, I want to give you the time and attention I need for You to teach me what You want me to learn. Let me not be distracted by anything, even a legitimate need.

SPIRITUAL BANQUET

THE MIRACLE STORY of Jesus found in Mark 6:30-44 was written about by all four gospel writers. Remember, each gospel was written to reach different people groups. They all felt this particular story was to be included in reaching the audience they were going after. This story is so common in the church world, it is important we look at it closely. Don't overlook it just because it may be a story you've heard since your youth.

Jesus and the apostles encounter a large group of people. Maybe the most important point is made in verse 34. Jesus had compassion on them because they were like sheep without a shepherd. He taught them many things. He taught so long that it grew late. The people had quite a day. Jesus the Christ was preaching and teaching them! Spiritual scales were falling from their eyes. It doesn't appear that anyone had eaten in a while. For many it might have been a long walk home. Yet, they stayed. They wanted more of Jesus. Jesus kept teaching and they kept listening. Truly, it was an act of faith.

These people depended on Jesus to give them spiritual food. Maybe they already had the understanding that they couldn't live on bread alone, but also needed the very words of God (Matthew 4:4). Then it came time to break up the party. It was late. Jesus' work was not done. It was time to give these people some physical nourishment. Jesus multiplies a little bread and a little fish. It fed all the people and everyone was full. It fed five thousand men, not including women and children. It may have been the final object lesson in Jesus' teaching that day. At the end of the day the people had a deep sense of Jesus' ability to take care of them physically and spiritually.

Mark 7

"Now when the Pharisees gathered to Him, with some of the scribes who had come from Jerusalem, they saw that some of His disciples ate with hands that were defiled, that is unwashed."

(Mark 7:1-2)

Point to Ponder

Letting go of religion enables us to hold on to Jesus.

Today's Journal

Am I holding onto religion instead of Jesus in some area of my life?

Prayer for the Day

Father, Enlighten me in the areas where my religious practices get in the way of Jesus.

SPIRITUAL LEADERS AND RELIGIOUS LEADERS

WHEN WE TALK about the difference between spiritual leaders and religious leaders, we must define what we are talking about. Religion is about keeping rules for the sake of the rules. For example, when it comes to prayer, religion would dictate the exact right times to pray along with a series of bowing, kneeling, standing, and sitting. If these things are done in the right spirit with the right heart, they are not bad things. Spirituality is mystical in that we can't see or touch the thing we are connected to. We relate to God through the Holy Spirit. Spirituality is negative if the thing you are connected to is not Jesus. It could mean opening yourself up to a whole world of new age gods, or ancient pagan deities.

The Pharisees were religious leaders. They wanted everything to be a certain way in an effort to please God. When a new spiritual leader came along it was expected that he would keep the religious rules of the Pharisees. They were used to cutting deals with the Romans, and making the rules for the people. It was a big change that people were following this man Jesus who loved scripture but didn't follow their rules. It angered them because deep down the spirit of religion wants to control others. People who are religious want control. Jesus could not be tamed. The Pharisees didn't care that the disciples' hands were dirty because people might get sick. They cared because this leader was not teaching their ways.

In church we all have to guard against holding our religion too tightly. Hold Jesus tightly. Your faith can't become wrecked if someone in leadership goes astray. You can't think the sky is falling if the music in church changes, or the sermon is preached at the beginning instead of the end, or if the pastor doesn't do an altar call. Whatever opinion you may have, you need to beware of one thing: We need Jesus. We need to understand Him as pure and holy. We can't let our religion block our relationship with Jesus.

Mark 8

Scribe to the Heart

"And He called to Him the crowd with His disciples and said to them, 'If anyone would come after Me, let him deny himself and take up his cross and follow Me.'"

(Mark 8:34)

Point to Ponder

Jesus wants us to follow Him, no matter where He goes.

Today's Journal

Is there something Jesus wants me to do that may be uncomfortable?

Prayer for the Day

Lord Jesus, I commit to following You through good times and bad. Even when it is uncomfortable or hurts. Help me when I have to make hard decisions.

PETER'S MOMENT

PETER HAD A lot of big moments during the earthly ministry of Jesus and after Jesus' ascension. In this chapter, beginning in verse 27 we read one of his defining moments. Jesus and the disciples are walking along the road. Have you ever noticed that a lot happens to the disciples and Jesus while they are on the way to somewhere else? Jesus asked the disciples to verbalize what people were saying about Him. He then asked, "Who do you say I am?" Peter pipes up and declares, "You are the Christ."

Now the story changes. Jesus tells them not to tell anyone, and He begins to speak of His up and coming death. Peter's adrenaline and the excitement is still pumping from answering correctly and knowing that Jesus is the Christ. He then pulls Jesus aside and begins to rebuke Him for talking of His death. Jesus cares for the disciples and the crowd by stopping Peter. He speaks to the source of Peter's comment, Satan. Satan, the prince of darkness, had influenced Peter's thoughts. Even though Peter vocalized it, all of the disciples likely saw Jesus' reign as an earthly conquering king at that point, because that was the dominate view of the Messiah's role at that time.

Jesus not only rebukes Peter, but He also gives Peter and the apostles a glimpse into their own fate. If you don't take up your own cross and follow me... (v. 34). Not only was Jesus going to die for this, but His followers would as well. We know later Peter was crucified upside down. The upside-down part was at his own request, because he finally understood. He knew he didn't deserve to die in the same way Jesus did. With the exception of John (and Judas Iscariot), the other apostles were all martyred. But it wasn't that they didn't try to kill John. Even though he'd been boiled in oil, Jesus had plans for him to stick around for a time.

But imagine the moment the disciples had in this passage. The realization that He was the Christ, and He was right there! He was to die and He was stating they would be asked to give their lives, too.

Mark 9

"*But they did not understand the saying, and were afraid to ask Him.*"

(Mark 9:32)

Point to Ponder

Allow God to stretch your ideas about Him!

Today's Journal

Have I ever not understood my circumstances because I did not understand God?

Prayer for the Day

Father God, Let me understand Your purposes for me. Give me courage to ask boldly when I do not understand.

SPEECHLESS

I WANT YOU to think of that person. It could be you. I know sometimes I am that guy. I'm talking about that person who always has an answer for everything. He or she will go down with the ship, even if ridiculously wrong about the issue. Sometimes, he will even keep going when he knows he's wrong, to try to salvage the contest or save face.

I believe Peter had a touch of this attitude. In the last chapter, Peter spoke up. He had a lot to say, and publicly. Jesus set him straight. He needed to, so Peter and the others present would understand. Here we see the same topic arise. Jesus speaks of His own death. He also speaks of a resurrection after three days. The disciples do not understand, but Scripture says they were afraid to ask Him. Even Peter was afraid to speak up. Peter may have recalled how he was called out for speaking incorrectly and thought it best to keep quiet.

It would have been very hard for the disciples to hear these words. Popular cultural theology said the Messiah was going to conquer. He was not going to die! It would have been hard even to hear the hope of the resurrection because they had a completely different idea of what Jesus' mission was.

The disciples' fear seems ridiculous to us because we know what really was going on, but here is the challenge. Maybe there are certain doctrines in our culture that at the highest levels of both conservative and liberal (and everything in between) biblical thinking are ridiculous and unbiblical. What if we miss out on God's best by not wrestling through our own theology? Often, we have others do the work for us. This is spiritually dangerous. Incomplete theology is an incomplete view of God. Dig deep and allow God to stretch you.

Mark 10

Scribe to the Heart

"For even the Son of Man came not to be served but to serve, and to give his life as a ransom for many."

(Mark 10:45)

Point to Ponder

Jesus calls us to humility and service in an upside- down kingdom.

Today's Journal

How can I better participate in the upside-down kingdom?

Prayer for the Day

Jesus, Show me what it looks like in my life to love with humility and service as my main goals. Keep me "upside down" from how the world views things.

THE UPSIDE-DOWN KINGDOM

THE BIBLE CHAPTER numbers, verses, and headings were not in the original texts. Mark's gospel was on a scroll. So, when we talk about a situation unfolding chapter by chapter, we run the risk of giving an inaccurate portrayal. However, the narrative is written in a way for us to see some repetition. Jesus foretold of His death in chapter 8. Peter then has words with Jesus and Jesus calls him Satan. In chapter 9, Jesus again tells of His death and resurrection and the disciples are confused but keep quiet. No one wanted the tongue lashing that Peter got.

In Mark 10, Jesus is about to enter Jerusalem, with the cross in sight. It is important to notice how stories are grouped together. Jesus challenges them to a very different type of thinking: humility and service. Read the subtitles in your Bible. They include titles like: Let the Children Come to Me, The Rich Young Man, Jesus Foretells His Death a Third Time and The Request of James and John. The first two deal with humility and service. Jesus teaches that they must not make it hard for others, especially children, to come to Him. We must put nothing ahead of following Jesus. But see then how the disciples still missed it? Right after these teachings, James and John lobby for the most prominent places in the Kingdom. Their actions still reflected the exact opposite of the vision Jesus was casting.

The gospel is so counter-cultural that sometimes we can miss it even if we are beside Jesus Himself! We know we are to be humble servants, but it is a constant battle because the world does things differently. Here are three conversations about Jesus' going to the cross and the disciples still couldn't get out of a status mindset. The other disciples were upset with James and John, but probably because they weren't bold enough to ask for themselves. This is an upside-down kingdom. It is not a top down organization. To please God, get down and wash feet. Get to know someone who needs your help. Don't think in terms of status. Be nice to people regardless of their social state. Love your neighbor as yourself. These things are the best way to begin to understand the upside-down kingdom.

Day 60

Mark 11

Scribe to the Heart

"And He was teaching them and saying to them, 'Is it not written, My house shall be called a house of prayer for all the nations? But you have made it a den of robbers.'"

(Mark 11:17)

Point to Ponder

God wants us to have a pure faith.

Today's Journal

I believe to have a pure faith I need to...

Prayer for the Day

Lord Jesus, Purify me in my thoughts and how I approach You, that I will draw others to You.

JESUS: MEAN AND WILD

THE MARKIAN VERSION of the gospel to the Roman gentiles continues to move very fast. By chapter 10 we are already getting ready for Jesus to go to the cross. Jesus, to the fulfillment of prophecy, rode into town on a colt no one had ever ridden. He was praised greatly in the streets; being hailed as the Messiah. They cried, "Blessed is He who comes in the name of the Lord!" It is hard to believe that He was going to Jerusalem to die. It is hard to believe this same crowd would be chanting for Him to be crucified in only five short days.

Not long ago I read a book with the title *Jesus Mean and Wild: The Unexpected Love of an Untamable God*. It was written by Mark Galli, an editor at *Christianity Today*. Now of course Jesus loves us all. However, religion redefines love. When we look closely at the life of Jesus, He said and did some shockingly bold things. Shortly after coming to town he visited the temple. The ungodly activity that was happening there forced a reaction. He was tired of the rich making it hard for the poor. He was tired of the religious elite controlling the activities of the temple and exploiting the poor. He overturned money tables and discouraged the selling of animals for profit in the temple.

Jesus is recorded as saying something interesting that Matthew didn't record, but Mark did. "My house is to be a house of prayer for all nations." Jesus was looking out for the poor, who couldn't afford expensive animals to sacrifice, and the gentile converts, for both then and in the future.

This was a turning point and it heightened the Pharisees' need to rid their lives of Jesus. God wants us to have a pure faith. There is no room for mixing the world's selfishness into how we approach God. We are not to be focused on what we can get from our service or who sees us. We are to be focused on worshipping God and drawing others into that same worship.

Mark 12

Scribe to the Heart

"Truly I say to you, this poor widow has put in more than all those who are contributing to the offering box. For they all contributed out of their abundance, but she out of her poverty has put in everything she had, all she had to live on."

(Mark 12:44)

Point to Ponder

God owns everything. We just get to use it for now.

Today's Journal

How can I be faithful to God with everything I've been given?

Prayer for the Day

Lord Jesus, I want to be faithful with all I've been given. Keep me in the recognition that 100% of what I have is yours.

MY HEART IS WHERE MY TREASURE LIES

"**MY HEART IS** where my treasure lies," starts the chorus of Tree63's song "Treasure." Doctrines of giving are very interesting. Tithing is taught in the Old Testament. It was a requirement, much like a tax. It kept the nation functioning as a people. It wasn't about currency, but crops. If we add up all of the required giving in the Old Testament, the nation of Israel tithed over 30% of each income.

Now, we are not the nation of Israel and we have our own taxes we have to pay. We also go to church and try to be faithful stewards of our finances with God. Tithing of 10% is what churches ask of their members. It is a great place to be. Without tithers, today many churches would simply die.

I don't want to knock the 10% tithe. I want to highlight why Jesus taught giving differently. This woman in Mark 12 gave it all. She was a widow, which means she didn't have a husband to support her. It doesn't look like she had much, but she still wanted to give to God. A single mother with five kids who is a new Christian may hear about tithing every week and go away feeling guilty. However, she is a new creature in Christ and she cries out to God to be able to be faithful. Sitting just one row in front of her is a high official of a major company who, by listening to the same teaching for years, is comfortable (a place God rarely wants us) and easily writes a check for 10%, and is under the delusion that the other 90% is his. If he just turned around, he may see someone God wants him to help. I realize many people in high financial positions already live this way. Which brings me to the main point. God wants your heart.

A noteworthy example of good stewardship is Pastor Rick Warren. Rick Warren has given back every penny he ever made from Saddleback Church. He works at the church for free. He lives on less than 10% of his book sales, speaking engagements, etc. No one expected this from him, except maybe God did. The man is high on the list of philanthropists, with people who bring in much, much more than he does. Rick keeps it about his heart. God owns everything. We just get to use it for now. When a person really understands this, everything changes. Personally, I am still trying.

Mark 13

Scribe to the Heart

"But be on your guard. For they will deliver you over to councils, and you will be beaten in synagogues, and you will stand before governors and kings for my sake, to bear witness before them."

(Mark 13:9)

Point to Ponder

Storms will come. Trust God to help.

Today's Journal

A storm in my life that God helped me through was...

Prayer for the Day

Holy Spirit, Work through me today and every day, particularly when the storms of life require Your extra help and guidance.

BE ON YOUR GUARD

ONE OF THE tough parts in studying the "end things" (eschatology) in the gospels is we are observing interactions between Jesus and the disciples that were layered conversations. There are statements very specific to things they would experience personally. There are also references to events that wouldn't take place until long after their lifetime.

How the disciples received and processed this information is an important consideration. In Mark 13 Jesus tells the disciples of a coming time when they would experience persecution by authorities both religious and political. They would be persecuted. They will be hated. It was time to get really prayed up and prepared. They were told to be on their guard. We should be cautious as well. We are not exempt from persecution when we are truly living out the gospel message. In fact, Jesus tells us to expect it.

Many only want to talk about the positive aspects of our faith. This is incomplete. Jesus gave us a faith that prepares us for hard things. Hard times are in store for each and every one of us. Jesus wants us to lean on Him in hard times. Notice they had a responsibility to be faithful under persecution—as do we. Jesus also told them that Holy Spirit would be there to help them. God Himself would be there to give them the words to say. Sometimes we are in over our heads, sometimes hard things come our way, but by leaning on God we are able to do anything we need to do.

Mark 14

Scribe to the Heart

"Watch and pray that you may not enter into temptation. The spirit indeed is willing, but the flesh is weak."

(Mark 14:38)

Point to Ponder

The Spirit within you is willing. The flesh, however, is weak.

Today's Journal

How can I better live through the Spirit and not fall victim to my flesh?

Prayer for the Day

Holy Spirit, Teach me about Your power. Help me to stay connected to You. Strengthen my resolve to not live in the flesh.

WILLING SPIRIT, WEAK FLESH

BECAUSE WE ARE Christian, we wouldn't hesitate to declare that we desperately want to do the right thing. Often times, however, we try to accomplish good godly objectives through the wrong means. Romans 8:14 teaches we are to live life by the Spirit. This means we are to go about our business with the Spirit guiding our actions. If you are a sheep of the Good Shepherd you will follow His voice (John 10:3).

Jesus knows what is coming in this chapter. He wants to pray by Himself. He asks the disciples to pray also so they might not fall into temptation. Scripture records just how intense His prayers were. He pours Himself out before the Father. He even asked God if there was another way. (Even though He knew there wasn't.) He is going through a very human experience of knowing He is going to suffer a brutal death, and He knew it. His death was for the sake of the entire world. His Spirit needed to be strengthened. He needed to go to battle in the spiritual realm. He knew that He needed to seek the presence of the Father. That is what we are called to. Jesus is our example.

Look at the contrast seen here in the disciples. Peter, who insisted he would never deny the Lord, is found sleeping. As are the others. Jesus wanted them to pray so they could be strong. They were open to temptation because they did not fight the battle in the spiritual realm.

We can't expect to do God's will without prayer and connection with Him. It just doesn't work. We are not to trust in our own abilities. There is no positive word anywhere in the New Testament about our flesh. We must overcome the flesh with our Spirit. This only happens with our new nature. As a new creation in Christ we are able to ask God to work through us to do the right thing, for the right reasons.

Mark 15

Scribe to the Heart

"And they compelled a passerby, Simon of Cyrene, who was coming in from the country, the father of Alexander and Rufus, to carry His cross."

(Mark 15:21)

Point to Ponder

Eyewitness testimony to the activity of Jesus in a person's life is powerful.

Today's Journal

How would I answer if someone asked me: "Can you tell me about the power of Jesus in your life?"

Prayer for the Day

Holy Spirit, I pray that other people would see the power of Christ when they see how I live my life. Thank You for empowering me to be a witness.

BRINGING THE STORY TO LIFE

THE PASSING DOWN of stories from the people who lived them is how we know much of what we know about human history. We also better understand events that happen in our own lifetime when we hear firsthand accounts. For example, we gain much insight into what happened on 9/11 through the accounts of people who lived through the tragedy. Eyewitness accounts are powerful. We have no grounds to tell someone that an event didn't happen when they have the scars to prove that it did.

Understanding that biblical texts are reliable documents is partially due to the fact that people who wrote them or publicly spoke were held to a high social accountability. If someone retold a story that Jesus told or shared an event from His life, they did so knowing others would interrupt and correct them if necessary. In this culture, getting things right was taken seriously.

In Mark 15 we see a man named Simon who lived in the town of Cyrene. He had two children who would have been adults at the writing of this text. When a first century recorder of history mentions Alexander and Rufus (Simon's children) in the story it is an invitation to the original audience. He's saying, "Hey, these people are still around and you can go ask them to verify what I am saying is true."

Jesus is controversial. Everyone has an opinion. Some people are followers. Some are not. Some are on the fence as they work through their doubts. But the amazing thing about Jesus is that so many have been affected by Him still today. Because we are Christians, it is important that we are willing to be asked. We are to be available and open to declare how He still changes our lives today.

Day 65

Mark 16

Scribe to the Heart

"And they went out and fled from the tomb, for trembling and astonishment had seized them, and they said nothing to anyone, for they were afraid."

(Mark 16:8)

Point to Ponder

God's word is the original text.

Today's Journal

Is my view of scripture in contradiction to the content of this entry? Why or why not?

Prayer for the Day

Lord Jesus, Teach me more deeply about Your Word.

UNCOMFORTABLE DISCUSSIONS

THE INTENTION OF theology is to describe God. Things are tested and proved through various methods just as things are in other sciences. However, we cannot take faith out of the methodology. Jesus was dead and He became alive again. A virgin teenager had a baby. The Holy Spirit comes to live inside of us. All of these things (as well as others) must be believed by faith. At the same time Theology is the science practiced to have a complete idea of who God is.

When you study the canonization of the Protestant Bible you learn why certain books are left out and why others were included. One of the best examples is James. The sources and the evidence showed the author to have been James, the half-brother of Jesus. There are many reasons why the book of James is included in the Bible. However, Martin Luther tried to exclude it. Why? Because James simply didn't fit into the nice neat mold of Luther's theology.

Now for the hard part. Original manuscripts did not include verses 9-20 in this chapter of Mark. They were added in later manuscripts. That brings us to some questions. Yes, I am a Bible loving Christian. I wrote *The New Testament Challenge* under the conviction that the New Testament is the Word of God. However, I believe it is more like John Mark to end this book abruptly at verse eight. The last 11 verses create some potential problems. It would seem that Jesus declares the need to be baptized for salvation (v. 16). There is also mention of drinking deadly poison and handling snakes in Jesus' name (v. 18).

There are many questions to be asked over these verses. There is much more information to be given, but not enough room on this page. Learning about canonization and how the Bible came to be gave me more faith in the Bible, and not less.

If you stop reading at verse eight, you see an ending indicative of the spirit and writing style of the author of this gospel, John Mark. God's Word is the original text.

Luke 1

Scribe to the Heart

"And Mary said, 'My soul magnifies the Lord, and my spirit rejoices in God my Savior.'"

(Luke 1:46-47)

Point to Ponder

Even Mary needed a Savior.

Today's Journal

How can my soul magnify the Lord today? How can my spirit rejoice in my savior?

Prayer for the Day

Holy Spirit, Work through me so I can strongly declare, like Mary did, "My soul magnifies the Lord!"

EVEN MARY

LUKE WAS AN extremely technical writer. He was a physician. As a doctor, he cared about facts and obviously believed his audience did too. In his gospel, Luke explains important details which help to set the scene in its proper time and place. He starts his writing with the events of the miraculous birth of John the Baptist. John was a relative of Jesus, born of a priestly line to a couple who were not supposed to be able to have children. John's father Zechariah was asked by the angel Gabriel to believe he and his wife would have a child in spite of their age. When he didn't believe, he was struck speechless for the duration of the pregnancy.

A virgin girl named Mary was asked to mother the Son of God. What great faith this girl had. She was very special to have received the favor of God in such an extraordinary fashion. Mary must have been one of those followers of God who believed and lived so strongly that in her presence you experienced God's grace.

Mary's age (probably teenaged) and her gender made her socially insignificant for the time. She would have been overlooked for leadership in the synagogue. Even today she would not have had a vote in your church or mine, but Mary found the favor of God. God saw her, and she knew it.

Many would have been filled with pride over such an awesome experience, but not Mary. She exclaimed to Elizabeth in private, "For he has looked on the humble estate of his servant." Perhaps the most important verse in all of what Mary spoke was said when she first opened her mouth, "And Mary said, 'My soul magnifies the Lord, and my spirit rejoices in God my Savior.'" That's right. Even Mary needed a Savior. Her righteousness started with the fact that she knew she needed a Savior. Mary knew she fell short and she knew God was bigger. She didn't have all the details as to how God would use the Messiah to complete her, but her faith told her He had to, and she was willing to do her part.

Luke 2

Scribe to the Heart

"Lord, now you are letting your servant depart in peace, according to your word; for my eyes have seen your salvation that you have prepared in the presence of all peoples, a light for revelation to the Gentiles, and for glory to your people Israel."

(Luke 2:29-32)

Point to Ponder

Closeness to Jesus can be closeness to pain.

Today's Journal

When I think about the baby Jesus as my king, the following thoughts come to mind...

Prayer for the Day

Father, Give me insight into the bigger picture for my life. As Simeon saw the bigger picture, I long to see a glimpse of Jesus in the bigger picture, too.

A SWORD THAT PIERCES THE SOUL

DR. LUKE GIVES us many things to think about in this second chapter. He mentions a few new characters in regards to Jesus' birth story and early childhood, one of which is a man named Simeon. Simeon was a prophet. God told him he wouldn't die until he saw the Savior with his own eyes. God showed him the Savior one day in the temple where Mary and Joseph were having the child circumcised.

When Simeon sees the baby Jesus, he has much to say. He probably said more than what is recorded. Peace came over him that told him to trust in the baby because this child would grow up to be the Messiah. It seems that Simeon had a better understanding than most people of the type of Messiah they were waiting for.

Simeon understood this baby would be a means of salvation for all people, a light to the gentiles, and a messenger to the people of Israel. He understood that not everyone would accept Him, and that there would be great tension over this Messiah. He told Mary, *"Behold this child is appointed for the fall and rising of many in Israel, and for a sign that is opposed (and a sword will pierce through your own soul also), so that thoughts from many hearts may be revealed"* (Luke 2:34b-35). He knew that in Israel many will believe and many won't. Before all was said and done, Mary will be at the foot of a bloody cross. Simeon saw that the mother of Jesus would experience great pain, like a sword piercing her soul. However, Mary got to play a special part in the life of Jesus; she raised Him from infancy. Jesus emptied Himself, and learned how to live as one of us. Jesus was sinless, yet He needed to be raised from birth. Mary got to be His mother.

While she believed in Him and trusted in Him to take away her sins, she was still His mother. Mary surely had her own unique cross to bear. She was there when He was crucified, and maybe only truly understood what Simeon meant when Jesus cried out, "It is finished" (John 19:30b). A sword pierced her soul. But after the heartache, she watched her son conquer death.

Luke 3

Scribe to the Heart

"during the high priesthood of Annas and Caiaphas, the word of God came to John the Son of Zechariah in the wilderness."

(Luke 3:2)

Point to Ponder

With all of the seemingly important people in the world, the Word of God came through John.

Today's Journal

What was it about John that made him so usable by God? Do I display any of those same qualities?

Prayer for the Day

Lord Jesus, Teach me to follow You, no matter what anyone else thinks.

IN THE YEAR OF...

CHAPTER THREE STARTS by identifying the exact timing of these events. Those receiving this gospel letter would have recognized Luke's list of people as important people of the time. There was a certain Caesar named Tiberius, a governor named Pontius Pilate. He mentions the religious leaders Annas and Caiaphas. We do the same today. We identify events by who was the president or in leadership. Could someone say today: *During the presidency of Donald Trump, the media era of Anderson Cooper and Sean Hannity, and the time of Pope Francis, the Word of God came to   (your name).*

Could it be you? Every time the wind changes directions, we have a new American Idol, or a politician making promises that can't be delivered. We witness the rise and fall of religious leaders. The tabloids are not short on gossip stories or dirty dealings of people. BUT... in the midst of it all, Jesus wants to speak. He wants you to get to know Him better. When you read His Word, like you are doing in this challenge, you begin to recognize what His voice sounds like. Those who know Him hear His voice.

John the Baptist was not a likely candidate to prepare the way for Jesus. Sure, his dad was a priest, which made him the Jewish equivalent of a pastor's kid. We know from chapter one that his family loved God, but John the Baptizer was not polished. He had long hair, he was dirty, and didn't use proper manners when he ate. Think about it. Would this guy even be allowed in your church, much less the pulpit? He was untamable and unpredictable. Yet, God wanted to send a wakeup call; He didn't want to send another religious rule-giver. He used a prophet; someone who only cared about what God thought of him. That is who John was.

Followers of Jesus hear from God in different ways. He may speak to you in your mind. He may use other believers to speak to you. He may even speak to you while you are sleeping. He will always speak to you when you read His Word. In the time of Donald Trump, Anderson Cooper and Pope Francis, what if God wants to speak through you? Are you ready for this magnificent responsibility?

Luke 4

Scribe to the Heart

"And when the devil had ended every temptation, he departed from him until an opportune time."

(Luke 4:13)

Point to Ponder

Satan is strategic. He will wait for an opportune time.

Today's Journal

How can I keep Satan from having an opportunity in my life?

Prayer for the Day

Holy Spirit, Show me how I can better worship God and not give the devil an opportunity.

OPPORTUNE TIMES

IT IS FASCINATING to me that the devil even tried to attack Jesus. I would have thought he'd know he couldn't succeed. Jesus had just been baptized to signify the beginning of His adult ministry. Then, as this chapter begins, He was led out into the wilderness for the purpose of being tested. This was a time of strengthening for Him.

When we are weak it is often because we are not committing our daily activities to God. This creates an opportunity for Satan to attack. However, when we hold fast to the Lord and declare our dependence on God, we will be strengthened. Satan, in all of his pride, believed this was the opportune time to attack Jesus. Jesus was hungry and vulnerable. Satan thought he could cause Jesus to sin and, in doing so, foil God's entire redemptive plan.

The Word of God was close to Jesus' heart the entire time. Satan told Him lie after lie, but Christ brought forth the truth of scripture by quoting it right to His enemy's face. We are then told that Satan left, until an opportune time.

We gain some insight into how the devil works. When you are weak, lonely, hungry, or depressed, he sees an opportunity. Have you ever noticed that when things hit rock bottom, often there is someone right there to add to it? I am not about to blame everything that happens to us on the devil, but I find it to be very plausible that the father of lies will show up in our lives at opportune times to wreak havoc. Why? Because he can't have our souls. If you are follower of Jesus, God owns you. Then why does Satan bother? He does it because if he steals your joy then you will not have a positive witness to give to this world. He wants to blind your view of your glorious Savior. He also wants you to put your light under a blanket so it cannot be seen by others.

Luke 5

Scribe to the Heart

"And when he saw their faith, he said, 'Man, your sins are forgiven you.'"

(Luke 5:20)

Point to Ponder

Our first response should be to act in faith on behalf of others.

Today's Journal

Who needs me to dig deep for Jesus?

Prayer for the Day

Lord Jesus, Bring to mind those for whom I need to dig deep in prayer.

DIG DEEP FOR JESUS

IN VERSE 17, a story begins: *"On one of those days..."* Luke lets us know that it was just another ordinary day. He isn't necessarily putting things in chronological order like he usually does, but he seems to be saying, "Oh yea, and another thing that happened..." Or, "On just another day at the office, when Jesus was out healing and preaching, this happened..." There is a sense that the activity to follow should be expected or considered ordinary for Jesus.

Often times, we talk to God the most when *we* have great needs. However, this time, a group of men carried a paralyzed *friend* on a mat. They couldn't get to Jesus, so they climbed up on the roof. They figured out how to dig through the roof without causing too much confusion. Then, they slowly lowered the man on a mat down to Jesus.

These men were probably sweaty and sore. They needed to work together, as their arms and legs were getting tired. They felt so bad for their friend, but they knew they were not the answer to the problem; Jesus was the answer to his problem. See this: It wasn't for them; it was for their friend. Luke tells us that Jesus saw *their* faith. We don't know anything about the faith of the man on the mat. Maybe he believed, and maybe he didn't, but the man was healed because of the faith of his friends. They took him to Jesus and left him in His hands. Once they let go of the mat there was nothing more they could do.

Often, the healing stories of the gospel teach us about personal times of desperation, when a person can only call out to God for healing. They are out of options. They are done. I wonder if going to Jesus was an early option for these guys? They weren't the ones who needed the healing, but they acted and worked hard in great faith on behalf of their friend. How we handle the brokenness and needs of others may say more about what we believe about God than when we call out to Him for ourselves. When someone has a need, is Jesus your first response? Would you be willing to dig deep for Jesus the Christ on behalf of someone else?

Day 71

Luke 6

Scribe to the Heart

*"he is like a man building a house, who dug deep
and laid the foundation on the rock.
And when a flood arose, the stream broke against that house
and could not shake it, because it had been well built."*

(Luke 6:48)

Point to Ponder

*Dig deep to build your spiritual house on the
firm foundation of Jesus Christ.*

Today's Journal

Am I digging deep to build a firm foundation? On what is my foundation built upon?

Prayer for the Day

Lord Jesus, Strengthen my foundation. Show me how to always build upon You.

GROUND TO BUILD ON

MOST OF MY early life was lived in Western Pennsylvania. My dad is a contractor. He builds and repairs houses, builds additions, garages, porches, and other projects of that nature. Before you build in Pennsylvania, you must create a firm foundation that extends deep into the soil. It requires a lot of digging. You only see the building that is above ground, but a sound structure extends ten to fifteen feet below the surface.

Now that I'm grown, I own a home in Texas. Most houses around here are like ours. The foundation doesn't extend into the ground. Houses are built on top of a cement slab. Even so, we need to water the foundation because if neglected, the house or the foundation could crack.

As a Christian you have the option to dig down deep. You have the option to build your spiritual house on the rock, Jesus Christ. To do this we must focus on our spiritual condition. Seek God in prayer and personal study. Get yourself around strong Christian people. Work on becoming a disciple of Christ. Above ground is the product of what we see, but the firm foundation is what makes the house strong. Notice the passage says "when" the storm comes. The storms will come. Dig down deep and allow God to establish your foundation and your house so you are prepared for the storms.

Day 72

Luke 7

Scribe to the Heart

"And when the Lord saw her, he had compassion on her and said to her, "Do not weep."

(Luke 7:13)

Point to Ponder

God cares for us during our darkest hours.

Today's Journal

Do I trust God with my deepest hurts? Have I asked Him to heal any anger or pain I have from past hurtful situations?

Prayer for the Day

God, Comfort me with Your presence during my darkest hours. Give me Your peace when I have a hurt in my life. I trust You for my healing.

GREAT PAIN IN NAIN

WE KNOW FROM the book of John that Jesus only does what He sees the Father doing (John 5:19-20). Jesus, directed by Holy Spirit, ends up in this little insignificant town called Nain. In Nain He encounters a funeral procession. I don't know a lot about the funeral processions of Jesus' day but I would imagine interrupting the funeral was not something that was socially acceptable.

Let's face it, the woman had been through enough. Her husband was dead. Now her son was dead. It is important to note it was her only son. Luke carefully records this detail because it speaks to her immediate future financial state. The woman would have no income. Women were not part of the workforce. They basically belonged to their husbands. If a woman didn't have a husband, a son could provide for her financially. She no longer had that security. How confused she must have felt. *God how could this have happened? God where were you? I loved my husband! I loved my son! Now I have nothing, and to top it all off I will never be able to take care of myself. What am I supposed to do?*

This truly was her darkest hour. We do not know if there may have been friends or relatives around. They would have helped in her immediate sadness, but at some point, she'd be left with a decision and the feeling of being completely alone. Just when all hope was lost, faith was fleeting, times were at their worst... Jesus showed up.

Day 73

Luke 8

Scribe to the Heart

"...Mary, called Magdelene, from whom seven demons had gone out, and Joanna, the wife of Chuza, Herod's household manager, and Susanna, and many others, who provided for them out of their means."

(Luke 8:2-3)

Point to Ponder

Women gave of their time, talent, and treasure to partner with Jesus.

Today's Journal

How have I seen God use women in my church or in my life in powerful ways?

Prayer for the Day

Lord, Teach me how to give of my time, talent, and treasure for Your glory.

BEHIND EVERY GOD MAN

IN THE LAST chapter we saw how God showed compassion to a widow who lost her only son. It was not only the loss of a child, which is possibly the greatest loss of all, but she also had lost the breadwinner in her house. She lost her remaining source of income and her closest family member.

At the beginning of this chapter we learn of three women who had also been touched by the grace of God through Jesus Christ. A woman named Mary Magdalene had seven demons come out of her. She was redeemed from a life of prostitution. Joanna was the wife of Chuza, who was Herod's household manager. It was counter-cultural and risky for Joanna to be associated with someone like Jesus, and to be providing for Him and his disciples. Then we see Susanna. She is mentioned only by first name, which tells us she was well-known to the original audience. Most likely she was wealthy.

Luke mentions the twelve disciples and these women only, when there were also others there. Why doesn't he give details about the others? It isn't because Luke wasn't detail-driven. Luke is very thorough. Surely he didn't get lazy in his recording. I believe he is making a counter-cultural point. These women had ministries and they were providing financially for Jesus and the apostles. These women were giving of their resources and traveling with Jesus because their lives had been touched by Him.

Jesus left heaven to become like us. He went through the entire human experience without sin (Hebrews 4:15). Part of that experience included His needing help at times. He didn't have the finances. Others gave and contributed so He could focus on His ministry. Could He have done it without them? Yes, but as the story goes Jesus employed the help of women for their time, talent, and treasure. This actually speaks volumes of a Savior who came to rescue us from boxed-in religion, and was thousands of years ahead of His time in regards to liberating women.

Luke 9

Scribe to the Heart

"Herod said, 'John I beheaded, but who is this about whom I hear such things?' And he sought to see him."

(Luke 9:9)

Point to Ponder

The mystery of Jesus draws in the curious.

Today's Journal

How can I make people curious about Jesus?

Prayer for the Day

Lord Jesus, Shine through me in such a way that it makes people want to know more about the God I serve.

CURIOUS HEROD?

IN CHAPTER 8 we encountered someone with a tie to Herod; Joanna, who was the wife of Chuza (Herod's household manager). (Luke 8:3) In this very next chapter we read that Herod becomes curious about Jesus. He'd had John the Baptist beheaded. The prophet Elijah was long gone. So, he's wondering, *"What's this guy's story?"* Herod was not a pious man. He was not someone you would look to for religious or moral guidance. But the stories he was hearing were incredible.

Could this word have gotten back to him through Chuza? Probably not from Chuza's wife since she would have had limited interaction with Herod. Either way, Jesus was influencing the highest of society. Jesus talked in parables. Why? Well, if Jesus went around saying plainly, He was the Messiah, someone like Herod could have taken Him out before He finished His mission. It would have been threatening to Herod to hear such a thing. Jesus provokes people to curiosity. He wants us to seek Him. If a non-Christian asked the typical evangelical in America how to get to heaven, there is a good chance the Christian would make it seem as if the Kingdom needs them. We sometimes present the gospel as if God needs the other person in order to be complete. The fact is: God doesn't need a single one of us to be complete. He wants us to draw close to Him because He loves us.

God may have called you to do something. You get to be a part of what He is doing because of His love, but He could do the same thing through a donkey if He wanted to. What we do matters, but God doesn't *need* us.

Jesus was and still is mysterious. He wants us to want to draw close to Him. He allows us to see things to puzzle us so we can grow. Herod heard about Jesus, but no one seemed to have a clear idea who this person was at this point. This passage doesn't suggest Herod was threatened in any way. He was probably more threatened by John the Baptist screaming, "Repent!" and personally criticizing his family. The mystery of Jesus had hard-hearted rulers thinking and wondering. It is quite amazing, isn't it?

Luke 10

Scribe to the Heart

"Nevertheless, do not rejoice in this, that the spirits are subject to you, but rejoice that your names are written in heaven."

(Luke 10:20)

Point to Ponder

Rejoice that your name is written in heaven.

Today's Journal

Do I truly rejoice that my name is written in heaven? Do I understand the miracle of that blessing?

Prayer for the Day

Holy Spirit, Allow me to better understand the miracle that my name is written in heaven. Thank You, God, that it is so.

NAMES WRITTEN IN HEAVEN

JESUS WILL ALWAYS show us something from a different angle than we are used to. There always seems to be a slight twist in the story. When Jesus sent out the seventy-two disciples, he gave them instructions. He told them where to go, who to talk to, what to say, what to take, and what to do.

To their surprise, they see miraculous things happen. They returned with great joy exclaiming to Jesus that, *"Even the demons are subject to us in your name."* It was a growth moment for the followers of Christ to realize the power and authority that Jesus had granted them in His name. For the disciples the question was answered. Do they have authority over the devil in this life? The answer was, "Yes!" What an amazing experience to see people delivered from darkness. People were healed from diseases. They were teaching and gathering more who wanted to follow after the Messiah. They had purpose, power, and authority.

Then here comes the twist. Jesus tells them: *"I saw Satan fall like lightning from heaven. Behold, I have given you authority to tread on serpents and scorpions, and over all the power of the enemy, and nothing shall hurt you. Nevertheless, do not rejoice in this, that the spirits are subject to you, but rejoice that your names are written in heaven" (Luke 10: 18-20).*

Never loose sight of the greatest miracle. The greatest miracle that has happened to those who are in Christ is that your name is written in heaven. God came to earth in the flesh, died and rose again for the sake of you. That is an amazing miracle. You, a sinner, can have your name written in heaven. Rejoice in that today!

Day 76

Luke 11

Scribe to the Heart

"Woe to you lawyers! For you have taken away the key of knowledge. You did not enter yourselves, and you hindered those who were entering."

(Luke 11:52)

Point to Ponder

Religion without God makes Him say, "Woe!"

Today's Journal

How does the Christian community I am a part of show love in the way God wants us to? Is there something we should be doing differently?

Prayer for the Day

Lord Jesus, Teach me the difference between religion and knowing God.

JESUS SAYS, "WOE!"

OUT OF THE many options in this chapter, I have chosen to take a look at what makes Jesus say, "Woe." Jesus is the Son of God. He is God Himself. When we experience Jesus and understand who He is, our jaws drop in awe. We may say, "Whoa!"

However, can Jesus ever be surprised or taken back? I don't believe He was surprised, but He did point out with amazement the hypocrisy of the religious leaders of the day. He wanted to emphasize for everyone that there is a major difference between true worship and dead religion.

Jesus reprimanded the Pharisees and Sadducees for tithing without love. It is as if Jesus was saying, "I see you doing your duty, but what about showing people who God is by how you love them, or Him?" Jesus talked to them about giving God the glory and not saving the glory for themselves. Jesus points out that if God is to get the glory then why did they love having the best seat in the synagogue, or the special treatment they received in public?

Jesus goes on to explain how they consult the traditions of the fathers, but they are to blame for killing God's prophets. He finished His pointed message telling them they have taken away the key of knowledge and are hindering people from entering the Kingdom. After this we see the Pharisees lie in wait, trying to trap Jesus in something that He would say.

Their hearts were hard. Jesus would have let them repent and empowered them to lead others. But they loved being important. It was too hard for them to give this up. It is very scary if we don't recognize the similarities between the church today and the Pharisees. The Pharisees started out with very good intentions. They were working class people who studied and taught the law. They memorized scripture unparalleled to almost anyone today. They were evangelical and God-focused. But religion looked so similar. Over time they grew to love tradition and religion more than even God Himself. When He stood in front of them, it made Him say "Woe!" His woe was also to tell them that they were doomed if they didn't change their ways.

Luke 12

Scribe to the Heart

"In the meantime, when so many thousands of the people had gathered together that they were trampling one another, he began to say to His disciples first, 'Beware of the leaven of the Pharisees, which is hypocrisy.'"

(Luke 12:1)

Point to Ponder

Learn from people who love God.

Today's Journal

Do the people I admire love God? Do they try to live according to how He instructs in His word?

Prayer for the Day

Holy Spirit, Lead me to good mentors who will help me in my spiritual growth.

FINDING MENTORS

REMEMBER WHEN THE book of Luke was written it didn't include chapter and verse breaks. Chapters and verses were placed in the Bible later to help us find what we need more easily. We must remember this when we are reading. Dr. Luke explains the dead religion of the Pharisees at the end of the last chapter. This chapter is a continuation of that.

Jesus says, *"Beware of the leaven of the Pharisees which is hypocrisy."* Jesus is referring to leaven or yeast used for baking bread. Yeast is worked throughout the dough prior to baking. It spreads through the whole dough, causing an effect. When Jesus calls us to *"Beware of the leaven of the Pharisees,"* He is telling us not to let them work their teaching into us. Don't fall for legalism. Don't fall for pointless religion that leaves you feeling empty, and please do not fall for hypocrisy. If you do, it will work its way into your dough, and it will ruin you. It will have a negative effect on you.

He then shifts away from the Pharisees and for the rest of the chapter talks about how we should be. He teaches we should not be greedy for money, but have our eyes focused on God. He instructs that we should not be anxious, but be ready to meet your maker at all times. He said that truly following Him will not be popular at times, and will cause division with family and friends.

When seeking a Christian mentor, you should seek one who follows God in these areas. He or she should not be a hypocrite like the Pharisees. A mentor should be good leaven, and when this leaven is worked into you, you will come out better than when you started. You will love God and believe Him. You will love people and want to be a good witness to others through your words and your actions. In the end you will become good yeast that will help to influence the world through someone else.

Luke 13

Scribe to the Heart

"Strive to enter through the narrow door. For many, I tell you, will seek to enter and will not be able."

(Luke 13:24)

Point to Ponder

Jesus will not be manipulated.

Today's Journal

Do I ever try to manipulate God? How?

Prayer for the Day

Lord Jesus, I am sorry for the times I try to manipulate You. Give me the resolve to continue on the narrow path.

THE NARROW DOOR

THERE ARE SO many who have learned to manipulate their way through life. I am sure you know what I mean. They know how to say the right things at the right times. It may be a corrupt teenager who knows how to put on the right front for a friend's parents. It may be a person who knows how to move up the corporate ladder of success by kissing up to the boss. If we are all honest in one way or another, we ourselves have been taught and molded into little manipulators. We know how to say the right things at the right times. We know how to word things on a resume or in a speech that makes us look a little smarter than normal. Sadly, manipulation is part of our lifestyle. It is part of how we are taught to survive.

With this in mind, it is no surprise that many of us have come to believe that we can approach God the same way. Think about it, we try to approach Jesus (The Light of the World) in a way that is dark and manipulative. He wants us to worship in Spirit and in truth. He sees everything, and we think we can get away with manipulating Him.

Because of our unfortunate human condition, Jesus speaks plainly to us about how to get to heaven. The manipulative human condition is what makes it hard. Jesus paid the price for us. He made it easy. We just need to be committed to Him. So, why is it Jesus refers to heaven as having a narrow door that only a few enter through? The reason is simple. We all try to manipulate. We try to be religious. We try to say the right things. We try to enter a side door or go in the window. Many will not enter through the narrow door because to do so you must be committed. You must commit your life to Jesus. Allow Him to live through you. Entering the narrow door is hard. It is hard only because we try to do it ourselves. We are self-reliant and manipulative. Commit your life to Jesus. Enter through the narrow door by trusting Him.

Day 79

Luke 14

Scribe to the Heart

"Whoever does not bear his own cross and come after me cannot be my disciple."

(Luke 14:27)

Point to Ponder

Jesus calls us to love the unlovable.

Today's Journal

Who am I called to love that I truly do not feel loving towards? How can I love them like Jesus?

Prayer for the Day

Lord Jesus, Love the unlovable through me. Show me what that looks like in my life.

WHO DO YOU LOVE?

IN THIS SECTION of the book of Luke we see Jesus going to great lengths to explain that following after Him is not easy. We learned in Luke 13 that Jesus will not be manipulated. It is against His nature. For Jesus, right is right and wrong is wrong. He calls us to righteousness. Since we can't achieve righteousness on our own, He must do it for us. That is why He lived a perfect life, died a perfected death, and rose to life to return to a perfect state. He paid for us. Yet what He calls for in us is intimacy. He calls us to truly love Him. He continually calls us to seek and obey Him in every area of our lives.

Jesus is very clear. He tells us, *"Whoever does not bear his own cross and come after me cannot be my disciple."* Jesus bore a cross for us, yet he calls us to bear our own cross. He calls us to love the unlovable. He calls us to reach out to people who can't ever repay us. Earlier in the chapter we read a parable where Jesus speaks of a banquet. Many made excuses as to why they couldn't attend the great banquet. The Master got angry and invited the poor, the blind, the crippled, and the lame.

Jesus wants us to do for those who can't help themselves. He wants us to love the people who were just like us–lost in their sin. Jesus didn't have to die for us. He didn't have to love us to the furthest extent of the word. But, He did. It wasn't because we were so lovable, or that we were people who would give Him something He didn't have. He loved us because He wanted to love. He created us to express His love.

We all know someone who needs to see the love of Christ. I am not talking about telling them about the love of Christ. I am talking about truly showing them. There is someone who gets picked on at school, who has no friends. There is someone you have to deal with at work who wears you out. God calls you to love like He loved–sacrificially. Who are you supposed to love today? Pick up your cross and follow after Jesus; even if it is not the popular thing to do.

Luke 15

Scribe to the Heart

"Just so, I tell you, there is joy before the angels of God over one sinner who repents."

(Luke 15:10)

Point to Ponder

We are of great value to God.

Today's Journal

I am of great value to God because...

Prayer for the Day

Father, Thank You that you see value in me. Teach me to see what You see. Let me see the value in those around me like You see them.

OVER A COIN

JESUS' WORDS IN Luke 15 are possibly the most straightforward words that talk about God's loving intent towards His people in all of scripture. Entire books have been written on this concept and if it were my intent, I could write an entire devotional on just this chapter. Consider the dumb sheep who wandered out on its own. Think about the Good Shepherd who would leave the ninety-nine to go and find that one sheep. How much rejoicing is there in heaven over one lost sheep who repents? Ponder the Prodigal Son. Focus on the story of the careless youth. He squandered his father's fortune, only to return home completely broke. The father took him in and treated him like royalty.

Finally, let's think of the lost coin. This story seems to be peculiarly positioned and out of place. To understand it we must understand the culture of Jesus' listeners. If a woman had ten coins, they were probably not ten ordinary coins. When a woman was betrothed to be married, the groom paid a dowry to the father. The father would then take the coins and have them fashioned into a necklace, so the coins could be worn around the neck of the future bride. If one of these coins were lost, it would mean that the necklace was incomplete. This would be comparable to losing part of an engagement ring. It would cause the bride to feel serious guilt and emotional pain. It could cause a strain in this future marriage.

The groom paid ten coins, not nine. The bride was to take care of her things and not lose them. She would have torn the entire place apart to find this coin. The coin is of great value to her. In contrast since it is a silver coin, it most likely wasn't worth much in the way of actual monetary value. There certainly would have been nicer necklaces in town. However, this coin belonged to *her* necklace. God created us and values us, just like the bride would her coin. He will tear this whole place apart to get our attention and lead us in the way that brings us back to Him.

Luke 16

Scribe to the Heart

"He said to him, 'If they do not hear Moses and the Prophets, neither will they be convinced if someone should rise from the dead.'"

(Luke 16:31)

Point to Ponder

If you belong to God, then He knows your name.

Today's Journal

Do I look up to anyone for reasons that are not godly? Who do I respect for godly reasons?

Prayer for the Day

Father, Let me be active doing the things You care about.

NO ONE KNEW HIS NAME

I BEGAN MY walk with Christ shortly after hearing a message on this passage of scripture. I have read it many times since. However, one detail was always hidden from me. Then one day in my personal study it jumped right out at me. Jesus does not tell us this rich man's name. Of course, he would have had a name. His father and brothers also had names that went unmentioned. If he was so rich, he was most likely locally or even nationally elite. People passed by his house, and saw the fine linen he wore from a distance. To the people of the day this man and his family had names that would have been known. We know the rich of our day, don't we? Trump, Gates, Hilton, and the list goes on. We buy magazines that talk about them. We follow their marriages, their divorces, and their investments. They are of great interest to us.

Lazarus, the poor man, was named in this story.

After his death, the rich man is in torment and sees Lazarus. He longs for Lazarus to give him a drop of water on the end of his finger, but it is too late. A great chasm has been fixed between them. The man of great earthly honor even begged for Lazarus to be sent to his family to warn them. He thought if Lazarus came back from the dead they will believe and repent. Abraham lets him know that if they will not listen to Moses and the Prophets, they will not listen even if someone rises from the dead. People often think that if they knew for sure that someone could rise from the dead, then they'll get their life right with God. Jesus is telling this story in reference to Himself. He knew that He would soon rise from the dead Himself, and that even though the Prophets foretold of His resurrection, once it happened, many still wouldn't believe.

But take note: God loves us all and wants us all to have our names written in the Book of Life. (Rev 20:15) At some point a poor man cried out for God's help. He must have repented and decided to follow God no matter what the future held. God then knew Lazarus (which means, "God is my help"). On earth, everyone knew the rich man's name. He never bowed the knee to anyone but himself. No matter what your financial state here on earth, if you don't repent, you, too, will end up like the rich man. In the end, no one knew his name.

Luke 17

Scribe to the Heart

"Then Jesus answered, 'Were not ten cleansed? Where are the nine? Was no one found to return and give praise to God except this foreigner?' Then he said to him, 'Rise and go your way; your faith has made you well.'"

(Luke 17:17-19)

Point to Ponder

Jesus gets the credit.

Today's Journal

Do I recall a time when Jesus worked in my life and I returned to praise Him? What did I do? Did I tell others?

Prayer for the Day

Lord Jesus, Thank You for working in my life. I pray that I will always give You the glory. Amen!

THE LONELY LEPER

THERE ARE NINE simple verses devoted to Jesus' story about the lepers. They were most likely cast aside by their friends and families. Everyone feared leprosy as it was highly contagious, so the lepers had no one who wanted to be around them. They were forced to carry each other's pain and sorrow. In this story the lepers cried out from a distance because they were used to not getting close to people.

Jesus instructed them to go present themselves at the temple and He chose to heal them as they were on their way. It wasn't wrong that the other nine continued on to the temple. It's what Jesus told them. We get the sense though that they didn't come back at all. A foreigner, a Samaritan, came back. The Samaritan wouldn't have been welcome at the temple. The others, who may or may not have all been Jews, would have been allowed in the temple. Perhaps once they got there they were so thrilled to once again be accepted into the culture and return to their place in society that they forgot about Jesus who actually healed them. They forgot the one who changed their lives. They forgot Jesus Christ!

Jesus knew His audience would be offended by these events. The Samaritans were unclean lowlifes to the Jews. In this story the Samaritan could have gone on back to Samaria, but instead he returned to Jesus. He was ready to tell others what Jesus did for him. For this reason, he was counted righteous, and the others, who were physically healed, were not. They had the temple. All the Samaritan had was Jesus. Jesus didn't treat the Samaritan as second class.

As a high school and college wrestler I remember several times I prayed for God's hand in accomplishing my goals. A few times I was given public opportunity to give God the glory and I forgot Him. Two times that I specifically remember were a newspaper interview and our team banquet my senior year of college. It was so easy to depend on God and ask for His help, but for some reason it wasn't as easy to return the rightful credit to Him.

Luke 18

Scribe to the Heart

"And will not God give justice to his elect, who cry to him day and night? Will he delay long over them? I tell you, he will give justice to them speedily. Nevertheless, when the Son of Man comes, will He find faith on the earth."

(Luke 18:7-8)

Point to Ponder

Persistent prayer is heard by God.

Today's Journal

Have I given up on prayer about something?

Prayer for the Day

Holy Spirit, Remind me about something that I've given up praying about.

PERSISTENT PRAYER

THIS CHAPTER STARTS with Jesus telling a parable. He explains that in a certain town there was a man who didn't care about God, and didn't care about people. Most likely he was self-indulgent and worked his way up the political ladder. He was a judge, however, he didn't care about justice. He didn't care about right or wrong. He only cared about getting paid. He cared about his status in the community, his 401K, and his new convertible. (OK, some of that didn't exist yet.)

A woman came to the judge with much persistence. We don't know much about her except she was probably of insignificant status in the community. We also know someone had treated her unjustly. She went to the judge and nagged. Day and night she nagged him. The judge finally got tired of listening to her and gave her what she wanted. He didn't care about her or the situation. It was just easier to give in.

We see this all the time. A wife wants something and will continually tell her husband. The husband will eventually do it, not out of love, but just because it is easier to do it than not to do it. Kids do it to their parents when they want something, and often parents will give in to persistence. Jesus ends this story by telling us that those who cry out to Him day and night will receive justice. That's good news!

A good parent will attend to an infant who is crying and try to figure out what is wrong. God hears us and will care for us the same way. He will do so out of love, not just because we are persistent. He promises that we will find justice if we have been wronged. Pray, seek Him, and never give up asking for justice. I don't think many of us persist like this woman did. Many don't ever find justice because they quit. That is why Jesus asks the question, *"When the Son of Man comes, will he find faith on the earth?"*

A current tragic event may even bring about immense good in your life. Don't lose heart. Our vision is limited. We need to take it one step at a time. There is unbridled power in persistent prayer.

Luke 19

Scribe to the Heart

"Today salvation has come to this house, since he also is a son of Abraham."

(Luke 19:9)

Point to Ponder

Take your mess openly to Jesus and allow Him to clean it up.

Today's Journal

Can I relate to Zacchaeus? Can I relate to the people who didn't think Jesus should have anything to do with him?

Prayer for the Day

Holy Spirit, Give me strong faith to allow Jesus to clean up my messes.

ZACCHAEUS' HOUSE OR A CLEAN HOUSE?

LUKE RECORDS ANOTHER interesting account that is unique to his gospel. It is the account of Zacchaeus. Zacchaeus was a chief tax collector and he was wealthy. To be a good tax collector in those days meant you were cheating people out of their money. He was a leader among other tax collectors, which meant he was not only good at cheating people out of money, but he taught others to do the same.

We are told he was short. I have in mind a Danny DeVito type of character, like maybe the role he played in the movie *Twins*. He was short, deviant, and crafty. He probably learned how to survive this way from a very early age. His father may have been a tax collector. If that was true, the natural progression would be for him to do the same. After all, who would want to hire the son of a tax collector?

When Jesus saw this insignificant man, He took an interest in Him. There was something about Jesus that made Zacchaeus feel he could trust Him. In an unlikely event, Jesus invited Himself to the short tax collector's house. Now Zacchaeus is faced with a choice: Do I go home and clean up first? Do I decline because I am ashamed of my house? Or do I just allow Jesus to see me as I am?

Zacchaeus jumps on it! He probably almost fell out of his tree, and he took Jesus to the house. Jesus was well aware of how Zacchaeus acquired his possessions. I am sure there were a lot of things about Zacchaeus' home that were uncomfortable to have out in front of Jesus. However, he saw that Jesus loved Him.

This love did something. This man declared he was giving half of his possessions to the poor and paying back anyone he'd cheated four times the amount. The story ends with Jesus declaring that salvation had come to the house of Zacchaeus, because Jesus came to seek and save what was lost. Think about it. He gave up everything. By paying back four times what he cheated people, he owed way more than he could pay. But, no longer was he going to trust in wealth for security. Starting that moment he trusted Christ, and true salvation came to his house.

Luke 20

Scribe to the Heart

"But those who are considered worthy to attain to that age and to the resurrection from the dead neither marry nor are given in marriage, for they cannot die anymore, because they are equal to angels and are sons of God, being sons of the resurrection."

(Luke 20:35-36)

Point to Ponder

We are to have a heavenly vision.

Today's Journal

What vision do I have for what it will be like with Jesus and the resurrected church?

Prayer for the Day

Lord Jesus, I pray to have a heavenly vision.

SAD, YOU SEE

THE SADDUCEES WERE sad, you see. I mean, what did they have to be happy about? According to their beliefs there was no resurrection of the dead. I don't know how they couldn't have been sad. For them "dead is dead." This was a scriptural truth, and a doctrine to hold dear. Naturally they didn't like any of Jesus' teachings about the resurrection of the dead. So, one day they approached Jesus. They spoke of Moses' instruction that if a man died it was the duty of his brother to take his wife and give her children (Deuteronomy 25:5-10).

There are many reasons why that was a good idea in biblical times, and not so much anymore. It was much harder for a woman to survive without a husband, just for starters. To focus on the main point of this passage, they ask Him if a man has a wife and he dies, and she remarries a brother, and this happens seven times, then whose wife is she in the resurrection?

Jesus is able to answer this question because He has heavenly vision. Part of the problem with us people is often we can't see past our own point of view. Jesus simply explained the resurrection will be better than marriage. The fellowship we have with God and His followers will be much more intimate. It will be better than the best relationship you have with the person you are closest to on earth.

Now I like to believe we will continue on in the relationships we have here. I like to think we will have an even more fulfilling relationship with our loved ones. I want to know my wife in a more intimate way than I do even now, and personally I believe that to be part of this. It only makes sense to me that way. However, that part is not revealed. The revelation we are given is: There is a resurrection, and on the other side of that resurrection is intimacy with God and His saints, the church. So there is no need to be a Sadducee, and no need to be sad, you see.

Luke 21

Scribe to the Heart

*"And he said, 'Truly, I tell you, this poor widow
has put in more than all of them.
For they all contributed out of their abundance, but she
out of her poverty put in all she had to live on.'"*

(Luke 21:3-4)

Point to Ponder

Giving with a motive is buying, not giving.

Today's Journal

How do I try and buy influence? How do I give from a pure heart?

Prayer for the Day

Lord Jesus, Teach me how to be a giver and not a taker today.

SOLD OUT VS. BUYING

THIS CHAPTER OPENS up with a short story. Four short verses show us everything we need to see. Basically, there were rich people putting large gifts into the temple treasury. Jesus makes reference to how the rich gave from their wealth, and this poor widow gave two copper coins, and it was all she had to live on. It was hard for a widow in those days. She probably didn't know where her next meal would come from, so she had to trust God. She showed her trust in God by giving. Often those with more could give larger gifts than they do. If they truly trusted in the Lord, they would give much more.

A difference in the widow's giving and the attitude of many rich givers is intent. The widow's gift was between her and God. It wasn't impressive. Only God (Jesus) noticed it. However, there were probably many present, who made sure others saw how much they gave. In churches today people sometimes give with the intention of getting more say in where the money goes. The problem is that attitude is one of buying, not giving. Giving with the intent to gain influence is no different than buying enough stock in a company to be considered a decision-swaying share holder. It is business, not sacrifice.

God wants people to give from a place of faith. He designed His church to band together to be the hope of the world. He is not impressed with our large gifts. God is not after your money. He is after your heart. Yes, money can do a lot of good, but a fully committed believer is way more important to God. Sometimes the hardest thing for us to give up is money. God can use your money to feed poor people or to take the Gospel to new lands. Allow Him to be in charge of your finances, just like this widow did. There is freedom in knowing that God takes care of you when you are obedient. It is an emotionally fearful place to live if you are always trying to figure out how to take care of yourself.

Luke 22

Scribe to the Heart

"And he said to them, 'I have earnestly desired to eat this Passover with you before I suffer.'"

(Luke 22:15)

Point to Ponder

Jesus is our Passover lamb.

Today's Journal

What do I imagine it would have been like to be around the table of the Passover supper with Jesus and the disciples?

Prayer for the Day

Lord Jesus, Reveal to me what I need to know about receiving holy communion. Show me what it truly means.

PASSOVER

ONCE UPON A time God rescued the Jews from the evil and powerful Egyptian regime. As the story unfolds in Exodus, Moses continually confronted Pharaoh (the most powerful person on earth at that time) on behalf of the Lord to: "Let my people go."

Moses and Aaron warned Pharaoh of a series of coming plagues. The Pharaoh denied the request to let the Hebrew slaves go, and the plagues hit. The last and final plague was to be the most deadly of them all. The firstborn son of every household would die, unless you followed God's orders. A lamb was to be sacrificed that night and its blood smeared over the top of the door. In doing this, the destroyer would pass over that house and move on to the next one (Exodus 11-12).

In Jesus' day, any semi-observant Jew knew this story. Rabbis celebrated the Passover meal with their disciples. Families would do the same. In fact, it is still done among Jews today. How strange it must have been when Jesus took the bread at the Passover meal and said it was His body. How confusing when He lifted the cup and declared it to be His blood. Moving forward from that specific Passover, they were to do this in remembrance of Him. It was no longer just a story about their ancestors. It was now a story about them. It is a story about us. Christ is our Passover sacrifice. Just as the lambs were slain so death would pass over the house of Israel, the Lamb of God was slain for you and me. It was His blood and His body. It was His pain for my sin.

Now the destroyer will pass over me. I will not receive eternal death. I will live with Christ as a righteous one. I will live forever with His holy church, as if I never sinned. His blood has restored me. He kept me from eternal death, just as the blood of the Passover lamb kept the first born of every Jewish household free from physical death that night in Egypt. The next time you take communion, ponder the perfect Lamb that was slain. Ponder His pain, and ponder the fact that only He could rescue you from the destroyer.

Luke 23

Scribe to the Heart

"Then Jesus, calling out with a loud voice, said, 'Father, into your hands I commit my spirit!' And having said this he breathed his last."

(Luke 23:46)

Point to Ponder

Commit every breath to God.

Today's Journal

What would change if I were to commit every breath to God?

Prayer for the Day

Lord Jesus, Thank You for dying on the cross for me. I commit myself to You.

I COMMIT MY SPIRIT

"FATHER, INTO YOUR *hands I commit my spirit!" And having said this he breathed his last.*

Even in our modern world, thousands of people die for the name of Jesus every year. They have taken up the name of Christ where it is not only unpopular, but it is dangerous. They pay the ultimate price. Can you envision someone looking down the barrel of the gun, or into the eyes of their offender and declaring: "I will not deny my Savior, and into His hands I will commit my spirit."

There is a huge difference in Jesus' death and the death that any of us, even martyrs, face. What is the difference? Is it that Jesus died for God and Jesus died for us? These martyrs died for God, and as a witness to the rest of the world, and even to those who killed them. So, what is the difference? The difference can be found by pondering the last half of the verse: *"he breathed his last."* Jesus committed His Spirit to God the Father every breath of His entire life. That is part of what makes Him God. It is part of what made Him exceptionally different.

No matter how great the martyr, no matter how horrendous the story, martyrs didn't commit every breath to God. They became followers of Jesus understanding the need to give Him their whole hearts. They first needed to repent. They have all had many breaths that were independent and unsubmitted to God the Father. We all have. Consider this: Jesus never had one. And in this passage of Scripture we read that He committed His breath to God one last time.

Luke 24

Scribe to the Heart

"But Peter rose and ran to the tomb; stooping and looking in, he saw the linen cloths by themselves; and he went home marveling at what had happened."

(Luke 24:12)

Point to Ponder

Jesus died, was buried, but lives again.

Today's Journal

How does the thought that Jesus was dead and now He is not reasonate with me?

Prayer for the Day

Father, Guide me to a deeper understanding of the resurrection and how Jesus overcame death.

THE MAN WAS DEAD

MOST PREACHER TYPES devote much time to the crucifixion, and much time to the resurrection. What I am going to ask you to do today is to ponder something else. The man was dead. When Jesus died on the cross, the chemical changes of rigor mortis began to set in. His followers who were there prepared His body so that He would be preserved for burial. He lay helpless, and His body was destined to slowly wither away; or so it would seem.

Jesus was dead from Friday until early Sunday morning. His body was cold, stiff, and beginning to smell. Then by the power of God He came back to life. Notice, He didn't rise from the dead instantly after He died. He was dead for three days. Why would God allow Jesus to lay dead? Maybe He wanted to make sure that no one could say it was a hoax. Or He wanted His followers to have to fight for their faith. Followers and those on the fence may have needed a few days to understand what life would be like without Christ.

Early in the morning He got up. Death had no power over Him. What was Jesus' resurrected state like? We are left to wonder. However, we do know that some were kept from recognizing him. We read elsewhere that Jesus had the scars on His hands and feet after the Resurrection. (John 20:27) Some believe they will be the only scars in heaven. I am not sure. If we are all honest, without our scars we wouldn't have even found Christ. Scarring emotional pain and emptiness is what brought me to God. Having those scars to look at and remember may be one of the most amazing joys of heaven. When God shows us our scars, we can remember that just like Jesus we too were once dead. Our spiritual bodies were stiff and rigor mortis had set in. We were on the road to no place good. However, by what Jesus did, we didn't have to stay that way.

Acts 1

Scribe to the Heart

"In the first book, O Theophilus, I have dealt with all that Jesus began to do and teach, until the day when he was taken up, after he had given commands through the Holy Spirit to the apostles whom he had chosen."

(Acts 1:1-2)

Point to Ponder

Acts is Act II of Luke.

Today's Journal

How does Act II of Luke relate to me and my story?

Prayer for the Day

Lord Jesus, Involve me in Your story today.

LUKE: ACT II

TODAY'S ENTRY WILL help to give you a framework for the book of Acts. Luke referred to his first book (Luke) while opening up his second book (Acts). Acts is properly known as The Acts of the Apostles. Over the years, many theologians have advocated for other names for this collection of writing. Two of the most popular names suggested are Acts of Jesus, and Acts of The Holy Spirit. The gospel story of Luke gave us an orderly account of Jesus' life and ministry. This book begins where the book of Luke ends. Acts begins at the ascension of Jesus.

In Acts, you will find that the main character of the story is always changing. In the beginning there is a lot of focus on Peter. Then we are given snapshots of others, like Stephen and Philip. In chapter 9 we will read of the Apostle Paul's conversion and, as he reaches out to the gentiles, he becomes the central character of many of the passages.

I believe there is a reason why there is not a single main character, or a clear plot line. Acts tells the story of the continued ministry of Jesus. Jesus influenced His followers. In the book of Acts they become empowered by the Holy Spirit. Sit back and enjoy these stories. People are about to be healed. Many will receive eternal salvation, but don't think it will come without a price. There will be danger, pain, and imprisonment. Some will be martyred.

This is the story of the Christian Church. God wants to use the church. It has been part of His plan all along. Bill Hybels coined the phrase, "The local church is the hope of the world." We are the hope of the world, but it comes with a price. Luke invites his readers to enter the battle. As we begin our 5th book of study in *The New Testament Challenge*, I invite you to enter a world without the physical presence of Jesus, I invite you to experience the drama. Be willing to be a living sacrifice. This is our story; this is your story.

Day 91

Acts 2

Scribe to the Heart

"For these people are not drunk, as you suppose, since it is only the third hour of the day."

(Acts 2:15)

Point to Ponder

Wrestling through doubt is necessary to produce faith.

Today's Journal

I have faith in…
Things I doubt include…

Prayer for the Day

Lord Jesus, Give me faith today.

IT'S ONLY 9 IN THE MORNING!

IN ACTS CHAPTER 1, Jesus directed the disciples to go to Jerusalem and wait for God's presence. This second chapter opens with the arrival of that presence: The Holy Spirit. The word Pentecost is the Greek name for the Old Testament Jewish Feast of Weeks that took place fifty days after the Passover. God chose this day as the day to send His presence to the followers of Jesus. The indwelling of Holy Spirit amongst believers happened as they were gathered together per Jesus' instructions. The non-believers heard these Jews begin to speak in other languages. They weren't just any other languages, they were the exact languages of those who were looking on.

At first it was unbelievable. At second glance the skeptics began to explain it away. They said, "These people are drunk." Then Peter stood up. He addressed the crowd to tell them they were not drunk; it was only nine in the morning! As Christian leaders do, Peter began to explain what was happening, but the wonder of it all was unexplainable. They all asked, "What does this mean?"

The sight was spectacular, but doubters tried to explain it away. To have the choice of faith, you always have the choice of doubt. Faith and doubt go together. You must wrestle through doubt to get to faith. As Peter explained this phenomenon under the empowerment of Holy Spirit, 3,000 people were saved and baptized that very day.

God was able to answer their question: *"What does this mean?"* It was the power of God. It was the fulfillment of prophecy. It was the beginning of the church. This was one of the most exciting things to ever happen. Even in that moment, we are tempted to look on and say, "Pay no attention, they are drunk." In our walk with God we are challenged every day to trust Him. We are to trust Him and live for Him every second. Sometimes however, we act in sin and disbelief. We say, "What is this all about?" As we walk with God, and trust Him, we can allow Him to empower us. Others may doubt the power they see in you. They may tell you that you are drunk. With confidence you can tell them, "I am fine. Besides, it is much too early for drinking."

Acts 3

Scribe to the Heart

"Then Peter said, 'Silver or gold I do not have, but what I do have I give you. In the name of Jesus Christ of Nazareth, walk.'"

(Acts 3:6)

Point to Ponder

The answer is always Jesus.

Today's Journal

What do I have?

Prayer for the Day

Lord, Show me what I have that I am to give to others.

WHAT DO YOU HAVE?

THERE WAS ONCE a man. Like many other men, he was born with problems. He was crippled. All of his life people tried to help him. They took pity on him. As a young boy he dreamed of being able to walk. He had dreams of playing and running like other children. As he got older he dreamed of having a family. He wanted a wife and children.

At some point it became easier to accept the daily help everyone gave him and not look for anything else. It was easier not to hope too much anymore. The man just wanted food. He had those who would help him, who'd carry him to the outside of the temple where people were the most vulnerable to feeling guilt.

He begins to beg while his friends are carrying him towards the temple gate. He was a sad man, in a sad situation. He had been dealt a bad hand, and he was going to use it the best way he knew how.

On the road he meets up with two men. There were several people who wanted to talk to them. The man thinks these guys must be important. He yells out to them with a sad face. He expresses his need for spare change and humble crumbs from their table.

Then something happened that changed his life forever. Peter, the follower of Jesus, looked right at him to assess the situation. A Spirit-guided follower of Jesus must be able to see the real problem. The problem wasn't money, clothes, or food. The problem wasn't even his disability. The problem was he needed God! John and Peter remembered a time when Jesus healed a man who was born blind. Jesus told them that neither he nor his parents sinned, but sometimes people are born blind so that God can work in their life (John 9:3).

"Then Peter said, 'Silver or gold I do not have, but what I do have I give you. In the name of Jesus Christ of Nazareth, walk.'" The man's life was changed.

So, I ask you this question. When someone comes to you with a hurt, what do you have to give? The answer is always Jesus.

Acts 4

Scribe to the Heart

"greatly annoyed because they were teaching the people and proclaiming in Jesus the resurrection of the dead."

(Acts 4:2)

Point to Ponder

When you are annoyed, submit to God.

Today's Journal

In what way is God annoying me? Is it a sin to address or a challenge to face?

Prayer for the Day

Holy Spirit, Build in me a submissive heart.

GREATLY ANNOYED

*"**AND AS THEY** were speaking to the people, the priests and the captain of the temple and the Sadducees came upon them, **greatly annoyed** because they were teaching the people and proclaiming in Jesus the resurrection from the dead"* (Acts 4:1-2 emphasis mine).

The Sadducees and Pharisees didn't agree on anything, yet they were united in this feeling towards the apostles. First, they were annoyed because the apostles were teaching, second they were annoyed because of what they were teaching. They were teaching and proclaiming the resurrection of Jesus the Christ.

We must ask, why were they *really* annoyed? They were annoyed because they were losing their religious control. They had Jesus killed, not because they didn't believe He was the Messiah, they had Him killed because He didn't fit their description of the Messiah.

Even as Christians we treat God this way. We are OK at quitting someone else's sin, but we don't do so well at quitting our own. Often times we Christians focus so much energy on condemning the sins we don't understand. We don't understand them because they are not our sins. The church loves to condemn the homosexual community, while heterosexual people listening are shacking up out of wedlock and saying, "Amen to that, Pastor!" When Jesus came on the scene the Pharisees and Sadducees were not ready for Jesus to call them to a new standard. They weren't prepared to allow Jesus to publicly oppose their way of doing things. So, they took Him out. Or so they thought.

Now that He is gone, He has multiplied. Even though the Pharisees thought they put Him to death, Jesus was a willing sacrifice all along. He told the disciples it was better for Him to go away so they could be empowered by the Spirit (John 16:7). God now dwells within the hearts of believers and He has continued to multiply His presence in the world. Every once in a while, we are annoyed. God disrupts our way of living. He lets us be annoyed in order to address our sin or to call us to new challenges. We belong to Him. It isn't the other way around. When you feel annoyed, ask God to show you what it is all about.

Acts 5

Scribe to the Heart

"Great fear seized the whole church and all who heard about these events."

(Acts 5:11)

Point to Ponder

Do not ever forget that God is Holy.

Today's Journal

To me, God's holiness means...

Prayer for the Day

Holy Spirit, Show me how I can do a better job regarding God as Holy. Thank You for guiding me in my thoughts, my words, and my actions. Amen.

JESUS IS MY HOMEBOY?

DRIVING DOWN THE road a car in front of you has a sticker on the rear windshield that reads, "God is my Co-Pilot."

You drive by a church marquee and read, "You have a friend in Jesus."

You walk into the local high school and you see a teenage boy who is brave enough to wear the name of Jesus on His t-shirt. The shirt reads, "Jesus is my homeboy."

There are millions of other creative ideas that people have used to bring the message of Christianity into our culture. I affirm these slogans and the hearts behind them. However, sometimes in our slogans we leave out part of the message. T-shirts that read, "God is Holy," or "The Fear of God is the Beginning of Knowledge" (Proverbs 1:7a), just don't sell as well as "Jesus is my homeboy."

As our story unfolds in Acts, we read of many who join up with the first church. It is exciting. People are being saved, healed, and baptized. Lives are being turned upside down. Nothing like this has ever happened before. It was understood that believers were to give financially to take care of each other. In this chapter we read of a couple who decided to lie about what they had, and held back from the apostles. They thought they were only lying to men, but since God was in charge, and it was His command for these people, they were struck dead.

This couple forgot that God was holy. "We work hard for what we have, we will keep back a little extra," they think. "Who will know?" God knew. He struck them dead. It seems harsh, but look what happened afterward: *"Great fear seized the whole church and all who heard about these events."*

We read a few verses later that even though more people believed, they hesitated to join up with them. More people were saved, more were healed, and it brought the believers together in a stronger way. We can never forget that God is Holy. He is in charge. When this is in proper focus, great things happen.

Acts 6

Scribe to the Heart

"So the word of God spread. The number of disciples in Jerusalem increased rapidly, and a large number of priests became obedient to the faith."

(Acts 6:7)

Point to Ponder

A church is best grown naturally, under the caring hand of God.

Today's Journal

How does my church look like the church I read about in the book of Acts? In what ways is it different?

Prayer for the Day

Father, Show me a vision of what You want the church to look like today.

NATURAL CHURCH

JESUS COMMANDED US to preach the gospel. We are to be about the business of building His church. Sometimes we confuse that with building an organization and calling it a church, or building a building and calling it the church. Neither of these man- made concepts are what Jesus intended. Don't get me wrong, those things are used to further God's Kingdom, but these methods are not to be the end within themselves.

In this chapter, as the church is growing in number, we see a problem arise. There is an accusation. The widows of the Jewish Christians are being taken care of, but the Greek widows, who are gentile converts, are not being looked after. Whether or not the accusation was true or not isn't the issue. The problem that arose was that the church had grown, but the apostles had not yet defined leadership roles within.

At first the apostles could run around and lead everything. They could preach, teach, lead, direct, counsel people, distribute food, etc. Since it had grown, they needed to redefine who they were. Notice what happened: The apostles declared they were going to spend their time attending to prayer and preaching the Word. They decided it was time to appoint some new leaders. God directed this decision all along. There were seven men ready to step into the leadership role of distributing food. The whole group was pleased, and the result was two-fold. First, the church was pleased. Second, many more were saved, even Jewish priests.

Many pastors and leaders think it is their job to do the ministry. It is not. It is their job to teach people how to do ministry, and recognize when they are ready for ministry. When God directs the church, He is raising up leaders and turning people from darkness to light. It happens naturally. The church will grow naturally when it is fed and exercised correctly. Small groups of people become a church, and over time it grows. This may lead to starting another church, or sending missionaries overseas. A healthy church is a church that creates both leaders and converts and continues to multiply.

Acts 7

Scribe to the Heart

"While they were stoning him, Stephen prayed, 'Lord Jesus, receive my spirit.'"

(Acts 7:59)

Point to Ponder

When you handle persecution well, the world knows you are for real.

Today's Journal

How have I handled persecution poorly in the past?

Prayer for the Day

Lord, Teach me to follow You in all circumstances today.

WHY STEPHEN?

AT THIS POINT in the book of Acts you may be struck with an alarming reality: God may allow even His most devoted followers to experience great persecution. A faithful young Christ-follower may even die a brutal death for the name of Jesus. Stephen was a man full of the Spirit and wisdom. He was known as a worker of miracles and was full of grace. Even on trial before the Sanhedrin, his face was seen as like the face of an angel.

Stephen went into great detail about the prophets and how they pointed to the Messiah whom they awaited. Stephen spoke at length about how Jesus was the fulfillment of scripture. The Pharisees hated this talk so much they were grinding their teeth. While they were stoning him to death he looked up and could see Jesus. He cried out to Him and then fell asleep (died). A young Pharisee named Saul was giving approval to this death and was holding the coats of the ones stoning Stephen. At first glance it seems tragic. It seems as though God allowed this Christ-follower to be defeated. This event sparked revival that lasted through the centuries. Stephen's death glorified God. The church scattered under persecution. When Christians scatter, the message spreads.

I'd like you to notice and remember that Saul was there to give approval to the death Stephen. People think of Paul's conversion as instantaneous on the road to Damascus. However, were these seeds planted for a later instantaneous change? No one could wrangle with Paul in theological dialogue. He watched Stephen stoned to death like a criminal. He saw the humiliation and the tragedy of a life cut way short. And he saw him die at peace. At the time that was a peace Saul/Paul knew nothing about. It seems as though this must have affected Paul in deep way.

The world around us looks on as we are faced with horrendous choices. Hopefully we will never have to make the ultimate choice like this, however, the world looks at us to see if we are truly following Jesus.

Acts 8

"On that day a great persecution broke out against the church at Jerusalem, and all except the apostles were scattered throughout Judea and Samaria."

(Acts 8:1)

Point to Ponder

The Church thrives under persecution.

Today's Journal

How has God called me to lift up His name during something hard?

Prayer for the Day

Lord Jesus, My desire is to lift Your name when it is unpopular to do so. Strengthen me during these times. Amen.

GREMLINS

GREMLINS WAS THE name of a movie that was popular when I was a child. It was a movie about little creatures. A teenaged boy was given one of these creatures as a pet. The pet was named Gizmo. Gizmo was extremely cute and cuddly. However, Gizmo came with special instructions. Don't get him wet and don't feed after midnight were two of the most important instructions. If the instructions weren't followed, something very bad would happen. And, as you can guess, the instructions weren't followed. Gizmo multiplied. The newly spawned "Gizmos" weren't all cute and cuddly like he was. They were devilish. They were dangerous, angry, and wreaked all kinds of havoc.

If you were someone who wanted to stop the church from growing, there are certain things you mustn't do. One of which is persecution. Don't persecute the church because that is when you find out who is for real. When the world sees the church living out its mission, even when Christians go to jail or are killed for it, more people will want to know what Christianity is about. It defeats the one doing the persecuting.

When the church is persecuted, the Christians will scatter. When they scatter, many more will hear the gospel. The outbreak of persecution found in Acts chapter 8 was the beginning of serious evangelism. Many were hearing the gospel. Localized bodies were about to be formed. Lives were being changed on account of the response to the persecution. An effort to kill the church only made it stronger, just like the gremlins became stronger and scattered. The difference is that the havoc we make is havoc upon Satan's schemes. We are to shake people up spiritually for the cause of Christ. That makes us dangerous to the devil's plans.

Acts 9

"I will show him how much he must suffer for my name."

(Acts 9:16)

We have a ministry to those who we used to be like.

Today's Journal

What type of non-Christian person do I relate to best? Why?

Prayer for the Day

Lord Jesus, Reveal to me those to whom I must reach out.

A CALL TO SUFFER

HAVE YOU EVER met someone who is always angry? Someone for whom anger is the normal state? To this type of person, you may look at him or her and ask, "What happened to you? What are you mad about?" Some know why they are mad. Some of them do not. It could be that they were abused as children. Maybe their marriage isn't going like they thought it would. There are countless reasons why people are angry. At some point each of us gets angry, but not everyone gets over it. Saul of Damascus became an angry guy. He was very religious and devout in his faith.

In his devotion to keep the Jewish faith, he came across something new. There were those who claimed to be followers of the way of Jesus. They claimed Jesus was the Messiah the Jews were waiting for. This infuriated Saul. Saul actually stood and gave approval for the death of Stephen. He watched while Stephen was willing to die, and heard as Stephen asked God to forgive his oppressors (Acts 7:60-8:1).

Saul then began to persecute the followers of Jesus of Nazareth. Saul was dragging out entire families and imprisoning them. One day God showed up in his life in a way he'd never experienced. God seems to show up when we least expect Him, doesn't He? Saul was in search of more Christians to condemn when suddenly He was struck blind. All along God was calling him. Now it was loud and clear. Saul is now known as Paul. His life was changed. He was never the same again.

God called a Christian brother named Ananias to pray with Paul. When Ananias questioned the Lord, God said something interesting. He told him about how much the man Paul would suffer for His name. How fitting? Paul inflicted suffering on Christians, now he must suffer as a Christian. What goes around comes around, I guess? But wait a minute. Paul is forgiven. God doesn't hold that against him anymore. Why then must he suffer? The answer is that no one would have understood what it was like to be a persecutor of Christians more than Paul. No one would have known what it meant to hate and be angry more than Paul did. God needed someone who understood what it was like. Paul was able to relate to the very people God needed him to reach.

Acts 10

"*The voice spoke to him a second time, 'Do not call anything impure that God has made clean.'*"

(Acts 10:15)

Point to Ponder

God's will can be found when we love Jesus more than anything else.

Today's Journal

What is the gospel? What things do I focus on more than I do the gospel?

Prayer for the Day

Lord Jesus, Help me take the gospel to the ends of the earth.

WHAT IS THE GOSPEL?

IN CHRISTIAN CIRCLES you will hear the term gospel used often. That's because gospel is the Greek word for "good news." The good news is that Jesus Christ rescued us from our sin. He lived a sinless life. He died for our sins, then rose from the dead. He lives forever, and those who follow Him will live forever in fellowship of His Holy Church. That is the good news that we are to tell. Jesus left the earth and His heart commands us to "Go into all the world and preach the gospel (Mark 16:15)." I realize we had a conversation about that verse already, but you can't hear it enough. This is the heart of Christ.

I have a friend named Jimbo. Jimbo came to Christ through dramatic circumstances. He loves Jesus. His wife, who has gone on to be with the Lord, loved Jesus too and fervently prayed for his ministry. Jimbo is an evangelist. He tells people the good news. One thing he always says is: "I just give them the gospel." He doesn't talk to them about baptism, confirmation, communion, if women can be ordained, or if you can lose your salvation. He tells them to believe on Christ. He recruits church leaders to disciple new believers into good doctrine. For Him it is only about the gospel.

Doctrine is important. We are to know God, and know Him well, but don't allow issues that God allows to be vague to distract you from reaching someone for Christ. When Jesus was walking with the disciples, He declared all food clean (Mark 7:19). Peter, who is in charge now, must have still been hung up on eating kosher foods and keeping with Jewish tradition. Jesus just wanted people to meet Him. He will begin to change them after their initial meeting. The first thing people need to know is that they are sinners. The second thing is that Jesus is the answer to this sin problem. Thus the journey begins.

Last Sunday morning, people argued in Sunday school classes all across North America about the proper structure of church government, or if we can lose our salvation once we have it, or if we have free-will or not. All the while these same people know of friends who have broken marriages, can't pay their bills, or are angry at God, and bitter. Jesus wants us to love our neighbors. In this chapter Peter is called out of his comfort zone. He might have to eat food he isn't used to. He may have to go places he hasn't been before. But that's not important: People needed the gospel.

Acts 11

Scribe to the Heart

"When they heard this, they had no further objections and praised God, saying, 'So then, God has granted even the Gentiles repentance unto life.'"

(Acts 11:18)

Point to Ponder

It is important to see Jesus clearly.

Today's Journal

What if Jesus came back? What do I think He would do?

Prayer for the Day

Lord Jesus, Give me eyes to see You clearly.

WHAT IF JESUS CAME BACK?

WHAT IF JESUS *came back?* I am not talking about the way we are expecting Him to. We know He is coming back and will judge the earth. I'd like us to speculate: What if He came back to walk the earth again, like He did the first time? I often think most of our pictures of what that would look like are ridiculous. Would He appear to the religious and don Himself in robes and a noticeable fancy hat? Would He hold special services where He sprinkles water on the people and they use big words like Potentate, Ecclesiology, and Anathema?

What if Jesus came back? Would He stand on the corner and preach? Would He carry a large sign that has a giant list of all the reasons people are going to hell? Would He preach about the fires of hell to scare people?

What if Jesus came back? Would He hold special meetings for the academically elite to discuss the deeper meaning of His parables, and proper Eschatology expounded from the book of Revelation?

What if Jesus came back? It would be just like the first time. He would love people. He would give us His all. He would ask us to follow Him. He would ask us to pray like Him, love like Him, and do what He did. Isn't it funny the strange ideas we have about Jesus? Don't feel bad. The disciples didn't understand either. When Peter came back and spoke to the Church about God's command to take Jesus' message to the gentiles, they had an interesting response.

"When they heard this, they had no further objections and praised God, saying, 'So then, God has granted even the Gentiles repentance unto life.'" Wow! It must have been a common perception that Jesus didn't care about the gentiles and this even seemed like a new idea. This should cause us to ask: What ways do I misunderstand Jesus?

Acts 12

Scribe to the Heart

"'You're out of your mind,' they told her. When she kept insisting that It was so, they said, 'It must be his angel.'"

(Acts 12:15)

Point to Ponder

Faith is believing with our mind, heart, and actions.

Today's Journal

Is there something I do that looks like faith, but is really fear? Do I spiritualize my faith at the expense of good news?

Prayer for the Day

Lord, My desire is to live through faith in You alone. Deepen my faith.

FALSE FAITH DECEPTION

IF I WERE the devil, I would create a false faith deception. That is truly what the battle is about, right? It is about faith. It is about who we put our faith in. It is about what you put your faith in. The true and living Christ asks that we put our faith in Him. Putting your faith in Him is a decision to live according to the light. To follow after Him, seek His voice and live a life of righteousness and peace.

The devil doesn't want us to see Jesus as He is. So, he is forced to create something false and try to convince us to put our faith in that. Anytime we decide to go against God by sinning we are believing that going the way of the devil will bring about the right result. If I were the devil, I would dress that sin up and make it look so good! He is able to trap many by the standard trappings of the world; sex, drugs, jealousy and gossip to name a few.

For those who aren't as easily swayed the devil needs to create another avenue of temptation. If I were the devil, the only way to get these hard cases would be to sit down with the other demons and create something spiritually false. It would need to be something that looks like it is Christian. We see it every day. Turn on the T.V., you will see people prophesying that you need to send them money for your own financial security. Many churches preach messages that focus on the latest headlines. Because of this week's headline Jesus is obviously coming very soon.

In this chapter, at the dawn of Christianity a group of disciples are sitting in a room praying for the Apostle Peter. There were probably heavy prayers that were possibly even declaring the release of Peter from prison in the name of Christ. When he came to the door and knocked, it was easier to believe the visitor to be spiritual. They declared it must be his angel. His angel? Like I said, it sounds spiritual. Notice something, it is faithless. They were praying for Peter to be delivered. He was! That is good news! That is great news! Why would you want even his angel present, if it didn't bring about anything positive for him?

Acts 13

Scribe to the Heart

"While they were worshiping the Lord and fasting, the Holy Spirit said, 'Set apart for me Barnabas and Saul for the work to which I called them.'"

(Acts 13:2)

Point to Ponder

God's calling is different from His sending.

Today's Journal

How have I been called? How have I been sent? What's the difference?

Prayer for the Day

Lord Jesus, Teach me about Your calling and Your sending for my life.

CALLED AND SENT

IN ACTS CHAPTER 9 we saw that Saul of Tarsus, who was persecuting Christians, became a Christian himself. Luke the author wants us to read between the lines. Saul, a very educated and devout Pharisee, is now a Christian. Surely that qualifies him as a great missionary or pastor. After all, he is more educated than the other followers and is now committed to Christianity.

It doesn't always work that way. God took some extra time with Paul. Why did he take extra time with Paul? It is hard to say. One thing is for certain. God knows what He is doing. Maybe Paul needed to experience worship under the leadership of others first. Maybe God just wanted to teach Paul patience. Whatever it was, it is important to understand the difference between being called and being sent. It seems in this passage that Paul and Barnabas knew it was coming, but God had not permitted them to move forward with the plan yet.

They were in a state of worship with other believers and they agreed the Spirit was telling them to go forward. Christians often find their calling. There is much talk about being called to do this or that. God burdens some to be pastors, leaders or missionaries. He may call you to be a mother, or to adopt a child. However, being called and being sent are not the same thing. A person may spend many years feeling the burden for something before God sets them free to actually pursue their life's calling.

Day 103

Acts 14

Scribe to the Heart

"But when the apostles Barnabas and Paul heard of this, they tore their clothes and rushed into the crowd, shouting: 'Men, why are you doing this? We too are only men, human like you.'"

(Acts 14:14-15a)

Point to Ponder

Always point to God.

Today's Journal

In what ways do I give God the glory? How can I do better?

Prayer for the Day

Father God, I give You the glory today.

A GREAT PREACHER, BUT NO MAN OF GOD

I KNELT TO pray as I had many times before. As a wrestler, my prayer was always similar. I prayed not to get injured. I prayed for success. And, as always, I prayed that spiritual prayer that I would give God the glory. My senior season as a college wrestler He gave me three opportunities to do so. The first time was at a big match. Everything came together. I had to lose a lot of weight in order to wrestle in my weight class, 174 lbs. At the weigh-in they drew 184 lbs. as the weight class that would wrestle first. That meant my weight class would go last, giving me a lot of time between the weigh-in and my match. God provided for me.

Our team out-wrestled our undefeated opponents and I was more than ready to go when it was time to wrestle a former high school teammate who was very accomplished. I wrestled possibly the best match I ever wrestled that night. The local sports editor stopped me after the match. He asked me all kinds of questions. It was the perfect opportunity to give God the glory. I missed it. Even after God allowed me to have a successful night, and allowed everything to go my way, I still missed it.

About a month later I took fourth place at the mid-season conference tournament. I was interviewed again after losing my last match. I was too self-consumed to see the opportunity to give God the glory. Once again, I missed it. My last chance came at the end of the year. At our senior banquet, I gave my speech and had a perfect opportunity to share how Jesus was alive and well in my life, and how important He was in getting me to this stage. I thanked everyone but Him. This future pastor gave a great speech. That day you could have called me a preacher, but no man of God.

We are all tempted in many ways. The measure of a true man or woman of God is to whom they give the credit. In this chapter of Acts, Paul and Barnabas were being worshipped for working in God's name. Who wouldn't like that? They didn't. The Bible says, "They tore their clothes." Paul and Barnabas understood Jesus deserved the credit.

Acts 15

Scribe to the Heart

"It is my judgment, therefore, that we should not make it difficult for the Gentiles who are turning to God."

(Acts 15:9)

Point to Ponder

The law is meant to point us to God.

Today's Journal

In what way am I legalistic about my faith? How does it keep me from pointing people to Jesus?

Prayer for the Day

Lord Jesus, Let me represent You well today. Help me not be too legalistic, but also help me not to be too lenient in how I follow You.

OUT WITH THE OLD

IT IS NO secret that people are slow to change. The church is no different. Change scares us. It messes with us. In this chapter we are dealing with very weighty subject matter. To get a deep understanding of this subject, take some time and examine the text. Also, have a look in the Old Testament at the last three books of Moses (Leviticus, Numbers, and Deuteronomy). Basically, Moses gave the Jews many laws and customs to abide by. Some were for moral reasons. Some served a purpose for a time. Some were for other reasons. Overall, the purpose of every law was to point us to God.

The main item on the agenda at the Jerusalem Council meeting was the topic of circumcision. Jews were circumcised as a matter of national identity as God's people. Many of these first Christians saw circumcision as something all gentile converts must do. They believed that is how "they" (the gentiles) would identify with "us" (the Christians). However, Jesus didn't call Christians to go into the world and circumcise. He called us to go into the world and baptize. Some of the Old Law served its purpose. Some of it is still very relevant. There is no indication, for example, that the Ten Commandments are something we should ignore. We are to follow them to the T.

In getting rid of some of the old that pointed to Jesus coming to earth, Jesus also instituted some new things to help us in remembering He was here. One of those is communion. As New Testament believers, the Lord's Supper helps us to identify with the risen Christ. He is with us in communion, as a local body of believers remembering Him. Baptism is also something that Jesus instituted for new believers to identify themselves with Him.

Acts 16

Scribe to the Heart

"During the night Paul had a vision of a man standing and begging him, 'Come over to Macedonia and help us.'"

(Acts 16:9)

Point to Ponder

God sometimes uses dreams and visions.

Today's Journal

What do I believe about God speaking through dreams and visions? Use well thought out biblical reasoning to answer. Don't give your "opinion."

Prayer for the Day

Lord Jesus, Give me Your vision for my life today.

JUST ENOUGH LIGHT

I HAVE MANAGED to work through the first part of this book avoiding a very important yet controversial topic among many pastors and Christian writers. That topic is dreams and visions. There are many good-hearted, well-versed, and accomplished Bible teachers who avoid this topic. Some will tell you that dreams and visions ceased with the death of the apostles. Others find ways around it, and call it one of those areas of theology we don't know much about. Some declare that we are in possession of God's written Word so we are no longer in need of dreams or visions.

The fact is throughout scripture, dreams and visions are a natural part of the lives of the people of faith. When Peter quoted Joel in his sermon in Acts 2, the Apostle Peter declared these to be the last days and in these last days old men will dream dreams, young men will see visions, and men and women both will prophesy (Acts 2:17). When Peter declares these days to be the last days, he was talking of the church age.

I understand why many pastors and Bible teachers would want us to just rely on the Bible and not on dreams and visions. The fact is, it is risky, and there are all kinds of whack jobs on TV and everywhere else declaring they had a revelation about the money you are to send them. What is to stop someone from declaring Jesus' return this week based on a vision? I get the skepticism.

His personal revelation to you will never contradict His Word. If your vision or dream doesn't line up with His written Word it's not Him. Another consideration, why would God give a vision? In Paul's case, God wasn't revealing anything new to Paul to be canonized or preserved through generations. It was for him.

God needed to teach Paul something specific about how he was to live out his personal calling. God wanted the people in Macedonia to hear the gospel and He chose to get Paul and Barnabas there through a dream. You may pray for a family member, and God may show you in a dream or vision how to talk or pray for them. Warning: This doesn't mean all dreams are from God. It also doesn't mean you will ever experience a dream or vision from God. But, don't count it out. We serve a living God!

Day 106

Acts 17

Scribe to the Heart

"Now when they heard of the resurrection of the dead, some mocked. But others said, 'We will hear you again about this.'"

(Acts 17:32)

Point to Ponder

The gospel reaches the minds and hearts of real people.

Today's Journal

What type of worldview does my closest non-Christian friend have? How does knowing this help me present Jesus to him / her?

Prayer for the Day

Lord Jesus, Show me how to take Your message to those around me.

REAL PEOPLE

EVERY ONCE IN awhile we are struck with the realization that these were real people. The Bible is filled with real people with real problems. They followed local religions. They embraced the worldview of their local region.

As Dr. Luke gives us an orderly account of the travels of Paul in this last half of Acts, he reminds us of some real people that were influenced by Paul's preaching. *"Now when they heard of the resurrection of the dead, some mocked. But others said, 'We will hear you again about this.' So Paul went out from their midst. But some men joined him and believed, among whom also were Dionysius the Areopagite and a woman named Damaris and others with them"* (Acts 17:32-34).

Paul faced something all preachers have faced since the beginning of preaching. Real people were laughing. However, Luke wanted to make mention of those who still were not sure and some who even believed after seemingly only one hearing of the gospel. To the untrained eye these new converts are glanced over. It is the only mention of these people in the entire Bible. To the original first century reader these may have been people many of the first century readers would have known.

Notice Luke also mentions Dionysius was a member of the Areopagus. This was divided into two schools of Greek philosophers. The Epicureans believed nothing in the world was lasting or stable. The Stoics believed that everything was determined by a universal mind or reason. Why is this important to us? It is important to us because we need to see the gospel transcends time, space, and worldviews of past and present. Yes, some laughed, but let's not miss that some listened.

Acts 18

Scribe to the Heart

"And when they opposed and reviled him, he shook out his garments and said to them, 'Your blood be on your own heads! I am innocent. From now on I will go to the Gentiles.'"

(Acts 18:6)

Point to Ponder

Like Paul, we are made perfectly for the ministry God has for us.

Today's Journal

"God calls us to ministries that we wouldn't necessarily think of for ourselves." How does that statement sit with me? Have I seen this is my life? How?

Prayer for the Day

Holy Spirit, Show me the ministry that I am called to. Let me be bold to step into it.

WHY PAUL FOR THE GENTILES?

IF WE WERE to decide what ministry a given person was called to, I am sure we would come up with different scenarios than God does. However, He is good, right and perfect. He also acts with great intention. Paul especially had a heart for Jews to know Jesus. He himself was a Jew. He was a respected Pharisee who studied under Gamaliel. He spent his life following rules and memorizing scripture. To me Paul is the perfect apostle to focus on converting Jews to the way.

Peter, on the other hand, was a fisherman. He was less educated aside from his personal hands-on experience with Jesus. I think he would have been the perfect person to go to the gentiles. Interestingly enough, God gave them both amazing ministries that were focused on the opposite people group to what we might think.

In this chapter Paul is focused on persuading people within the synagogue in Corinth on the Sabbath. In the cited verses to the left, we see what Paul had to say when he was rejected in the synagogue. It was the strong opposition of Paul's message by the Jews which gave him the ear of the gentiles. Paul was obviously tempted to feel frustrated or in danger. God simply told him to stay because of all the people in the city that belong to Him. God was talking of future converts, since the city had very few Christians in it.

Paul actually went next door to a house where they could meet to talk about Jesus. The message of the way set up shop right beside the synagogue. Many gentiles were open to the message and investigating because of the conflict between Paul and the synagogue. Paul's deep knowledge of the Jewish scriptures and tradition is a quality that made him worthy of an audience.

Acts 19

Scribe to the Heart

"But the evil spirit answered them, 'Jesus I know, and Paul I recognize, but who are you?'"

(Acts 19:15)

Point to Ponder

Our power for spiritual warfare comes from knowing Jesus.

Today's Journal

Do the demons know who I am?

Prayer for the Day

Holy Spirit, Keep me in close connection with You. Help me to battle in prayer.

BUT WHO ARE YOU?

THERE IS A real battle which exists in the spiritual realm. In this chapter we see the heightened spiritual battle in the city of Ephesus. At the time Ephesus was a busy port city. Local worship was centered heavily around the goddess Artemis. Paul finds the city very upset with him as he spoke against the city's fertility god. The local economy was heavily dependent upon the making and selling of Artemis idols. It was deeply ingrained in the culture.

There is an interesting story thrown in here I want to focus on today. There were seven sons, referred to as sons of a high priest, who were performing exorcisms. On paper they seem to be ideal for the job. They came from the right family. They grew up learning the religion trade. But when these seven sons encountered a demon-possessed man, the man beat them and tore off all of their clothes.

In the spiritual realm these seven sons were no-names. The spirit knew he had to listen to Paul the apostle. The demon knew he was at war with true followers of Jesus. Even though these guys were part of a high priestly family, and in the world of religion they were well-known and maybe even considered to be important, in actuality they were not.

The demon simply says to them, "Who are you?" However, the demons knew Paul. When you are at war you know who your enemy is. The contrast here is that even pieces of clothing that touched Paul appeared to have supernatural power. The sons of the high priest were not connected to Jesus, so they had no power in the spiritual realm.

Acts 20

"Therefore I testify to you this day that I am innocent of the blood of all of you, for I did not shrink from declaring to you the whole counsel of God."

(Acts 20:26-27)

Point to Ponder

We have a responsibility to mentor people into understanding all of God's Word.

Today's Journal

What responsibility do I feel about understanding all of God's Word?

Prayer for the Day

Holy Spirit, Deepen my understanding of God's Word. Allow me to proclaim God's Word. Allow me to fulfill my ministry and be innocent of the blood of those You send me to proclaim to.

THE GOAL OF INNOCENCE

PART OF LIVING out our godly mission is that we feel a heightened responsibility for others to receive from us something we are able to give them. I am talking about our calling. When we don't live out our calling, it can even make us physically sick, because we have a conviction that we are supposed to be living for God.

Paul was an expert in the Jewish Law. He was highly educated and now a converted Apostle of Jesus the Christ. Paul had a lot to give. His education and experience made him very knowledgeable when it came to preaching the entire Word of God. Because he knew he was always mentoring these elders in Ephesus, no matter how it went for them he was innocent of their blood. He equipped them to go to battle in a very dark place. It would have been lonely to follow Jesus in Ephesus, but through the Word of God and Paul's instruction he had gotten these people ready.

The battle would be hard and maybe some wouldn't make it, but Paul was innocent because he had been faithful with what he was called to. What does Paul mean by the "Whole Counsel of God?" Paul couldn't pick the parts of God's Word to teach and leave some parts out. All of God's Word matters. To be innocent and as a teacher of God's Word, we must teach all of God's Word. We can't just talk about things we like. We need to talk about the areas we are not as strong in. We need to talk about the things we don't even naturally agree with. It is important to be faithful with the entire Word of God.

Acts 21

Scribe to the Heart

"After these days we got ready and went up to Jerusalem."

(Acts 21:15)

Point to Ponder

It is important that we draw close to God to discern the will of God.

Today's Journal

God works in our lives according to seasons. What is He teaching me about my life right now?

Prayer for the Day

Holy Spirit, Let me be flexible and discerning about the changes of seasons in my life.

RIVER

THE CHRISTIAN JOURNEY can be compared to many things. One example would be a river. Every year people head to rivers for their entertainment. Some rivers contain raging rapids and are known for rushing waters with dangerous curves and drops. Individuals or entire groups of people take on rapids for fun. During the journey down the river there are times where the water flows differently. It will be calm for a little while, during which you'll catch your breath. You may even have to paddle. Other times it may seem as though you are hanging on for your very life.

At the beginning of this chapter there is much activity. Luke records several events. He talks about prayer times and meeting up with Phillip, one of the seven, who has four daughters who are all now prophetesses. Paul's ministry was very active. He sought God and aggressively spread the Christian message in his world.

At the end of this chapter we see a new door opening for Paul. Paul may have the opportunity to preach to the world's most powerful people. He was arrested and it was discovered after the arrest he was a Roman citizen. Paul has a new opportunity, which now involves a lot of waiting. He isn't coming and going anymore. The river he was traveling had changed. Paul needed to adapt and stay close to God to understand so he could discern exactly what move he was to make next in his ministry.

Following God is like this. He keeps us on our toes. It is only by our close connection to Him that we can see when something is an opportunity and when it is a roadblock.

Acts 22

Scribe to the Heart

"And He said to me, 'Go, for I will send you far away to the Gentiles.'"

(Acts 22:21)

Point to Ponder

God calls us to do things we don't understand. We just need to obey.

Today's Journal

Has God ever asked me to do something I felt was strange?

Prayer for the Day

Holy Spirit, Let me follow You faithfully, even when I don't understand You.

INTERESTING CALLING

WHEN WE THINK about the power of the gospel, we think of people becoming who they were meant to be. We think of boldness and courage. We think of someone like Peter who, many years after the events recorded in this book, was crucified. His last request was to be crucified upside down. He didn't feel worthy to be crucified like our Lord. I think of people suffering for the faith all around the world, even today.

In this chapter, Paul has the opportunity to boldly share his story. While Paul is prepared to be bold with his testimony, God actually told him to leave. Obedience to God in this circumstance was to get away from the people who would try to hurt him. God was going to send him far away where many gentiles would need to hear the message. Paul was called by God to run for his life.

Discerning God's will is very hard. We must stay faithful to Him. We must live Holy lives and humbly seek His face. When we seek His face, He gives us His hands. Obviously, God could have made it so Paul didn't have to run. Maybe Paul needed it though. Maybe he needed to understand what he actually put people through before his conversion. Understanding God is hard. When we think we understand Him, that is a pride that will bite us back. We must be humble. We must realize we are limited in what we can see and understand. We also know God exists outside of time, and knows much more than us. In this case, Paul was called to run for his life. I find that interesting.

Acts 23

"*Paul called one of the centurions and said, 'Take this young man to the tribune, for he has something to tell him.'*"

(Acts 23:17)

God's favor is connected to our ability to love Him and others.

Today's Journal

How do I get the favor of God on my life?

Prayer for the Day

Holy Spirit, Teach me about Your favor. Let me love God and love others.

GOD'S FAVOR

WE SEE IN this chapter Paul has a sister. Her son, Paul's nephew, heard of the Pharisees and Sadducees' plot to kill Paul. God used him to be in the right place at the right time, to do the right thing. He went to Paul with a message. Paul had already built a relationship with one of the Roman guards. It was passed on to him that they were seeking his life, even though he did nothing worthy of death. The Romans didn't care much about the Jewish laws, but they had to contend with them.

Not only did God's favor help Paul by saving his life, it also set up another opportunity to preach and represent God before the governor. How do we find the favor of God? It is talked about often. What does the Bible teach about God's favor?

Well if you want to please someone, a good place to start would be caring about what they care about. God cares that we love Him, love others, and spread His Word. Paul represented God well and with love, in spite of bad treatment or seemingly unfortunate circumstances.

Sometimes people fast or pray extra-long for God's favor. Those are not bad things. But what about forgiving people? What about loving people? What about helping others? What about worshiping God with thankfulness no matter what? Of course, pray for favor. But, seek God. Love others. People are drawn to that and want to love you back. Don't make it harder for God to want to bless you with favor. What if He wants to give you favor to do what He calls you to, but has to discipline you instead? The Roman guard wanted to help Paul because they had a good experience with him.

Acts 24

Scribe to the Heart

"When two years had elapsed, Felix was succeeded by Porcius Festus. And desiring to do the Jews a favor, Felix left Paul in prison."

(Acts 24:27)

Point to Ponder

Live to be seen by God. Be God-focused.

Today's Journal

Have I ever felt I was truly only seeking God's approval? Have I been disappointed by my pursuit of the approval of man?

Prayer for the Day

Father, My desire is to live for an audience of One. You.

THE EASY WAY OUT

PAUL, LIKE MANY Christian missionaries after him, was falsely accused of several things. He wasn't stirring up trouble. He was merely spreading the message of Jesus, which is divisive in nature due to our own sinfulness. We want things our own way. We don't want to answer to the true and living God, to whom we will all one day give an account.

One of the most fascinating tidbits in this section deals with Felix. He called for Paul often. The Bible teaches us in this chapter that he wanted to give Paul a chance to give him a bribe. Now Paul was settled in his spirit. You know Paul knew what was happening, but he was prayerful. He wanted to be where God was, and this is where God wanted him. On a very regular basis he witnessed to Felix and built a relationship with him.

There is no evidence that Felix was converted. There is no evidence that it did any good at all. In fact, Felix left Paul in prison when he left office because he needed to do a favor for the Jews. Paul completely got hosed in the deal. Humanly speaking, he should have been angry and hurt. He could have felt used. Was he just a source of entertainment for Felix? The difference between Paul and most men is that Paul was God-focused. God saw what Paul was doing. God knew his heart and his intentions, and God was setting the scene for Paul to witness on the largest stage known to the first century world. Focus on Jesus and He will use you where you are. Be God-focused.

Acts 25

Scribe to the Heart

"Then Festus, when he had conferred with his council, answered, 'To Caesar you have appealed; to Caesar you shall go.'"

(Acts 25:12)

Point to Ponder

Take comfort when you or God is on trial for doing the right thing.

Today's Journal

What comes to mind when I think about the Holy Spirit empowering Paul to be bold?

Prayer for the Day

Father, Let me be emboldened by the Holy Spirit.

TAKE COMFORT IN THE TRIAL

MANY ARE AFRAID to put their theology or their God on trial. In this chapter, we're talking about Paul being on trial for witnessing and being falsely accused of several things. We are not necessarily talking about God being on trial here. I couldn't help but think how bold Paul was. First, he spent two years talking to Felix, only to be thrown aside like trash at the end. Now he is talking with Festus and continues to climb the ladder of the courts. Paul, a follower of Christ Jesus, wants to stand before Caesar and proclaim Christ. He wants to stand before the most powerful man in the world.

He continues to appeal and stays in prison. It could have ended his life early. This decision could keep him from visiting churches and building them up. This decision was either made by faith or absolute lunacy. I will go with the former. It is by faith that Paul continues to strive forward following after Jesus regardless of what it means. Ironically, had Paul gone the other route there were people trying to ambush him. There is a good chance he would have been put to death in Jerusalem. But he continued in boldness and spoke to anyone in front of him who would listen.

Under persecution he continued to represent Christ by witnessing to those around him. He built relationships with guards and people in authority. Jesus the Christ was shining through him. God was all over him. He was amazing. The path God put this educated powerful man on was a path of witnessing to very powerful people. Paul kept the course. So, when you or your God is on trial, keep the faith. Jesus Christ is with you and He is truth. That's the truth that will and does always set you free.

Day 115

Acts 26

Scribe to the Heart

"And Agrippa said to Festus, 'This man could have been set free if he had not appealed to Caesar.'"

(Acts 26:32)

Point to Ponder

True freedom and boldness is found while doing the will of God through Christ.

Today's Journal

Do I have freedom to do the will of God regardless of the circumstances?

Prayer for the Day

Father, Teach me boldness and obedience as I seek to do Your will.

COULD HAVE BEEN SET FREE?

WE CAN LEARN a lot about how to give a conversion testimony from this chapter. It is important to note, Paul cites his own shortcomings often as he gives his testimony. He talks about the evil he committed against Christians before becoming one. He speaks of Jesus calling him, and tells how much he will suffer for the name of Christ. This chapter is very fascinating because he is on trial. He chose to be on trial. No one in his right mind would have done such a thing. Paul did, and he boldly proclaimed the crucified and risen Christ.

It is interesting that at the end of the chapter, Agrippa says to Festus that Paul could have been set free, had he not appealed to Caesar. Paul wants to stand before powerful people and reason with them. Paul was an extremely educated man and these people would have been in that category as well.

The truth was that the man was already free. He was free the moment he met Jesus Christ. He couldn't do anything but live for Jesus. Paul doesn't seem to fear death. He continues to push forward. He was not someone who thought he could skim by fearfully, barely proclaiming his faith. He proclaimed Jesus as if he was accountable to a real and living Christ. And He was.

Day 116

Acts 27

Scribe to the Heart

"Therefore I urge you to take some food. It will give you strength, for not a hair is to perish from the head of any of you."

(Acts 27:34)

Point to Ponder

Part of being missional is believing God will put you in many circumstances and will use you in all of them.

Today's Journal

How does God set the scene for me to witness for Him in bold and creative ways?

Prayer for the Day

Father, Let me represent You well and discern Your will no matter where I go.

MISSIONAL PAUL

I HAVE A feeling Paul was one of those guys who was a friend, but you wouldn't like to admit he was. Right? You might have wanted to smack him. Now I realize Paul was an apostle and humble, but his persistence is uncanny. In this chapter there is a situation on the ship where Paul is trying to help, but they do not want to take his advice. Who would blame them really? We know Paul was on a mission, but Paul was just a prisoner to these people. He was being transported. They don't know his motives. They don't know his angle. They just want him to be quiet.

Paul gains favor and a voice in the situation. He gives them advice about eating. As Paul gains a hearing, notice what happens. He took bread and broke it. There was a communion type of moment where God was given thanks, and we get the picture that people got it. They understood what was happening. Paul was the bold representative of Jesus the Christ again. There was a moment where the people looked to him. There was something different about him, and he lets them know it is His God. They recognize it and what a moment it is.

Sometimes we go through really hard things. Paul even chose this, knowing the risk because it seemed like God wanted him to. Even though he is a prisoner in this chapter, he is still giving it over to God. Many of us would not only have not chosen this, but we would be mad that God wasn't bailing us out of the situation. All along, God wants us to have a "Paul moment" in the midst of our struggle.

Acts 28

Scribe to the Heart

"He lived there two whole years at his own expense, and welcomed all who came to him, proclaiming the kingdom of God and teaching about the Lord Jesus Christ with all boldness and without hindrance."

(Acts 28:30-31)

Point to Ponder

*A God-fearing person is hard to stop—
especially when he or she persists.*

Today's Journal

How does fearing God keep me from fearing people or obstacles in this world?

Prayer for the Day

Father, Empower me to be God-fearing enough to be fearless in this world and fearless against the people in it.

HOW DO YOU STOP THE FEARLESS?

THERE IS A principle that holds true in sports, sales, business—pretty much all areas of life: People without fear are hard to stop. It is our own fear and self-pity that holds us back. Paul has done enough already by appealing to Caesar. He has made friends and witnessed for Christ everywhere he went. He has excelled. If Paul rotted in prison for the next few years waiting to die, he still would have had a very powerful story. In spite of new circumstances, Paul was still extremely productive. He witnessed to people and wrote letters to Christians in other parts of the Roman Empire. He chose to be powerful, and not pitiful. He chose to know Jesus and the power of His resurrection and fellowship of His suffering. These were Paul's own words (Philippians 3:10).

Think about a salesman who hears "no" all day but continues to push and push until he gets a yes. Think about the mother praying relentlessly for her kids who have lost their way. When we do not fear even death, we become powerful. Did Paul fear anything? I believe he did, but we don't see anything here but the fear of God. The man was powerful— powerful through Jesus the Christ.

Everywhere he went God gave him favor with guards, shipman, and even kings. Even while under house arrest waiting to get an opportunity before Caesar he is powerful. You can't bring the man down.

They had no record from Judea in regards to him. He then lived there for two years at his own expense. The man was a machine. He was fearless, but not godless. He was godly and that is what made him fearless.

Romans 1

Scribe to the Heart

"For I am not ashamed of the gospel, for it is the power of God for salvation to everyone who believes, to the Jew first and also to the Greek."

(Rom. 1:16)

Point to Ponder

How we reach out to homosexuals is influenced by what we believe to be true about God's word.

Today's Journal

How can I better reach out to homosexuals with love and with truth?

Prayer for the Day

Lord, Show me how to be true to You by reaching out to everyone with love, and love people who are not like me. Amen.

TWO QUESTIONS

MANY PEOPLE DECIDE what they think about an author based on what he or she presents regarding the message in this chapter. In our culture, we are bombarded with the message that homosexuality is an acceptable, even natural, thing. This message comes in many forms: "They were born that way." "Who would really choose that lifestyle?"

God's Word doesn't always tell us what we want to hear. The issue needs to be divided into 2 questions. 1.) Is homosexuality a sinful or an acceptable lifestyle before God? The biblical answer is that homosexuality is not God's will for any person. Your starting point to come to this conclusion is found in Romans 1. If you believe God is behind the inspiration of scripture, then this is the only possible academic Christian position. We can't look at the text and its context and try to make it something it is not.

Christians do an excellent job of quitting the sins of others and seeing their own sins as lesser evils. This creates a wall and makes it hard for the message of love and grace to reach this community. In I Corinthians 6 homosexuality is mentioned with the sexually immoral, which includes people who are living together. It also tells us that many of the readers were like this before they were redeemed. The power of the gospel penetrated the hearts of homosexuals living in the corrupt Corinthian culture. They were some of the recipients of that letter. This same power is still available today, and many can attest to it personally.

Question 2.) Based on my first answer, how do I respond? Homosexuals have been beaten down enough. People are won over with love and grace. They have to be won to the true message, and how we respect and treat people matters. I have worked in several jobs and know many different kinds of people. Two friendships with co-workers come to mind. One was male and one female. They respected my viewpoint because I told them, "I am not your judge. I am only to love you." I was always very clear it is not God's intention for their life that they remain living as homosexuals. My approach created opportunities where I could freely love and apologize for all of the ways Christians hurt them. All people, regardless of the sin, can be changed by God's love.

Romans 2

Scribe to the Heart

"For all who have sinned without the law will also perish without the law, and all who have sinned under the law will be judged by the law."

(Rom. 2:12)

Point to Ponder

Our concern is faithfulness to God, not finding fault in others.

Today's Journal

Does judgment and fault-finding infiltrate my Christianity? How?

Prayer for the Day

Holy Spirit, Help me to not be judgmental, but obedient to Your word.

CLOSE YOUR EYES

I HAD A friend who felt that everyone should close their eyes when praying. Since I pray while I drive, I already went against this belief. It was religion no one could afford. However, my friend was so set on people praying with their eyes closed he would make sure people's eyes were closed and tell them to close them if they weren't.

One time we were at a prayer meeting and he kept telling me to close my eyes. Finally, I put my head down, thinking I ended the insanity, and he actually got under my face looked at me. In an exaggerated way he shut his eyes real hard so that I would close mine. At this point, I gave in and closed my eyes. The irony of this story is that he had to have his eyes open to see if the eyes of others were open or shut.

In this chapter Paul is writing to the Roman believers and is telling them, "practice what you preach." Do not judge someone for a sin and then turn around and do the same thing. You must be actively looking, tasting, and smelling like Jesus. Your knowledge is not what will make you effective in spreading this message. It is your obedience that lifts Christ up.

If you only needed knowledge, then spreading the gospel would be simple. It would be a godless act based solely on our ability to outsmart a prospect of the faith. Simply go to seminary and when you get out, use your knowledge to spread the gospel. Seminary was great for me, but our obedience is what God is looking for and the obedient person is the one He is going to work through. Is this true in your life? If so, there is much you can learn from the lesson in this chapter.

Romans 3

Scribe to the Heart

"For all have sinned and fall short of the glory of God, and are justified by His grace as a gift, through the redemption that is in Christ Jesus."

(Rom. 3:23-24)

Point to Ponder

Jesus Christ died in our place because He loves us and because someone had to pay.

Today's Journal

Someone had to pay for my sin. Jesus chose to. How do I feel about that?

Prayer for the Day

Lord Jesus, Thank You for Your willingness to pay the price for my sins. Teach me more about what that means. Amen.

JUSTICE FOR ALL

EVERY MORNING, STUDENTS all across the country, young and old, put their hands on their hearts and say the pledge of allegiance to the American flag. At the very end of the pledge we hear the words, "With liberty and justice for all." We have an innate desire for justice. When someone does wrong, we want to see payment. When someone does right, we think they should be noticed.

As part of the curse of sin, humans began to judge one another. The problem with our judgment is that we judge things according to our sinful minds. In this chapter we get to know a little bit of God's justice. We see a description of the human heart through a collection of Old Testament quotes from Isaiah, Psalms, and Proverbs.

Romans 3:23 is a famous verse that is often quoted; I want you to recognize the next verse in context with it. I believe Paul wanted his readers to understand the text in this way. Everyone has fallen short. Everyone has sinned. Yet, everyone has been freely justified. Jesus died for everyone. His death was in place of the death we deserved. Yet not everyone goes to heaven or has the life on earth they were meant to have. We must come to the place where we choose to humbly repent and accept what He did for us at Calvary. We then choose to follow Him with our own lives.

Justice was served at the cross. We deserved to die. We deserved to be on that cross instead of Jesus. When someone wrongs you, you intuitively want that person to pay. When you wrong someone else, the other person thinks you should pay. When you feel guilty for your sin, you are trying to pay for it. Only one had the ability to pay, and the intention of His payment was to make you free from that life, and a liberated follower of the King of Kings—Jesus Christ the Righteous.

Romans 4

Scribe to the Heart

"For what does the Scripture say? 'Abraham believed God, and it was counted to him as righteous- ness.'"

(Rom. 4:3)

Point to Ponder

Believing God is counted as righteousness.

Today's Journal

Do I believe God?

Prayer for the Day

Holy Spirit, I pray that my belief would be strong and true. I pray that I will always believe the promises of God.

STAND AND BE COUNTED

A BELIEF IN someone or something can drive us to do all kinds of crazy things. *Jerry Maguire* was a movie about a sports management representative who, after being fired from his job, starts his own sports management firm. On his way out the door from his old company, he gives the office onlookers a bit of a speech about morals and ethics and starting fresh. He then asks, "Who is coming with me?" His assistant didn't even budge. He was truly alone. But in a moment of inspiration one woman, Dorothy Boyd, stands to her feet and blurts out, "I will go with you!"

Starting the new company isn't easy, and she begins to question if she made the right choice. When he asks her later about her choice, she tells him that the mission statement he wrote, which ironically was the thing that got him fired, inspired her. By the end of the movie, they ultimately were successful and got married in an all-good Hollywood fashion.

In this chapter of Romans, Paul devotes a lot of time to Abraham. Abraham believed God, and God counted that as righteousness. When we believe God, we don't have to tell lies. We don't steal or do things we know we shouldn't do out of fear and reverence for God. We believe God will get us through whatever situation we are in. We follow Him out of first believing Him. When we truly believe God it is counted to us as righteousness, and it also leads to a deeper connection with Him.

Faith in God may lead to behavior that seems irrational. (Like leaving a perfectly good job with an established company because you are inspired by someone who is being fired). However, when we trust God and truly hear from Him, we do not need to worry about what lies ahead. Dorothy believed Jerry. Abraham believed God. Do you believe God and are you willing to stand to your feet and say fearlessly, "I will go with you"?

Romans 5

Scribe to the Heart

"For while we were still weak, at the right time Christ died for the ungodly."

(Rom. 5:6)

Point to Ponder

Jesus gave His life for us, His enemies.

Today's Journal

What does it mean to me that Jesus died for those who oppose Him?

Prayer for the Day

Lord Jesus, Give me a heart for those who oppose You. I pray that I would be able to show them that You died for them.

WE ARE AT WAR

IN EVERY GENERATION in recent history, our country has endured war. Many men and women die every single year in combat for our country. In churches, schools, and around our communities we see pictures of those who died for our freedom. Often the faces are very young. It is a sad reality, and these people are heroes. Thank God people are willing to risk their lives for the people and the country they love. They are willing so their children will have a good life, a free life. Many will do it because they have a deep understanding of what this country has done for them.

In this chapter Jesus is described as someone who would die for sinners. Essentially, we were God's enemies and He was willing to die for us. It is the equivalent of a soldier dying for the opposing country. That is an interesting thought, isn't it? As a disobedient sinner we bring nothing good to the table. We are tainted and sinfully nasty before God.

God doesn't need us. He simply looks at us and sees we need help. Read these verses again:

"For while we were still weak, at the right time Christ died for the ungodly. For one will scarcely die for a righteous person- though perhaps for a good person one would dare even to die – but God shows His love for us in that while we were still sinners Christ died for us" (Romans 5:6-8).

In our unlovable state we are trying to live our own lives. We are trying to live life apart from God. The idea that God would love us even then is unbelievable. Yes, we can be redeemed and transformed, but God's love is not about what is in it for Him. God's love is amazing. Jesus gave His life for us, His enemies. Are we willing to do the same?

Romans 6

Scribe to the Heart

"For the wages of sin is death, but the free gift of God is eternal life in Christ Jesus our Lord."

(Rom. 6:23)

Point to Ponder

We are not to keep sinning. By grace we are to live as holy before God.

Today's Journal

What does it mean to have reverence for the holy life I am called to live?

Prayer for the Day

Holy Spirit, Teach me what it looks like to live a life that is worthy of my calling.

THE COST OF SIN

PAUL KICKS OFF this chapter with some important statements: *"What shall we say then? Are we to continue in sin that grace may abound? By no means! How can we who died to sin still live in it?"*

We are to have respect for our redeemed lives. We can't keep on sinning. That doesn't glorify God. We are to work against the grain of the world, and live for Jesus. Our obedience pleases Jesus. Our sin is what He had to die a brutal death for.

Paul ends this chapter with a verse you've likely heard: *"For the wages of sin is death, but the free gift of God is eternal life in Christ Jesus our Lord."*

Sin costs you everything. It will hurt you. Paul teaches us here that the wages of sin is death. When we see the word "wages" we have to ask ourselves, "What does that mean?" Well, it is talking about the cost. Ultimately, sin costs us our lives. Thanks be to God through our Lord Jesus Christ that Jesus paid the penalty for us. We do not have to go to hell, and we can live forever with God.

When we don't have a reverence for the holy life we are called to live, we should take note and be concerned. I am not saying you should walk around afraid, but you must realize, you are free. Jesus set you free from sin. With Holy Spirit walking with you, you now have power over sin. It has no power over you anymore. When you are disobedient, you empower sin to rule. You give it an aggressive role in your life when you continue on in it.

Think of it this way: the more you obey, the less power sin has. You have the ability to squash it. I am not saying you will not still sin or stumble, but you truly have no excuse to fall into habitual sin anymore. If you know Jesus you have the power.

Romans 7

"For I know that nothing good dwells within me, that is, my flesh. For I have the desire to do what is right, but not the ability to carry it out."

(Rom. 7:18)

Our flesh is bad.

Today's Journal

Is it wrong to live by the flesh? How can I avoid it?

Prayer for the Day

Holy Spirit, Tame my flesh. Feed my spirit and soul.

OUR FLESH IS BAD

THERE ARE SOME things we know in our heads, but do not know in our hearts. One of these things is that our flesh is bad. Basically, we are made up of three parts. Our soul is our inner being. Then, we have a Spirit that is brought to life through meeting and walking with Jesus Christ. And the third portion is our flesh. Nowhere in the New Testament is the flesh recognized as good. Paul lays out his struggle of wanting to do right, but temptation is always right there to trip him up. He says this trip up comes from the flesh. It is a relief for me to know that Paul had a constant battle with sin. We must stay humble because even Paul was capable of sin.

The messages we often tell kids present the flesh as something positive or special. Think about these sayings: "You can do anything you set your mind to."

"Discipline will get you anything." "If you can dream it, you can do it."

Many people see these statements as good, even Christian. The problem is: It is Christianity without Christ. We are set up to be our own savior. We're saying the power is up to you to succeed. I am not saying self-discipline and this type of rhetoric has no place, but Christ must be central. The flesh is not to rule your life, Christ is.

The truth is: We need Jesus. He keeps us from temptation. He helps us to do the right thing. He helps us to be disciplined. It is our connection and prayer life that helps us contend with our flesh. Our flesh must be crucified daily. We must deny it and open ourselves up with prayer and study of God's word. We need more of God feeding our Spirit and soul, and we need our flesh to take a back seat.

Romans 8

Scribe to the Heart

"There is therefore now no condemnation for those who are in Christ Jesus."

(Rom. 8:1)

Point to Ponder

There is no condemnation for those who are in Christ.

Today's Journal

What is the difference between atonement and forgiveness?

Prayer for the Day

Holy Spirit, Free me from condemnation. There is no condemnation in You.

YOU ARE FREE

THIS CHAPTER IS widely discussed in theological circles. The discussion has much to do with God's election and free will. It isn't an issue that can be settled for anyone on one page, so we won't even go there today. I do want to encourage you to wrestle through the issue however, no matter where you land in the discussion. Perhaps you've never even thought about whether we truly have free will or if God controls our decisions. If you do feel strongly about it you must understand why you believe the way you do.

I want to focus on the very first verse in this chapter. The devil is known as our accuser. On the other hand, Jesus is not an accuser. God is our judge. We are blessed with conviction and we might be convicted to confess our sin, or not do it again, but condemnation is not the work of God. Condemnation slows us down. It makes us feel worthless. It stays with you, and cripples you from having any influence. It has no place in the life of a Christian.

On any given day, you can turn on the news and there is some kind of trial going on that has made headlines. Celebrities, sports icons, politicians, everyday men and women; someone is always on trial and it is newsworthy. People are accused of awful crimes, and some of them are so shocking we struggle to believe it. And if they are determined "not guilty," and they walk free from the courtroom, we are horrified. We think justice wasn't served. The system failed. We get angry because we believe someone has to pay; especially if the crime the person is freed from is one that is punishable by death.

Consider this: our crimes against God are also punishable by death. Someone has to pay. When we walk free, it is an injustice. Only it is not. Jesus Christ the Righteous paid for us. Justice was served and we have been given grace. He atoned for our sin. That atonement is way bigger than being forgiven! North American Christianity talks about Christ in terms of forgiveness. Consider His atonement. Atonement is the act of Jesus paying for your sins, so you can be declared innocent. We need to stop trying to pay for it. What He did was enough. Condemnation slows you down. There is no condemnation for those who are in Christ.

Day 126

Romans 9

Scribe to the Heart

"What shall we say, then? That Gentiles who did not pursue righteousness have attained it, that is, a righteousness that is by faith."

(Rom. 9:30)

Point to Ponder

Whether Jew or gentile, everyone needs a relationship with Jesus.

Today's Journal

What does the Old Testament help me better understand about my faith?

Prayer for the Day

Holy Spirit, Show me what it means to be a gentile or Jewish believer. (Depending which you are.) Help me to better understand.

GENTILE FAITH

IN ROMANS 9 Paul continues to talk about deep topics. In this chapter, he devotes some time to Israel. He begins by emphasizing how he longs for his Jewish brothers and sisters to see the truth. It is important to him that the Jews accept Jesus as the long-awaited Messiah. He is deeply burdened for them.

He explains how the gentiles were not looking for salvation but found it because it is salvation by faith. The Jews were looking for salvation but didn't find it because they pursued it with works. If you believe you can achieve salvation through works, you do not have a need for a Savior.

It is important to understand that as gentiles we have been added into this faith. The message went to the Jews first and then to us. The Old Testament teaches us the history and the foundation of our faith leading up to the New Testament. We can't discount or neglect those roots, traditions, and foundations.

There is much confusion among people over proper Christian theology in regards to the Jews. (Although God is not confused by it at all.) We will seek to shine a light on this topic later. One thing is for sure: everyone, whether you are a Jew or a gentile, needs Jesus. We have all fallen short and Jesus came as the answer to our problem. We need Him. Thanks be to God He came not only for Israel, but for me too. Pay attention to these verses below:

"What shall we say, then? That Gentiles who did not pursue righteousness have attained it, that is, a righteousness that is by faith; but that Israel who pursued a law that would lead to righteousness did not succeed in reaching that law. Why? Because they did not pursue it by faith, but as if it were based on works. They have stumbled over the stumbling stone" (Romans 9:30-32).

Romans 10

Scribe to the Heart

"But of Israel he says, 'All day long I have held out my hands to a disobedient and contrary people.'"

(Rom. 10:21)

Point to Ponder

God worked through the Jewish people. This makes them more accountable.

Today's Journal

Am I more accountable to God because of how He has worked in my life?

Prayer for the Day

Lord Jesus, Let me represent You in this world like someone who has been touched by You.

THE RESPONSIBILITY OF THE CHOSEN

WHEN WE CHOOSE presidents and people for public office there is a great amount of pressure, we place on them to be perfect. They must fix our country, our economy, and our wars. They must side with our moral agendas. Our list of expectations and demands is extensive. We also put great pressure on them to be relatable and to have a family, which represents the ideal family picture as we see it in our country.

God chose Israel to be the people of the Messiah. They were chosen to be the nation through whom God would reveal Himself. Throughout the Old Testament the Jewish nation is held to a very high standard. God expects more from them than He does from the nations around them. They are disciplined over and over again. Their disobedience results in more discipline and in some cases, death.

The Jewish people were given God's presence all throughout history. They were given the Messiah. Because of this, they are not off the hook. In fact, it is much the opposite. They are God's people therefore they are accountable to God. Jewish people today still have a responsibility and need to recognize Jesus as their Messiah. It is what God desired from them back then, and it is what He desires now.

Jesus came to redeem them of their sins. Many didn't listen, and still don't today, but that doesn't take away their responsibility to listen and respond. You, too, have a responsibility to listen and respond.

Romans 11

Scribe to the Heart

"So I ask, did they stumble in order that they might fall? By no means! Rather through their trespass salvation has come to the Gentiles, so as to make Israel jealous."

(Rom. 11:11)

Point to Ponder

The gospel is divisive, which is something that draws people.

Today's Journal

How does God use jealousy to spread the message of the kingdom? Does this create tension in how I think about God?

Prayer for the Day

Holy Spirit, Show me how jealousy can draw people to You.

THE METHOD OF JEALOUSY

JUST SAY THE name out loud, "Jesus Christ." Or say it a different way, "Jesus the Christ." Do you realize there is power in that name? Jesus being named as the Messiah is a controversial topic. It especially was difficult for the Jews.

Remember back in the book of Acts when Paul left the synagogue to go next door to preach to the gentiles (Acts 18:6-7)? This controversy and the passion behind it helped to move the gospel through the gentiles. The gentiles were attracted to the gospel because of the stir it created among the Jews. It made them curious. We are not talking about boring Jewish law anymore. We are talking about a possible life-changing Messiah.

When gentiles began to flood the kingdom, it created more curiosity among the Jews. The gospel message doesn't change for anyone. It is what it is. It creates a stir. It creates emotion and that makes it attractive. People like to get involved in a stir. People like to form opinions. That is why the media can beat a story to death and people remain interested in the controversy. People like to feel involved in the action.

Romans 12

Scribe to the Heart

"Do not be conformed to this world, but be transformed by the renewal of your mind, that by testing you may discern what is the will of God, what is good and acceptable and perfect."

(Rom. 12:2)

Point to Ponder

Following Christ always goes against the grain of the culture.

Today's Journal

How do I live for Christ as a living sacrifice? In what ways do I fall into the patterns of this world?

Prayer for the Day

Holy Spirit, I offer myself as a living sacrifice. I pray that I would not conform to the patterns of this world. Stop me when I am tempted.

A LIVING SACRIFICE

IN THIS CHAPTER, which has much to say about Christian living, I am going to focus on the first two verses:

"I appeal to you therefore, brothers, by the mercies of God, to present your bodies as a living sacrifice, holy and acceptable to God which is your spiritual worship. Do not be conformed to this world, but be transformed by the renewal of your mind, that by testing you may discern what is the will of God, what is good and acceptable and perfect" (Romans 12:1-2).

Paul makes an appeal to these Roman gentile believers. In the last three entries we've highlighted how Paul explained their role in the kingdom as gentiles or Jewish believers in light of Jewish history. In understanding the Jewish rites of worship, they would have understood the call to be a living sacrifice. The sacrifice needed to be without blemish, perfect, and holy. It was how God outlined sacrifice to be in the Old Testament. There is a striving to be holy even to the point of shedding blood. This same example is how Paul describes they are to worship God; they are to live for Him wholly and holy.

In verse two some translations say not to be conformed to the "pattern of this world." I've always liked that description because I constantly find myself tempted into falling into the daily patterns, cares, and worries of this world. This world has many traps. Many Christians go down a road looking for money and power and completely lose sight of what is important. There is a temptation to be extremely busy and not have any time or energy for God or family in your everyday life.

Christianity always goes against the grain of the culture. It doesn't matter if you live in China or the Bible belt of the United States. No matter what, living for God will always go against the pattern of this world, and our life is the continual act of putting ourselves on the altar as living sacrifices for Jesus Christ. That is how we walk with God in a culture that encourages us to follow their pattern.

Romans 13

Scribe to the Heart

"Let every person be subject to the governing authorities. For there is no authority except from God, and those that exist have been instituted by God."

(Rom. 13:1)

Point to Ponder

Submit to authorities.
Truly love everyone. It may be a divine opportunity.

Today's Journal

Do I really believe that God is in charge? How can I better submit to and love those who are in authority above me here on earth?

Prayer for the Day

Holy Spirit, I pray that I will better love those who are in authority over me. Show me how to do that. Love them through me, as I submit in the way God wants me to.

WHO'S IN CHARGE?

THE PERSECUTION THAT happened under Roman rule in early Christianity was more intense at certain times than at others. But, it was always an important concern during the writing of Paul's epistles. We see the Apostle Paul encouraging Christians to subject themselves to authority. He even goes so far as to say these authorities are only permitted to exist by God Almighty Himself.

In others words, no matter who is ruling this world, God is still in charge. Paul then ties this theme to love. As Christians, we are to follow the commandments and love people regardless of our circumstances. We are not to seek revenge.

You may not always understand why people are in the positions they are in. You may not understand how it is that you can be smarter than your boss. You may not understand how even a pastor or teacher achieved their position. The point is that is not for you to determine. You are to delight in your day and submit to the authorities God allows you to have. Maybe by truly loving people and not judging them, God will use you to make that person's life better, and maybe even transform his or her life with Christ's message. Look at these as divine opportunities to influence the world. Do you really believe God is in charge? Do you live like it?

Romans 14

Scribe to the Heart

"Therefore let us not pass judgment on one another any longer, but rather decide never to put a stumbling block or hindrance in the way of a brother."

(Rom. 14:13)

Point to Ponder

It is sinful to cause people to be tempted.

Today's Journal

Do I cause people to stumble in any way? How? What can I do differently?

Prayer for the Day

Holy Spirit, Reveal to me anything in my life that may cause another to stumble.

PREVENT THE CAUSE

IT MAKES PERFECT sense to wear your seatbelt in a car. If there is an accident you are more likely to live through it and less likely to be seriously injured. Hours are spent every year helping new parents understand how to properly install a car seat for a newborn's safety. Prevention in this area is a normal and expected part of our culture.

In this chapter we see Paul talking about the complicated issue of eating food that has been sacrificed to idols. Food that was sacrificed to pagan idols was commonly sold in the marketplace. If you went to someone's house to eat, you might end up eating something that was sacrificed in worship to another deity. This was a major concern for the Christians, who knew from Old Testament law that they were not to eat such food. It is not necessarily our concern today, but what we glean from it is.

The main point of this lesson is that we are not to do anything to make a brother (or sister) stumble. For example, I have never understood the Amish culture. They are such humble people. They love God. But, one of the things they practice is not operating a car. They won't do it themselves, but they will allow a person who is not Amish to drive them around. It's a mixed message. In this way, they are causing others to stumble. This verse directly talks about that.

Another example on a practical level is how some Christian parents will encourage or permit their daughters to dress. They allow their daughters to wear provocative, skimpy clothing. Imagine being a sincere Christian boy who is trying to follow Jesus. He goes to youth group and talks to sincere girls who are following Jesus in most areas of their life, but their clothes send a different message. Worldly thoughts flood his mind. It is a confusing message. Women must stop encouraging temptation that causes their brothers to stumble. Both parties bear responsibility. We are responsible for the things we do and the things we permit those who are in our care to do.

Romans 15

Scribe to the Heart

"May the God of endurance and encouragement grant you to live in such harmony with one another, in accord with Christ Jesus."

(Rom. 15:5)

Point to Ponder

Love God and love each other. This can change the world.

Today's Journal

How can I better love God and love others in order to change the world?

Prayer for the Day

Holy Spirit, Teach me how to love.

MISSING INGREDIENT

IF YOU WERE to bake a cake, you would follow the instructions of the recipe. It may be a recipe that belonged to your grandmother. When she made it, it was perfect. You know if you do everything right, you will end up with a cake just like hers. Right? But at some point, you realize you do not have sugar. No one would try to bake the perfect cake without sugar. That throws off the whole plan. Sugar is a necessary ingredient.

As we get towards the end of Paul's very theologically deep letter to the Romans, we see him shifting gears. Paul wants to see them, but his time is limited. He may catch them on the way to somewhere else (v. 24), but his intention in this letter is to give them deep understanding. Paul knows this church needs some help, but he probably will not be able to stop and spend the time with them they need.

So, his focus shifts to encouraging them to get along. Living in harmony is the needed ingredient in this world. It's the sugar to the perfect cake. He wants to love them, and for them to love God and love each other. Don't fight about meaningless stuff, but be in agreement with each other. Feuding churches are doomed because it is hard enough to follow Christ in a world that rejects Him. It's near impossible when there is division in the Body of Christ.

A church that doesn't do the main thing is like a cake with no sugar. God wants us to love Him and love each other. That is the main thing. Love changes the world.

Day 133

Romans 16

Scribe to the Heart

"I commend to you our sister Phoebe, a servant of the church at Cenchreae"

(Rom. 16:1)

Point to Ponder

We must read and interpret Scripture for what it says; not for what we are most comfortable with it saying.

Today's Journal

Can women be church leaders? How did I reach my conclusion? *(How you reach the conclusion may be more important than the conclusion itself.)*

Prayer for the Day

Holy Spirit, Teach me to read Your word for what it actually is.

APOSTLE

IT IS IMPORTANT not to neglect the final chapters of Paul's letters. He has many greetings and thank you statements. They might seem like something you can skip over. In the letter endings, we are reminded that Paul was a real person, and we are reading his mail. The only way to read such a document is by seeking to understand how the original audience would have heard the message.

I want to focus in on the first two verses of the chapter:

"I commend to you our sister Phoebe, a servant of the church at Cenchreae, that you may welcome her in the Lord in a way worthy of the saints, and help her in whatever she may need from you, for she has been a patron of many and of myself as well" (Romans 16:1-2).

This will stretch the theology of some. Even if you don't agree with me it is important for you to know why. This same word "servant" or a variation of this word is translated to describe a man as a minister, deacon, or something like that. Our English translations for this verse seem to give her the designation of servant. But note: Phoebe is commended here as a church leader. They were to help her in what she needed, and she obviously had helped many. Pricilla and Aquilla are mentioned next and Paul mentions Pricilla first, which seems to give her the seat of more importance over Aquilla in that relationship.

Our theology on the role of women in the church is important. Playing it safe sometimes is the work of the devil. Translators play it safe and only call Phoebe a servant because everyone is OK with a woman serving; just don't let her teach or be in charge of any men. If we hinder women who are called by God to preach and teach we are working against God.

What does the Bible truly teach about these matters? It is important that you truly investigate. What if God is calling your daughter to preach or lead a church? Are you convinced God would never do that? How sure are you? Have you investigated your position biblically and thorough enough to know what you should do to help your daughter or a daughter of the church on that journey?

Day 134

1 Cor. 1

Scribe to the Heart

"so that, as it is written, 'Let the one who boasts, boast in the Lord.'"

(1 Cor. 1:31)

Point to Ponder

*You shouldn't follow a pastor or a denomination.
You should follow Jesus.*

Today's Journal

What can I do to better follow Jesus with my life today?

Prayer for the Day

Holy Spirit, Help me to follow You, even if no one else is doing so.

FOLLOW CHRIST

PAUL WAS THE first church planter. To understand Paul and the context of his letters we need to understand him in this way. He came into an area and preached the Gospel. He discipled and diligently taught the ways of Christ. He raised up leaders and then moved on to other areas. He would later come back to check on them. His goal was to equip them to lead themselves. He didn't need for them to need him.

The church in Corinth was probably not a huge church like we might think. I picture a church of a few hundred people or less. I think we sometimes think of these churches as the mega-churches in our modern neighborhoods. That would take away from the message. The message was to live out the countercultural teaching of Christ in this pagan world you find yourself in. You are no longer one of them. You are now in the minority, so live in a way that makes the majority want what you have. Many in the area participated in pagan worship with male prostitutes. To say living for Jesus was going against the grain of society was an understatement. It is also important to note that Paul was talking to a group with many young believers who used to live like this. The church in Corinth had very strong discipleship needs.

The first issue Paul addresses is a schism in the church. Following Christ in this environment requires strong unity among believers. Some in the church are claiming to follow Peter, Apollos, Paul, or even Jesus. Paul wants them all to realize they all are on the same team. We must all follow Jesus together. He reiterates the gospel message. Paul has no interest in trying to win them back to following him in any way. He is interested in helping them follow Jesus. You have heard it before, but in other words Paul was saying, "The Gospel is not about me. The Gospel is about Jesus." We must live the same way. We are not to follow anything or anyone but Jesus.

Day 135

1 Cor. 2

Scribe to the Heart

"The natural person does not accept the things of the Spirit of God, for they are folly to him, and he is not able to understand them because they are spiritually discerned."

(1 Cor. 2:14)

Point to Ponder

The basic message of the gospel is not meant to be hard to understand.

Today's Journal

How would I explain the basic message of the gospel to someone who has developed an overly complicated worldview?

Prayer for the Day

Holy Spirit, Let me better understand, proclaim, and live out the truth of the gospel message.

SUPER PASTORS

WHEN I THINK of the Apostle Paul, I typically think of someone who was extremely well-educated. I think of someone who knew Scripture. He was well-traveled. He grew up more advantaged than the other apostles. All evidence would indicate that Paul was a very good speaker. God gifted this man to be able to go into hostile pagan areas, talk to people, and start churches. He was equipped to be the man behind the Christian movement going to the gentiles.

The Corinthian people were no strangers to good speakers. Greek philosophers were common in Corinth. By the time this letter was written, Paul had been gone for a time from Corinth. As often happens when time goes by, many would have been intrigued by the next flavor of the week. Some other speakers or philosophers had gotten the people's attention and Paul's memory had become a little distant.

Does that sound fickle? Yes. But we often do the same thing. We want our pastors to speak like someone we respect on T.V. or to entertain us. Notice Paul took a different approach. He basically told them he *wasn't* the best speaker. He doesn't use fancy words. He gave them Christ, and Christ crucified. What he talks about is simple to understand, but hard to follow!

Paul didn't want the message to be hard to understand. He wanted them to know Christ. He also humbled himself and was not looking to be seen as a great apostle. He wanted to be seen as someone preaching the message of Christ crucified and that was it.

Day 136

1 Cor. 3

Scribe to the Heart

"I planted, Apollos watered, but God gave the growth. So neither he who plants nor he who waters is anything, but only God who gives the growth."

(1 Cor. 3:6-7)

Point to Ponder

We are nothing more than servants who have been called to be faithful.

Today's Journal

God uses many servants to build one Christian. In whose discipleship process am I currently involved? In my past, whose process have I been a part of? How?

Prayer for the Day

Holy Spirit, Show me how I am to be a part of someone else's discipleship process. Move me when I need to take my discipleship to another level in someone's life.

JUST SERVANTS

PAUL REFERS TO himself and Apollos as "servants through whom you believed." Paul probably can't figure out why they are even having this discussion. He is probably thinking, "Come on. What are we even talking about here? Are we really going to argue about who is the better preacher or who is the leader?" His whole message was centered around Jesus Christ. It had nothing to do with Paul, Cephas (Peter), or Apollos.

Paul then gives a very humbling example in the cited verse to the right. Paul planted the Gospel. Apollos came in and "watered" the believers by continuing on in the instruction, but God gave the growth. God is the only one who is anything. Paul and Apollos were faithful with the message and the calling they have been given, but the power of the Gospel comes from Christ.

Paul wanted them to know he was just someone being faithful to what he was called to do. This must have been so frustrating for Paul. He wants to move on and take them deeper. He was a deep theological thinker who liked to take people to the next level, and they are stuck on wondering if Apollos is better at proclaiming the message of Christ. He would have loved to instruct them deeply like he does in his letter to the Romans or even the Ephesians, who came from a similar cultural background as the Corinthians. However, this is the pastoral heart. Paul addresses them in this way because this is where they were. They needed instruction in this area. They were still in spiritual infancy. They needed milk for a little while longer.

Day 137

1 Cor. 4

Scribe to the Heart

"For though you have countless guides in Christ, you do not have many fathers. For I became your father in Christ Jesus through the gospel. I urge you, then, be imitators of me."

(1 Cor. 4:15-16)

Point to Ponder

Be a sold out fool for Christ.

Today's Journal

Do I let the voices in my day influence my life and my philosophies or am I sold-out for Christ?

Prayer for the Day

Jesus, Let me be a fool for You.

SCUM OF THE WORLD

I FIND IT fascinating to come across a phrase in the Bible that is used commonly in the world. There are many things non-believers say that actually were initially written in the Bible. For example, I have heard people refer to another person as being the "scum of the earth." Paul refers to himself and other apostles as scum of the world in verse 13 of this chapter. In verse 10, he refers to himself and the other apostles as fools for Christ. "Fools for" is a phrase I've also heard tossed out in various settings.

Paul of course is addressing the Corinthian church in light of their culture. The culture is obviously tempting them to gravitate towards other speakers. There were many well-spoken philosophers around. There were some who were more elegantly dressed and saying things that were probably not as divisive as the Christian Gospel.

Paul then does an interesting thing. It is quite a different word play. He talks about being a fool for Christ, and the scum of the earth. Then in verses 15 and 16, he urges them to be imitators of him.

It is not the best sales pitch. *Be the scum of the earth with me. Be a fool with me. Follow me as I follow Christ.* Paul was basically saying, "They make good points. We are not dressed like them. We are not as smooth as they are. They are wise. We are fools. But, we are fools for Christ." For Paul, his heart was in conversion and discipleship. He wasn't looking to compete and sell his brand of religion. He simply wanted them to see he had something that was different from everything else, and he was sold out for Christ. Follow Paul as he follows Christ.

1 Cor. 5

Scribe to the Heart

"You are to deliver this man to Satan for the destruction of the flesh, so that his spirit may be saved in the day of the Lord."

(1 Cor. 5:5)

Point to Ponder

Sometimes God's love is a very tough love.

Today's Journal

How have I been touched by my heavenly Father's tough love?

Prayer for the Day

Holy Spirit, Make me aware of the times You are applying tough love to someone's life so that I do not get in the way.

DIVINE TOUGH LOVE

IN THIS CHAPTER, Paul actually made the statement that a particular person was to be delivered to Satan. That seems pretty odd for the Bible, don't you think? This doesn't seem right. In our Christian subculture there is a lot of talk about deliverance. There are entire ministries built around delivering people and freeing them from demonic holds.

Yet here Paul says to deliver this person to Satan (not from), and it seems to be both for his good and the good of the church. We can learn much from the New Testament about church discipline. It seems when someone is disobedient and refuses to be reasoned with, there is a form of excommunication that can happen.

Remember there were no other churches to go to. This was *the* church. This person's friends were there. When Paul wants him delivered to Satan for his spirit to be saved, and flesh to be destroyed, it seems like it is for his own good. It also seems it would help the church to address this problem. This known sexual sin is hurting the church and Paul doesn't want that.

It sounds so unloving that Christian people would be called to pull away from someone with a problem. However, this person doesn't want the help he needs. Paul was addressing something that was not going to go away, and the only hope for this man is for God to break his Spirit and bring him to repentance. Could it be that it was hurting this man because the church was not applying discipline? We can have good intentions and still get in God's way sometimes. Sometimes God's love is a very tough love.

Day 139

1 Cor. 6

Scribe to the Heart

"I say this to your shame. Can it be that there is no one among you wise enough to settle a dispute between the brothers..."

(1 Cor. 6:5)

Point to Ponder

Remember where you came from to help bring others to where you are going.

Today's Journal

How does where I came from help me to influence others positively for the kingdom of God?

Prayer for the Day

Holy Spirit, Let me remember where You found me; particularly when I am tempted to judge others.

SOME OF YOU

IN THIS CHAPTER Paul lays it out there for the Corinthian believers. Read these verses again: *"Do not be deceived: neither the sexually immoral, nor idolaters, nor adulterers, nor men who practice homosexuality, nor thieves, nor the greedy, nor drunkards, nor revilers, nor swindlers will inherit the kingdom of God. And such were some of you. But you were washed, you were sanctified, you were justified in the name of the Lord Jesus Christ and by the Spirit of our God."*

Paul talks about several different types of people who are not on track to inherit the kingdom of God; homosexuals, along with the sexually immoral (this includes shacking up and pornographic sins), thieves, greedy people, and drunkards, to name a few.

Paul didn't name these things so that the Corinthian believers would look down on them like the Parable of the Pharisee and the Tax Collector (Luke 18: 9-14). He mentioned them to refer to the culture around them that needs Jesus. This was Corinth. These people may have been coming to church already. Many were involved the in sexual pagan worship of the city.

Paul also reminds them, "Some of you were like this. This is where you came from. Don't fall back into this sin, but go get them. Teach them how they should be, but most of all teach them about the love, grace, and goodness of Jesus Christ. They will not need any of these worldly activities if they find Jesus."

It is important to remember where you came from. You might not have been deep in paganism or sexual sin before becoming a Christian, but your need for salvation was as equally great. God hates gossip, pride, judgment, and many other sins that may hit home for you.

Remembering our testimony and how we came to Christ helps us to know it is God who has worked in our lives. We can't take credit for our own salvation and we shouldn't look down on those who are still far from God. The fact that we were once on the wrong path should give us sympathy for those who are still are. The Christian response to sin is to show the love of Jesus.

Day 140

1 Cor. 7

Scribe to the Heart

"But because of the temptation to sexual immorality, each man should have his own wife and each woman her own husband."

(1 Cor. 7:2)

Point to Ponder

Part of the reason God gave us marriage is so that we would not burn with lust.

Today's Journal

What are my honest feelings about God and marriage?

Prayer for the Day

Lord Jesus, Let me be fully in love with You. Let no relationship ever take a higher priority than my relationship with You.

TO MARRY OR NOT TO MARRY?

THE CORINTHIAN CHURCH had major problems that needed to be straightened out. In this chapter there is a hint of how heavily sexualized the culture was. Sexuality permeated everything. There were male cult prostitutes in the pagan temple just down the road. Everywhere they looked it was sex, sex, sex.

Getting married was a good thing for many because if they did not, they would burn with passion. Paul also talks about the special gift some have not to marry. This comment leads to some interesting questions. I recently read a study in *Christianity Today* comparing people who married young with those who waited until they were financially ready or done with grad school, etc.

In our culture there is an idea that waiting until you are mature enough and financially ready to marry sets you up more for success. However, the study didn't prove that. The study made a strong case for marrying earlier to live a more fruitful, healthy Christian life that doesn't fight against the reproductive nature we were blessed with. ("The Case for Early Marriage" *Christianity Today;* August 2009.)

In Corinth, lust of the flesh was keeping Christians from being all they could be for God and moving the gospel forward in their culture. Similarly, in our culture today sex is everywhere. Maybe getting married soon after you meet the right person is exactly what God wants. Maybe we are not to project our plan onto God. Please pray it through. That is my point. Don't use this entry to help you make an equally bad decision. You must search the heart of God. There is an old song by Toto called "Love Isn't Always on Time." Love is always on God's time.

1 Cor. 8

Scribe to the Heart

"Thus, sinning against your brothers and wounding their conscience when it is weak, you sin against Christ."

(1 Cor. 8:12)

Point to Ponder

God's will can be found when we love Jesus more than anything else.

Today's Journal

How do I understand God's instruction that I am not to cause another to stumble? (Use the Bible for your support)

Prayer for the Day

Lord Jesus, My desire is not to be a stumbling block for anyone. Give me discernment on the important matters in which I might cause someone to struggle.

PASS THE BBQ SAUCE

IN DISCUSSING ROMANS 14 we briefly talked about the subject of today's entry. I'm coming back to it because it is extremely relevant in our Christian walk. In general, most of today's readership of Paul's Corinthian letters are not faced with the temptation to eat meat that was sacrificed to idols. In Corinth they were faced with this problem just as the original audience of the Roman epistle. Animals were sacrificed to false gods and then it would show up as food in the marketplace or at a friend's house for dinner.

Just like in Romans, Paul tells the Corinthians that the important issue is about making others stumble. The actual eating of the meat is not something they should spend a lot of time worrying about. There are several discussions in modern Christianity that center around the question, "How do we participate in society and follow Christ wholeheartedly?"

Alcohol is one of those points of discussion where Christians can have greatly differing opinions. Alcohol is present at the majority of social events in our culture outside of the church. Jesus turned water into wine (John 2:1-11). Paul told Timothy wine would help his stomach (1 Timothy 5:23). The Bible condemns getting drunk (Ephesians 5:18). We are also condemned here regarding causing others to stumble (v. 9). Many questions arise out of this topic. First off, if you are under 21 it is against the law, and the Bible obligates you to follow the law of the land (Romans 13:1-2). That one is an easy matter to settle.

What does the Bible teach as a whole on the matter? What do you do with issues like these? My intention is not to settle anything for you. The question you must always ask is how do you keep from causing others to stumble? How do you stay faithful? How do you come to your conclusions about what the Bible teaches?

Day 142

1 Cor. 9

Scribe to the Heart

"For though I am free from all, I have made myself a servant of all, that I might win more of them."

(1 Cor. 9:19)

Point to Ponder

We are to provide for those who preach the gospel. Those who preach the gospel are not to take advantage of the church's provision.

Today's Journal

What does it look like to provide for God's leadership?

Prayer for the Day

Holy Spirit, Show me how I am to provide for God's leaders.

PECULIAR CALLING

SOMETIMES WATCHING GOD'S calling lived out is strange. God has specific intentions for us. Paul lays out for the people of Corinth the idea that pastors, missionaries, etc. are to make their living from preaching the gospel. People are to provide for them. At the same time, we see that it was very important to Paul that he never took any money.

Now think about this. Why is it important for Paul to both not be provided for by the people, and for the people to provide for others when they come? See, on the one hand Paul was not to look like a poor lunchroom bully saying, "Give me your food, I gave you the gospel." Instead Paul made tents and worked for his food in the ways that he could.

At the same time, it was important for Paul to go into detail about how the preachers of the gospel are to be provided for by the church, so later someone couldn't say, "Paul didn't need money or food from us. Yeah, you preach to us, but find a way to provide for your family through normal means." Paul wanted the people to know he was going above and beyond and it was not a scam for his gain. Because of Paul's teaching on this issue, the next leader is likely to get financial support that will free his time up to be focusing on the work of the ministry.

In my first ministry I was mentored by someone who had already built a strong base through another organization. He was not a young married man like me. He was a retired married man. He raised money during his time leading this ministry and everyone knew he didn't keep a penny. When he began to help me raise money he explained to people the need for a full-time person in my role, the work it took, and explained that they would be supporting someone young doing God's work. We were in different stages of life during our time serving this ministry. I was newly married and fresh out of college and burdened for college students. My mentor understood the difference in our situations. I thank God for people helping to support that first ministry to college students. I believe that is the heart of Paul's lesson in this section.

1 Cor. 10

Scribe to the Heart

"No temptation has overtaken you that is not common to man. God is faithful, and he will not let you be tempted beyond your ability, but with the temptation he will also provide the way of escape, that you may be able to endure it."

(1 Cor. 10:13)

Point to Ponder

God has a great plan for you.

Today's Journal

What do I need to allow God to take out of my life? Can I commit to Him and say, "No more excuses!"

Prayer for the Day

Holy Spirit, Allow me to understand the importance of my obedience. Empower me in my moment of temptation.

ADDICT

IF YOU HAVE ever known someone who is an addict of any kind, you have seen and possibly even felt times of sadness and confusion. A person can have the very best of intentions about living his or her life right. They can look you in the eye and tell you they have been changed. They recommit to Jesus, and only hours later they can fall right back into their sin. I am someone who likes to see Jesus get ahold of people. I am hopeful and excited to hear news like this, especially from an old friend. Then I hear of their fall again and it hurts. I don't get it.

There are studies and theories that try and explain addictions. You can find information showing that genetics can contribute to making someone more prone to addiction. Addictions are often labeled as diseases. These things may be worth mentioning. However, when it comes down to it, addictions often begin because we (humans) are selfish creatures and sometimes we need to call addiction what it is. It is the devil's plan for a life. It is the way of destruction. This action is based in self-loathing. It is an action that takes no care in others. It is heinous and repulsive in the nostrils of God.

Yet God knows we are weak. He came to die for our sins. He came to set us free and here is the amazing thing: He gave us the way of escape. He made a way. When someone meets Jesus Christ, they now have the power to say "no" to sin. They are no longer winging it in this life. They are given the same Holy Spirit that raised Jesus from the dead (Romans 8:11).

If you are facing an addiction today, can I encourage you to take steps to break it? You may need a trustworthy friend. Don't just talk to anyone; you need someone trustworthy. Be careful! Don't think for a second God wants you to stay there. What if there is a ministry for you that God is keeping from you until you are ready? What if your pulpit stays empty until you are ready for the responsibility that comes with it? Skills, gifts, talent, and education can help you be a great success for God. It is character that keeps you there for the long haul.

1 Cor. 11

Scribe to the Heart

"For as often as you eat this bread and drink the cup, you proclaim the Lord's death until he comes."

(1 Cor. 11:26)

Point to Ponder

Jesus commanded we celebrate communion and we should take it seriously.

Today's Journal

What is the most impacting communion experience I've had?

Prayer for the Day

Lord Jesus, Give me strong reverence for Your death and the importance of celebrating the resurrected Christian life.

HOLY COMMUNION

IN THIS DAY'S entry, I want to look at something Paul began to teach about beginning in verse 17—the Lord's Supper. What was this act of communion originally? The command to observe the Last Supper came right from Jesus. We see in the early church that communion was practiced. He admonishes them strongly because it seems here in Corinth there was some kind of meal going on, but people were not taking the act of communion seriously. People were getting drunk on wine. People were stuffing their faces. It was not done in a reverent way. It certainly wasn't what Christ intended.

The act of communion is a holy act. We are asked to remember the shedding of Jesus' blood for our sins. We are asked to remember the price He paid and reflect on our own sinful nature. It reminds us of our union with God and fellow believers.

We are not to have anger and bitterness in our hearts toward our neighbor. We are not to have unconfessed sin before God. It is a cleansing time. It is a time of renewal and remembrance.

Paul cared deeply that the church was taking seriously this act. We must not stomp on the grace of God! God did a great thing for us. Why would we not take this celebration seriously? It is an opportunity to get right with Him. It is an opportunity for worship.

Day 145

1 Cor. 12

Scribe to the Heart

"For just as the body is one and has many members, and all the members of the body, though many, are one body, so it is with Christ."

(1 Cor. 12:12)

Point to Ponder

We are all gifted in different ways for the unique purposes God calls us to.

Today's Journal

What am I gifted to do? What am I called to do?

Prayer for the Day

Holy Spirit, Teach me about my gifts and my calling for You.

BODY PARTS

IN WHAT SEEMS like a distant memory and can only be referred to as once upon a time, I was a collegiate level athlete. In my particular sport, wrestling, in the summer we would add muscle mass by spending hours in the weight room. When the season drew near we would change our lifting program to one of muscular endurance while shaving our weight down so we would have a low body fat percentage. Our bodies were finely tuned for the season.

What if we had the opportunity to interchange body parts with other athletes? What if a wrestler was able to change arms and legs with a swimmer? Would it work? No way. The thought is ridiculous. Both sports take a highly competitive athlete. Both take an extreme amount of muscular and respiratory endurance. Both take a certain level of mental toughness. There are many similarities.

But the wrestler's legs are trained for endurance in hand-to- hand combat. They need to lift and be strong and explosive late in the match. A swimmer needs speed and endurance. If you put a wrestler's leg on a swimmer's body, the swimmer would have to move too big of a leg. If you put a swimmer's arms on the body of the wrestler, you wouldn't have arms that could finish the takedown.

In this chapter Paul relates the church to a physical body. If you look at a local church, it is important to realize God often molds us specifically for our local body. A good pastor in Maryland would not necessarily make a good pastor in Texas and vice versa. That is why it is so important to stay close to God and listen to His voice. You want to be in His plan, doing what He created you to do.

In my life as a minister of the gospel I have occasionally looked around and thought, "Why am I different from other pastors and Christians I know?" Simply, it is because God made me different. I am not supposed to try to be like them. I am me, and I want to be the best me God intends me to be.

Day 146

1 Cor. 13

Scribe to the Heart

"Love bears all things, believes all things, hopes all things, endures all things. Love never ends. As for prophecies, they will pass away; as for tongues, they will cease; as for knowledge, it will pass away."

(1 Cor. 13:7-8)

Point to Ponder

Our gifts and talents are to help us love others better.

Today's Journal

How does love touch the heart of God and the world?

Prayer for the Day

Holy Spirit, I know I need You to give me the strength to love those who are difficult to love.

WEDDING RINGS AND WORSHIP LEADERS

AH, THE FAMOUS love chapter. The romantic reflects and says, "OK, now we are talking about love. We have left the conversation about gifts and talents in the dust. It is a new topic." Don't forget this letter was not broken up into chapters when Paul wrote it, and when we look at the very end of chapter 12, we see Paul promising to show us a better way (1 Corinthians 12:31b).

Love is that better way. Love is what brings us together. We see that we can be gifted and talented, but without love what is it worth? Paul teaches that it is not worth anything. It is sad to me what we have done in the church. We have made it a business. It is a polished program on Sunday and another on Wednesday. Don't get me wrong. There is nothing wrong with striving for excellence in our programs. Nothing, so long as it doesn't strangle out love.

Really test yourself on this point: Do you believe someone is godly based on scripture knowledge or because of a daily example of sacrificial giving? Do you believe someone is close to God because of exceptional worship leadership or because of a committed prayer life? Do you believe someone is special because of an ability to preach an outstanding message or because that message is lived out consistently?

Without love our message is powerless to the world. Love is what this message is about, not your gifts or talents. When we are focused on gifts and talents and not loving people, we mess up royally.

1 Cor. 14

Scribe to the Heart

"Pursue love, and earnestly desire the spiritual gifts, especially that you may prophesy."

(1 Cor. 14:1)

Point to Ponder

Faith in the text will reveal to us how God works today.

Today's Journal

Have I ever seen God work supernaturally through my life or through the life of another? How?

Prayer for the Day

Holy Spirit, Teach me how You function in this world. Reveal new things to me.

TO TONGUE OR NOT TO TONGUE?

WHEN I STARTED into this project, I had certain chapters in mind that I knew would be controversial chapters because they dealt with divisive topics. Part of writing a book like this and addressing every chapter in the New Testament is you must cover hard topics. However, in my initial thinking, I didn't even consider 1 Corinthians 14 as being on my list of tough topics. But when I read over this chapter in preparation for this lesson I thought, "An entire chapter on speaking in tongues and prophesy? Really?"

This topic causes division at the highest levels of church and Christian education. Some believe these gifts ceased with the apostles and we (the modern church are simply in a different dispensation. That means gifts like these are no longer necessary. If you are someone like me who believes Acts 2 through now is "these last days," then we can't divide up that time between now and then.

Theology done right examines the text divorced from personal attachment and emotion. We are to look at the evidence, which is the New Testament as a whole. Is the gift of tongues important for the church today? Whether it is something that still happens or not, I don't believe it is particularly important to us today. One thing I do believe is important however is how we come to the conclusions we come to.

We are told in these last days, *"Your young men shall see visions, and your old men shall dream dreams; even on my male servants and female servants in those days I will pour out my Spirit, and they shall prophesy"* (Acts 2:17-18). Supernatural gifting happens. If you are someone who believes this doesn't happen anymore, ask yourself why? Is it because you are a skeptic and "no" is your automatic answer? Is it because you haven't experienced such things? What is it?

Whether Christians speak in tongues or not today is not all that important to me. However, whether God still works supernaturally through extraordinary gifts is very important. How do we decide what God does and doesn't do? How we come to the theological conclusions about gifts says a lot about what we think about God. Is God a hands-off type of God, or is He there for us like He was in Corinth?

1 Cor. 15

Scribe to the Heart

"And if Christ has not been raised, your faith is futile and you are still in your sins."

(1 Cor. 15:17)

Point to Ponder

Without the resurrection there is no payment for sin.

Today's Journal

Christ defeated death for me through the resurrection. How does that make me feel when I think about it?

Prayer for the Day

Holy Spirit, Reveal something new to me today about the resurrection. Thank You, Jesus, for paying for my sins.

HE IS NOT FAIR!

ONE OF THE many issues Paul desperately needed to address shows up in this chapter. It is the last chapter of weighty theological material in this letter. He needed to speak of the Resurrection of Christ, and our hope in being resurrected. Some were obviously skeptical about the resurrection.

In American Christianity we focus heavily on the cross. However, we see in the cited passage to the right that without the resurrection we are still in our sins. There is no forgiveness of sin without it. Jesus defeated death. He took away the sting of death. He took away the victory of death. Like Paul did in his letter to the Romans, he revisits this idea about the second Adam with the Corinthians. Beginning in verse 45 Paul teaches that the first Adam passed down death to us, while the second is a life source.

The resurrection completed the transaction of payment for sin. It put the nail in the coffin of death and gave us eternal life. We can't look at the resurrection as anything but grace. God's defeat of death for us is remarkable. It had nothing to do with what we did. It had everything to do with what God did, and how valuable we are to Him.

Often times God is painted as being unfair, and many say the life He gave us is unfair. But think about this: Who wants fair? In fairness, I would have to pay for my own sin. Instead Jesus Christ rescued me from death by defeating it Himself. He paid my debt in full! He washed me clean! Now I can live a life to Him, and guided by the Holy Spirit. Thanks be to God that He is not fair, or I'd really be in trouble!

Day 149

1 Cor. 16

Scribe to the Heart

"Be watchful, stand firm in the faith, act like men, be strong."

(1 Cor. 16:13)

Point to Ponder

It is manly to follow Jesus.

Today's Journal

What does it mean that "real men follow Jesus"?

Prayer for the Day

Holy Spirit, Strengthen me in my faith and in my calling. Keep my feet firm and my eyes watchful.

BE STRONG

THIS LAST CHAPTER is typical of how Paul likes to end his letters. He is very encouraging as he gives final instructions. One thing I noticed in comparison to other letters, however, is that in this last chapter he does not thank as many people as he does elsewhere in Scripture. This letter was meant to straighten out and clarify a lot of the problems the Corinthians were having and I'd even say we can surmise this church was light on having strong leadership.

Remember, these people are new converts in a hostile pagan world. Being a Christian with all of the cultic activity going on around them would not have been easy. So, Paul tells them to act like men and be strong. Paul had a completely different spin on what it meant to "be a man" than what manliness meant in this culture. These pagans equated sexuality with manhood. Paul urges people to be strong, to be men, and to stand firm. Standing firm was a very hard thing to do. Paul was saying that being a real man meant (and still means) staying true. Be faithful. Husbands, be faithful to your wives. Don't get caught up in all of the sex in our culture.

Our culture today is overtaken with sex. It is in our movies, T.V., magazines, and billboards. It has completely taken over the internet. We are in deep. To be a Christian man or woman in this culture, like the Corinthian men, we must also stand firm. We must be strong. We are to be real men and follow only Jesus.

2 Cor. 1

Scribe to the Heart

"For as we share abundantly in Christ's sufferings, so through Christ we share abundantly in comfort too."

(2 Cor. 1:5)

Point to Ponder

God can use our pain to be someone else's gain.

Today's Journal

How does God want to use my pain to be someone else's gain?

Prayer for the Day

Holy Spirit, Show me what of my pain can be used for someone else's gain. Thank You for your comfort.

MY PAIN, YOUR GAIN

I DIDN'T HAVE to be in ministry very long before I understood that many times, we as people generally do not like these verses:

"Blessed be the God and Father of our Lord Jesus Christ, the Father of mercies and God of all comfort, who comforts us in all our affliction, so that we may be able to comfort those who are in any affliction, with the comfort with which we ourselves are comforted by God. For as we share abundantly in Christ's sufferings, so through Christ we share abundantly in comfort too" (2 Corinthians 1:3-5).

When my wife Heidi and I were young in ministry, there was a young woman going through some hard things. Heidi shared these verses with her because they not only fit the situation, but fit her as a person. Heidi had heard her say that her life was hard and things never went right for her. It was a continuous theme in this woman's life. She saw herself as a victim of life's circumstances. Heidi brought these verses up in an effort to lift her from the pit. Oddly, she wanted to stay there.

"You just don't understand. Things are really hard for me," she said. Heidi did understand, though. My wife has been through some hard things herself, and she was able to talk about how she wished certain things never happened in her life. She was (and still is) able to be a blessing and a godly voice to people who go through difficulties, especially those she can relate to directly.

People are often deeply committed to remaining a victim. God wants to comfort us, and wants us to be there for others through our testimony. Paul was despaired to the point of death. Whatever he was going through he wanted to die. Paul wasn't being dramatic. He hated life in those moments. But when it was over, he then knew what it was like, and could comfort others. I only understand depression from going through it. Most people would never think I was someone who would have experience with that, but I do. God uses that experience to help others through me.

Today, don't be the victim. Be victorious. It is OK to feel hurt when we go through hard things. But just ask, "How does God want to use this to help someone else?" Let Him bless you, so in turn you can be the blessing to someone else.

Day 151

2 Cor. 2

Scribe to the Heart

"For we are the aroma of Christ to God among those who are being saved and among those who are perishing,"

(2 Cor. 2:15)

Point to Ponder

The gospel smells either like hope or death—it depends on the smeller.

Today's Journal

How can I better view my world as a place where God is calling people to hope and repentence?

Prayer for the Day

Lord Jesus, Give me understanding as to how the gospel smells to those around me.

DO YOU SMELL THAT?

IN THIS CHAPTER Paul explains the power of the gospel message by relating it to smells and fragrances. Smells evoke memories. They can make an impression. I remember well the smell of my grandmother's baking. Fresh Christmas cookies have a warm, delicious smell. Catching a whiff of cookies can remind you of happy family times. Smells become part of our memories.

Hospitals and doctor offices also have a certain smell. It can be unpleasant and remind us of sickness. Those who have been in war speak of the horrific smells out on the battlefield.

With that in mind, Paul writes to the church in Corinth these verses: *"But thanks be to God, who in Christ always leads us in triumphal procession, and through us spreads the fragrance of the knowledge of him everywhere. For we are the aroma of Christ to God among those who are being saved and among those who are perishing, to one a fragrance from death to death, to the other a fragrance from life to life. Who is sufficient for these things"* (2 Corinthians 2:14-16?)

The gospel is powerful. It creates emotion and feelings in everyone. For some, it is the good news of salvation. It is like the smell of Christmas cookies right out of the oven. It is comforting and pleasant. For others, it is horrible. It is the smell of warfare. It is awful. For these people, it is the stench of death because they are rebelling against truth.

The gospel creates feelings. When I was a young college student, I used to make fun of a guy who tried to tell me about Jesus. Part of the reason I mocked him was because of what I smelled. I was deceived into thinking I was OK with God, but I wasn't. When he was around, I smelled the nasty stench of my death. It was the death of my fleshly desires. It was easier to dismiss than it was to deal with my sin.

2 Cor. 3

"And we all, with unveiled face, beholding the glory of the Lord, are being transformed into the same image from one degree of glory to another. For this comes from the Lord who is the Spirit."

(2 Cor. 3:18)

Point to Ponder

God makes something wonderful in spite of us.

Today's Journal

"God is making you into something wonderful." How do I feel about that statement? Do I believe it?

Prayer for the Day

Father, Reveal to me what You are recreating me to be.

GLORY TO GLORY

"AND WE ALL, *with unveiled face, beholding the glory of the Lord, are being transformed into the same image from one degree of glory to another...* " (2 Corinthians 3:18).

What a victorious statement this is! We, who are in desperate need of a Savior, are being transformed from one glory to another. How triumphant is our God? He can take people and raise them up, in spite of how unlovable they are. He loves me and raises me up not just to glory, but He continually will take me to new levels of glory. I am amazed He even wants to do this.

Underdog stories are inspiring, aren't they? Think of an athlete who came from underprivileged circumstances, or had to work hard to overcome a weakness, and went on to greatness in his or her sport. When we hear success stories about people with disabilities who persevere to reach a milestone, we smile inside for them. We love the underdog. We root for him (or her).

But what about overcoming our sin? What about overcoming the fact that we are unlovable, unusable, and selfish at the core? We are flawed. In the factory, we would have been thrown out. On the sports team, we would have been cut. But thanks be to God through our Lord Jesus Christ we were not. God saw you as one who needed His help to transform you from underdog to glory. And, you are not only being raised up to glory, but from one glory to another. It's a victory story to celebrate!

Day 153

2 Cor. 4

Scribe to the Heart

"In their case the god of this world has blinded the minds of the unbelievers, to keep them from seeing the light of the gospel of the glory of Christ, who is the image of God."

(2 Cor. 4:4)

Point to Ponder

We are at war. Wake up!

Today's Journal

How would I know if I was deceived?

Prayer for the Day

Holy Spirit, Give me understanding that I am in a battle. It is a battle that has already been won by Jesus Christ the Righteous. Let me stand in victory with Him every day. Amen.

WE ARE AT WAR

IT IS HARD to imagine, but the Bible refers to the devil in this chapter as the god of this world. No, he is not "God." But he is the god of this world. For a period of time he is able to tempt people and keep them in darkness. The devil is focused on veiling the eyes of people so they cannot believe God's promises. He also veils the eyes of believers so they are less committed in their faith.

Imagine fighting a war and the enemy was able to convince you that there was no war. What if the enemy was able to say to you, "That wasn't a missile, it was just a storm or a freak accident that happened." The enemy would then convince you that he wasn't killing you and your friends, it was just coincidence.

The god of this world has done exactly that. He has blinded people so much that it is common to believe that the devil is just a fairy tale. Many Christians don't believe the devil exists or at least they do not believe he is actively at war with us in this world today. Why does the devil want us to believe he doesn't exist?

Because if believers understand the reality of the devil, then it is over for him. We have the power over the devil at that point. He may be the god of this world, but we are servants of the creator of the Universe. Jesus Christ can extinguish the devil with the breath of His mouth. In Jesus Christ, you have power over the god of this world! He cannot defeat you.

You must know that you are at war. Wake up and put your armor on. Pray through the scriptures found in Ephesians 6. Seek God! Grow in His word. However, when you don't believe the devil is real, then he has power. The satanic realm can put all kinds of temptations in your path, and you will not see them as war. It will just be something strange happening. You'll think it is "just the way the world is." No! We are at war! Wake up!

2 Cor. 5

Scribe to the Heart

"Therefore, if anyone is in Christ, he is a new creation. The old has passed away; behold, the new has come."

(2 Cor. 5:17)

Point to Ponder

A Christian is a new creation in Jesus Christ.

Today's Journal

Have I been made new? Do I think of myself as new? Am I still stuck in my old thinking in any way? Do I see myself as an overcomer of sin and a new creation in Jesus Christ?

Prayer for the Day

Holy Spirit, Teach me about the new creation that I am in You.

A NEW CREATION

2 CORINTHIANS 5:17 is referenced often when describing our life in Jesus Christ. Unfortunately, when something is referenced often, it can lose its meaning to us. When we hear it over and over again, we may never truly take the time to try to understand it. Today, I want you to truly think about how powerful the truth from this verse is. Paul is talking to a group of believers at the church in Corinth. Many in this area came out of paganism. They were cultists. They were worldly people who were rescued from sexual sin (1 Corinthians 6:11). They fell into the trap of following the god of this world for most of their lives. Now they are told the life they have lived will not be counted against them because of the grace of God through Jesus Christ.

They were told they have been empowered to live a life that is beyond what was capable before. As we learned in the last chapter, we are at war, but now there is a battle plan. The Holy Spirit, God Himself, will live on the inside of you, and will walk with you, Christian brothers and sisters. You are something new. Now when you are tempted to sin, you will have someone helping you *not* to sin. You can now live a new life in the supernatural realm. You will be able to use your talents for serving God. You will be supernaturally enabled with spiritual gifts that you didn't have before. Everything has changed. The Holy Spirit is a complete game changer.

You may still look the same, but thanks be to God through our Lord Jesus Christ you are not the same. You are completely new. Old things are gone. The devil will try to convince you that you are still the same old dog, but you are not. You are remade in the image of God and have been supernaturally enabled to live the life you are called to. Do not glance over this common reference anymore. You are a new creation in Jesus Christ.

Day 155

2 Cor. 6

Scribe to the Heart

"We put no obstacle in anyone's way, so that no fault may be found with our ministry."

(2 Cor. 6:3)

Point to Ponder

The fruit of Paul's life was his most powerful talking point.

Today's Journal

Is the fruit of my life a good argument for Christianity? Do I focus on God working on me (grace), not me working for God (works)? What must I do differently?

Prayer for the Day

Lord Jesus, Allow my life to be a good argument for everything You stand for and the message You seek to give a broken world.

MATURE DECISION

AS A YOUNG man in charge of a college ministry on a medium sized campus of about 6,000 students, I was tempted in a way Paul doesn't appear to be here. At the time I'd only been a believer for a few years. I was extremely passionate and it was easy for me to believe that since the gospel is truth, I could win the masses over by teaching them deep truths and explaining what makes the gospel true.

Some worldly college students benefited from those presentations and discussions in apologetics that I offered. However, Paul takes a different approach here. Paul makes a mature decision. The people of Corinth were into philosophy and deep discussions. Talking to the Corinthians was probably much like talking to a college student. College students at their peak of study can truly push you and sharpen you because they think so deeply. That is what they are asked to do daily.

Paul was beyond biblically educated. If you were going to argue scripture with Paul you better have come to play. This guy had the ability to destroy any worldly argument in a battle of wits. Oddly though, the argument he chooses here is different. He asks the people of Corinth to look at the fruit of what he is doing. He says, "Look at what is going on here. We are enduring beatings and hardships and returning those things with blessings. We are going hungry and without sleep for the sake of the gospel. We are going through all of this for you and others to know and follow Jesus Christ." He shows that they are able to do all of this with such kindness because the message had truly changed their lives.

Paul gives a testimonial approach. He reasons in great detail throughout this letter, but his experience is key to the presentation of the gospel to these people. Paul and the others knew Christ. Paul knew this was evident and people looked at the sacrifices those with Paul were willing to make, and they stood in awe over it all.

Day 156

2 Cor. 7

Scribe to the Heart

"For godly grief produces a repentance that leads to salvation without regret, whereas worldly grief produces death."

(2 Cor. 7:10)

Point to Ponder

What we do with our pain says a lot about who we are and where we are going.

Today's Journal

How have I been hurt? How does my own sin hurt me? How have I handled my pain? What can I do differently?

Prayer for the Day

Lord Jesus, Let me always take my pain to You.

GOOD GRIEF

WITHOUT A DOUBT, emotional pain affects us. It makes us different than we were before the pain. We can choose to get better or we can choose to be bitter. Whether we are grieving over loss, an injustice towards us, or our own sin and inability to live for God, pain affects us. How we deal with our pain says a lot about us and who we are becoming. In 2 Corinthians 7:10, Paul refers to the difference between worldly grief and godly grief. When your grief over what you have done leads to repentance, you've experienced godly grief.

How do we handle our pain? There is only one way. We must take our pain to Jesus the Christ. Jesus came to earth and lived as one of us. He was tempted in every way we are tempted. (Hebrews 4:15) He went through the entire human experience without sin. He is amazing! He is my hero.

Because He became one of us, He empathizes with us. He is not a God that doesn't care, or doesn't see us. He gets involved. When Paul talks about processing your pain in the right way, that is the only way. Take it to Jesus. As we grow, we will experience this type of good grief. We will sin and do things that used to not bother us, but now we need to repent. We need to make things right. Do not walk in guilt today. There is no condemnation for those who are in Christ. The purpose of conviction is to produce good grief. We are not to stay there. We are to take our pain and our sin to Jesus.

2 Cor. 8

Scribe to the Heart

"Whoever gathered much had nothing left over, and whoever gathered little had no lack."

(2 Cor. 8:15)

Point to Ponder

We are called to help each other.

Today's Journal

Write about these two statements: Christians are called to help each other. We are accountable and should not take needlessly.

Prayer for the Day

Father, Let me always be a cheerful, obedient giver. Amen.

MONEY

WHETHER IN A positive or negative way, money always changes situations. In churches, it is no different. For example, people may think the amount they give to a church should give them special privilege when it comes to having say in what the church does with its donations. Sometimes people in the church treat those who have money differently than they treat those with less.

Most pastors do preach about tithing in their sermons or they will teach on stewardship. Often times though we (the body of Christ) miss the mark. In this chapter, Paul is teaching through a situation that came up to show them how to deal with the fact that some have more than others. Some in the church were financially comfortable while their Christian brothers and sisters were in need. Now here is where we often make it sticky. The Bible doesn't teach us to be socialists. Everyone else's problems are not ours all of the time. We don't strive to make more so we can even out society. However, we are supposed to share and, in a relational way, sometimes we are blessed to be able to help the people around us. Sometimes we have been given much so that we ourselves can have the joy of helping others through hard times. In this passage some have been given more and Paul is calling them to take more responsibility in helping to fund the financial need Paul is presenting.

I do believe sometimes God convicts people to leave churches because their tithe is being wasted. It is a mismatch that one person could be struggling to tithe in order to be obedient to God while those in charge of the church's tithe are mishandling it. It isn't uncommon that a church has some people complaining over petty spending issues while several families in that same church are in danger of losing their homes. The religious mindset messes with our biblical common sense. Tithing is not bad, but Paul here is taking a simple problem and presenting a simple solution. He simply explains, that some of them could help some of their Christian brothers and sisters. So, they should go ahead and do it.

2 Cor. 9

Scribe to the Heart

"The point is this: whoever sows sparingly will also reap sparingly, and whoever sows bountifully will also reap bountifully. Each one must give as he has decided in his heart, not reluctantly or under compulsion, for God loves a cheerful giver."

(2 Cor. 9:6-7)

Point to Ponder

God honors our faithfulness.

Today's Journal

How does Paul's teaching on giving in this chapter differ from what I hear from modern day prosperity preaching?

Prayer for the Day

Father, I pray that I will always be a reverent steward of the time, talent, and treasure You entrust me with.

SIMPLE SOWING AND REAPING

THIS LETTER WAS written at least a few years after the letter found in 1 Corinthians. These believers had grown. They were not new believers anymore. They had a responsibility to be giving financially to the kingdom of God. When I first read this chapter and pondered what it meant, I am not going to lie. I thought, "Paul sounds like one of these charlatans I see on T.V. who continually misuse scripture." You have seen them. They have been called "heretics" throughout church history.

Our church culture has a selfish mindset when it comes to finances. People tithe and give in order to *get*. Paul is asking for cheerful givers who want to take responsibility for moving the kingdom of God forward.

As I thought about these verses it came to me: Things were much simpler in that culture. This was an apostle speaking. He was proven. He was preaching the entire message of God. He wasn't making up new ideas about "giving $2,015 in the year 2015 so you can receive it back seven times over." It was simple and truthful. God does bless us for being a cheerful giver, and for being good stewards of what we have been given.

Again, in Paul's day this was a simple letter to maturing believers from an apostle. He wasn't begging them with the concept, "You must give to get." However, God does honor our faithfulness.

2 Cor. 10

Scribe to the Heart

"For the weapons of our warfare are not of the flesh but have divine power to destroy strongholds."

(2 Cor. 10:4)

Point to Ponder

We need to be reminded of the divine power of the God we know and serve.

Today's Journal

Has God ever reminded me to remember?

Prayer for the Day

Holy Spirit, Let me remember what it was like when I first believed and began to experience You in my life. Amen!

REMIND ME AGAIN

YOUNG BELIEVERS NEED more seasoned believers for discipleship. That fact is not as often overlooked as the fact that seasoned believers need young believers to remember. What do we need to remember? We need to remember what it was like. Have you ever seen the excitement in a teenager newly returned from a mission trip or heard a college student give a testimony about recently giving over his or her very life to Jesus Christ?

Why do these testimonies bring some of the most masculine Christian men to tears? They touch something in us. It hits us in a place that is not usually found. It hits way down deep. They cause us to remember what it was like; the original feeling of when it all began for us. They bring us back to that moment when we said, "Lord I am completely wrong and you are completely right. I want to go your way every day from now on."

That time when you first believed was your honeymoon with God. Remember you lived for yourself all those years. Then you realized it didn't have to be that way anymore. You were no longer trapped by lusts of the flesh. You had been rescued.

In the natural progression of this letter Paul is talking about giving, and it is no coincidence that we are now talking about the power of the gospel. These Corinthian believers were in a fleshly pagan culture. They had been rescued. Paul reminds them of the power of the gospel. It can pull down strongholds. What we have is powerful. It is divinely powerful in the spiritual realm. God wins and following Him is the most important and exciting thing in the world. This was just a reminder to remember. Amen.

Day 160

2 Cor. 11

Scribe to the Heart

"And no wonder, for even Satan disguises himself as an angel of light. So it is no surprise if his servants, also, disguises themselves as servants of righteousness. Their end will correspond to their deeds."

(2 Cor. 11:14-15)

Point to Ponder

Satan attacks when good deeds have wrong motives.

Today's Journal

If I was Satan, where would I hide?

Prayer for the Day

Holy Spirit, Help me to discern how the enemy is attacking, or can attack, my family, my church, or my friendships. Give me understanding and protection.

ANGELS OF LIGHT

IF YOU HAVE ever worked in a sales job where the products or services you sell are highly competitive, then you know how important it is to explain what makes your product different and better than all of the others out there that do a similar thing. It is a constant part of the sales rep's duty. Sadly, pastors and churches sometimes treat their church attendance like a sales situation.

Here's how it might play out: "We are better than this denomination because of our belief on this." "We are better than that church because we have a better youth ministry." "It is better to come to our church because our pastor is a better speaker."

Paul, who was probably an excellent speaker, talks down his speaking ability in this chapter, as he compares himself to some people who are in opposition to him.

Knowing that he was called of God to do what he was doing Paul goes so far as to call them servants of Satan. Satan disguises himself as an angel of light. He brings up an interesting concept. Satan hides himself in doing good deeds. If you were Satan where would you hide? The church! If you were at war with someone and you could get close to your enemy's army by being their friend, and actively working alongside them, wouldn't you?

Satan is at work. He is working through people with wrong motives serving in all different areas of the church. I am not trying to make you paranoid, but sometimes the Prince of Darkness hides very well. We shouldn't be surprised when it comes out. Pray and seek God in your relationships with people. Don't let your guard down, for your enemy the devil is a prowling lion looking for someone to devour (1 Peter 5:8).

2 Cor. 12

Scribe to the Heart

"Three times I pleaded with the Lord about this, that it should leave me. But he said to me, 'My grace is sufficient for you, for my power is make perfect in weakness.'"

(2 Cor. 12:8-9)

Point to Ponder

The power of God is manifested when we are weak and must lean on Him.

Today's Journal

Can I relate to Paul? Is there a thorn in my flesh? How does God want to use it to strengthen me? How have I seen Him working in this way?

Prayer for the Day

Holy Spirit, Give me revelation about the thorns You will not remove because they are for my benefit.

POPULAR JESUS

IN EACH GENERATION, young people are generally credited as the inventors of what is currently cool and in style. When something new becomes popular, the previous generation are labeled as the odd-balls. There has always been a temptation to present Jesus as the cool guy. After all, He came to solve all of your problems. We love talking about walking in the victory of Christ. We love talking about reigning with Him. We love it!

But the gospel isn't complete without Jesus redefining what we look at as cool. The message doesn't quite work without verses like today's Scribe to the Heart. Pain is part of our life. Sometimes we have to endure and depend on God. He doesn't always just take our problems away for our own comfort's sake. He didn't for Paul, so he might not for you either.

We don't know what was going on with Paul. It could have been a demonic attack. It could have been an illness or depression. He could be talking about his opponents. It could have been how he is being treated. We don't know. What we do know is Paul pleaded with God to take the problem away. It was like a thorn constantly poking Him in His flesh.

Even the Apostle Paul still needed work. God needed to keep this painful situation there. He needed to keep it there for Paul's sake. He was a better person for going through the pain.

Did God leave Paul? Absolutely not! Paul heard straight from God. God told him His grace was enough. The power of God is made perfect in our weakness. How is that possible? Paul may have been tempted to trust His own strength. Whatever it was, Paul was asked to trust God to take care of him.

Day 162

2 Cor. 13

Scribe to the Heart

"Finally, brothers, rejoice. Aim for restoration, comfort one another, agree with one another, live in peace; and the God of love and peace will be with you."

(2 Cor. 13:11)

Point to Ponder

Ready, aim, fire! Shoot for restoration.

Today's Journal

If it is true that God is aiming me to shoot for restoration, then what do I need to do? What is my personal assignment?

Prayer for the Day

Holy Spirit, Help me aim for restoration. Show me where I need it today and every day.

READY, AIM, FIRE!

WHERE YOU ARE aimed is where you will go. That is the rule for shooting a gun, driving a car, steering a boat, throwing a ball, whatever! You point before you shoot, that is the rule. If the nose of an airplane is only an inch lower than required, unless it is adjusted eventually the plane will crash. What you aim for is the determining factor of where you'll go.

We admire quarterbacks who can aim a ball down field and fire it into a receiver's arms for the perfect catch. If he is only inches off it leads to an interception or an incomplete pass. We love to watch the accuracy of the three-point shooter who, time after time, can bank the shot off the middle of the square from several feet down court.

It makes perfect sense that after Paul talks through all of the conflict and problems in this church, he ends this letter giving them a goal of restoration. "Aim for restoration," he says in verse 11. Here is a goal worth shooting for. Restore people to God. Show the world how Christians should treat each other. For those outside the church, make believers out of them.

His final instructions are to be unified under the authority of the Trinity. Here is something for all of us to shoot for. Aim for restoration. Unify people under the truth. Let's get together and love God and each other anyway. Let's do it in spite of our differences.

Day 163

Galatians 1

Scribe to the Heart

"But even if we or an angel from heaven should preach to you a gospel contrary to the one we preached to you, let him be accursed."

(Gal. 1:8)

Point to Ponder

We are saved by grace through faith.

Today's Journal

Do I struggle with adding to the gospel message when I am telling someone how to get to heaven?

Prayer for the Day

Lord Jesus, Teach me more about Your grace. Amen.

AND...

IF A SMALL child has a story to share, they'll often just run right up to you and start talking. Then, if you are not giving them the attention they desire, you'll start hearing, "and... and... and..." as they embellish their details, adding to the story for emphasis. They, of course, hope you will see just how extreme the situation is.

Paul wrote this letter to the Galatians to straighten out a scenario similar to that of an embellishing child. The believers in Galatia had received the gospel message that Paul preached. They understood they were saved by grace through faith in Jesus Christ. They were born again believers based on what Jesus did for them by dying on the cross and rising from the dead. In the end they put their faith in Him and were seeking to follow Him with their lives.

Some Judaizers came in and started to preach what Paul refers to in this chapter as another gospel. They added to the story. Their story said: Yes, you are saved by grace through faith, but you also have to comply with Jewish customs. You need to be circumcised and we ask you to comply with a number of other things. The reason why this was such a big deal was it was messing with the very foundation Paul had laid with these new believers.

You are called to trust Jesus. If you add anything to that, you missed the point. Paul even goes so far as to say that even if an angel preaches to you and gives you another message it is not from Jesus. He calls the message of the Judaizers a perversion. We are saved because Jesus did the work for us. We can't earn it. All we can do is accept that truth in our hearts and follow after Jesus. You can't add to the message so that you are more saved. What Jesus did, He did permanently and if a church or any person adds requirements beyond trusting Jesus they are in serious error.

Galatians 2

Scribe to the Heart

"I do not nullify the grace of God, for if righteousness were through the law, then Christ died for no purpose."

(Gal. 2:21)

Point to Ponder

Compromising what you believe hurts people and hinders your message.

Today's Journal

Am I more concerned with fitting in or representing Jesus well?

Prayer for the Day

Lord Jesus, My prayer today is to live my life authentically committed to You.

THE POWER OF COMPROMISE

THE DECISIONS WE face usually come with more than two options. As such, we can stay true to our convictions in part, while compromising a part of our beliefs so we don't make any waves. A slight compromise can have very serious consequences, causing big problems. It has been said, "Sin takes you further than you wanted to go, keeps you longer than you wanted to stay, and costs more than you wanted to pay."

Peter probably felt his sin wasn't going to hurt anyone. Peter allowed the Judaizers to influence how he treated the new gentile converts. He was sending them mixed messages. He should have known better. He walked with Jesus for three and a half years! He is leading this new movement called the church. But, on top of it all, in Acts 10 Peter had a dramatic encounter with God teaching him this very lesson, so he could effectively reach out to Cornelius and understand how to reach out to the gentile world. However, it still took a former Pharisee to point out this error to him.

What if Paul had not come along and corrected this error? Peter had great influence. Even Barnabas was led astray. If Peter continued in this compromise, the gospel would have been hindered. By allowing bad teaching to prevail, the leader of the church would have introduced works into the gospel equation. Barnabas and other key church leaders went right along with this heresy.

That is why Paul needed to rebuke Peter and the others in front of everyone. Paul respected Peter's authority and the position of the others, but the message was on the line. It was a question of loyalty to Christ. Afterwards, Peter and others had an opportunity to repent and correct their error.

This compromise could have hindered the advancement of the gospel. Paul had the foresight to understand the importance of teaching pure doctrine. When we compromise the gospel message by what we say or how we act towards the people around us it matters. We must live and teach a pure Christian message. That message is we are saved by grace through faith in Christ Jesus.

Day 165

Galatians 3

Scribe to the Heart

"And if you are Christ's, then you are Abraham's offspring, heirs according to promise."

(Gal. 3:29)

Point to Ponder

Faith in Jesus Christ makes you a spiritual descendent of Abraham.

Today's Journal

What does it mean to me to be a spiritual descendent of Abraham?

Prayer for the Day

Lord Jesus, Thank You for making me a spiritual descendent of Abraham. Show me at a deeper level what this means for my life.

ALL THE PEOPLES OF THE EARTH

THIS CHAPTER CARRIES enormous value that many do not understand. So far, Paul has addressed the Galatians very aggressively over the issue of, "What is the gospel?" He is teaching them that they are saved by grace through faith and are not to add anything to it, not even Jewish customs like circumcision.

Paul refers here to the promise of Abraham. In Genesis 12 God spoke to Abram (who is later renamed Abraham).

"And I will make of you a great nation, and I will bless you and make your name great, so that you will be a blessing. I will bless those who bless you, and him who dishonors you I will curse, and in you all the families of the earth shall be blessed" (Genesis 12:2-3).

These verses teach that not only was Abraham destined to be the father of a great nation, but every people group on the earth will experience blessing through Abraham in some way. In Paul's address to the Galatians we see clarification in this story. Paul begins to explain how believers in Christ are children of Abraham. This ancient promise is known as the Abrahamic Covenant. When God makes a promise, it is irrevocable. God always holds up His end of the deal. That is what makes it a covenant. Israel was accustomed to being this great nation with a special heritage. However, the fact that all people groups are blessed through Abraham's seed is way more significant than just being great. It is the nationality of our Messiah, King Jesus.

Those who put their faith in Christ are recipients of the promise of Abraham. You worship the God of Israel, and are part of the family. You are not less of a family member if you are not Jewish. In fact, it is only by faith in Jesus Christ that you can be a true recipient of the promise. For as verses 26-29 read:

"For in Christ Jesus you are all sons of God, through faith. For as many of you as were baptized into Christ have put on Christ. There is neither Jew nor Greek, there is neither slave nor free, there is no male and female, for you are all one in Christ Jesus. And if you are Christ's, then you are Abraham's offspring, heirs according to promise."

Galatians 4

"And because you are sons, God has sent the Spirit of his Son into our hearts, crying, 'Abba! Father!' So you are no longer a slave, but a son, and if a son, then an heir through God."

(Gal. 4:6-7)

Point to Ponder

We are given God's spirit to remind us that we are His children.

Today's Journal

What is the difference between how someone who is "religious" makes me feel compared to someone who lives by the Holy Spirit of God?

Prayer for the Day

Lord Jesus, Let me look and feel like I belong to You. I pray that others will know that I carry the Holy Spirit within me.

NO LONGER A SLAVE

SLAVERY IN OUR country ended as a result of the Civil War. That was a great day! Generations of innocent people had suffered. As a part of our country's history, it was brutal. For those whose families were enslaved, thinking about that time brings up feelings of anger and resentment on behalf of their descendants. Some don't even want to talk about it.

As Paul is addressing the believers in Galatia, he gives them a pointed analogy. In verses 6-7 he writes:

"And because you are sons, God has sent the Spirit of his Son into our hearts, crying, 'Abba! Father!' So you are no longer a slave, but a son, and if a son, then an heir through God."

Being around the Judaizers would have been a painful experience for a new convert. They could have made you feel like you were less of a believer if you hadn't been circumcised or weren't observant enough of Passover, the Feast of Weeks, or any number of Jewish traditions. Those traditions have their place. Paul addresses this by encouraging them that they were given something so much better. You were given God's Spirit. His Spirit makes you His child. You are no longer a slave. You have rights. You can come and go as you please. You are an heir and you have an inheritance.

In other words, do not let religious people make you feel like less of a follower of Jesus. You are God's child because He gave you His Spirit. Don't get caught up in religion. Get caught up in God, where your inheritance is great!

Day 167

Galatians 5

Scribe to the Heart

"But the fruit of the Spirit is love, joy, peace, patience, kindness, goodness, faithfulness, gentleness, self-control; against such things there is no law."

(Gal. 5:22-23)

Point to Ponder

Christians are to be spiritual nourishment to the world around them.

Today's Journal

How can I stay better connected to Jesus and bear fruit that will nourish the world around me?

Prayer for the Day

Lord Jesus, Use me to bear fruit that will nourish the world around me.

THE PURPOSE OF FRUIT

"BUT THE FRUIT *of the Spirit is love, joy, peace, patience, kindness, goodness, faithfulness, gentleness, self-control; against such things there is no law"* (Galatians 5:22-23).

These are the famous words of Galatians 5 known as the fruit of the Spirit. In the last chapter Paul addressed the Galatians as people who had received the Spirit. This was proof they belonged to God.

In this chapter Paul takes the idea a little further. God's Spirit will actually produce good things in your life if you cooperate with Him. Paul refers to this as bearing fruit. Jesus spoke similarly in John 15. Why does God want us to understand the result of our faith in terms of bearing fruit? We should ponder this.

When a tree produces fruit, someone then has the opportunity to take that fruit and eat it. It can be enjoyed. It can nourish. It can contribute to the sustenance of life. An unexpected discovery of fruit at the right moment might take stress off of a weary traveler, or someone in need. But none of those things can happen if the tree does not produce the fruit to begin with.

To consistently bear fruit we must continually stay connected to Jesus. We must allow Him to work through us. Allow Him to mold us and change us. This will produce sweet things in our life that others will benefit from.

Galatians 6

Scribe to the Heart

"But far be it from me to boast except in the cross of our Lord Jesus Christ, by which the world has been crucified to me, and I to the world."

(Gal. 6:14)

Point to Ponder

Brag about the grace of God.

Today's Journal

Do I boast about the life that God allows me to lead? How can I better brag about the grace of God?

Prayer for the Day

Lord Jesus, I appreciate Your grace more than I can express. Thank You for loving me.

THE LEVEL FIVE LEADER

HARVARD BUSINESS REVIEW published the results of a study of what they considered to be the most successful companies in the country. They called them "level five" companies. They came to the conclusion that all 18 level five companies had a level five leader in the highest leadership role. A level one leader proves to be a competent and effective under an identified set of conditions. Level two leaders have those skills plus others, and so on up the ladder.

Level four leaders operate with extreme confidence. They don't doubt themselves. Because they are confident and proven, the people around them believe in them as well. Level five leadership require this same confidence plus one more thing: humility. The CEOs of the top 18 companies in the U.S. in this study all demonstrated humility. Humility is not the opposite of confidence. They go together. A humble person simply knows their place in the world. They know they are not the center of the Universe. They listen to suggestions. They are open to the possibility that they still make mistakes.

In the last six days of *The New Testament Challenge*, we have been looking at Paul's message to the believers in Galatia. He wanted them to understand God's message of grace. To conclude the message Paul explains there is only one thing to brag about. Think of all the education, experience, and ability Paul possessed. He was a very accomplished individual. This is what He says, *"But far be it from me to boast except in the cross of our Lord Jesus Christ, by which the world has been crucified to me, and I to the world"* (Gal. 6:14). Out of everything Paul had seen and done in his life, he declares that he owed it all to God. What Jesus did for Him was all there was to brag about. Every opportunity or accomplishment was in some way provided by God. By grace Paul got to be who he was.

Ephesians 1

Scribe to the Heart

"In him you also, when you heard the word of truth, the gospel of your salvation, and believed in him, were sealed with the promised Holy Spirit, who is the guarantee of our inheritance until we acquire possession of it, to the praise of his glory."

(Eph. 1:13-14)

Point to Ponder

Receiving God's Spirit is only the beginning.

Today's Journal

What blessings are mine because I know God?

Prayer for the Day

Holy Spirit, I pray that I will know You better today than I did yesterday.

DEPOSIT PLEASE

GOD WAS DOING magnificent things in the city of Ephesus. Ephesus was a major trade city in the first century world. We saw in Acts 19 how the production of Artemis or Diana idols was intricate to the local economy in Ephesus. Sex, idol worship, and foolish philosophical thinking were a result. Paul's message of Christ collided with a culture that didn't want to change, because change could hurt their prosperity as a people.

In the middle of all of this, God did a wonderful work in this city. People came to know Jesus as their Lord. People stopped having casual sexual relationships. They stopped their idol worship. They became hungry for Jesus. The city as a whole went on in their vain pursuits, but some met Jesus and their lives were forever changed.

Paul began to call these people to something better. It wasn't good enough that they were different from their neighbors. Paul wanted their neighbors to meet Jesus too. He called them to great things. However, there were huge challenges. For the Ephesians, it could be dangerous to worship Jesus and refuse to worship the local fertility goddess Diana. It would be lonely living a righteous life in such an unrighteous place. The strange thing about this first chapter is Paul's excitement. Verses 3-10 are one long run on sentence. He uses words like "chosen" and "blessed." Paul is ecstatic about what is happening with these people.

It was hard to follow Jesus in this culture. Paul knows they are lonely and suffering so he gives them a beautiful reminder. *"In him you also, when you heard the word of truth, the gospel of your salvation, and believed in him, were sealed with the promised Holy Spirit, who is the guarantee of our inheritance until we acquire possession of it, to the praise of his glory"* (Eph. 1:13-14). Holy Spirit, God on the inside of you, is only a deposit. It is wonderful, but it is nothing compared to the glory to come.

Day 170

Ephesians 2

Scribe to the Heart

"For we are his workmanship, created in Christ Jesus for good works, which God prepared beforehand, that we should walk in them."

(Eph. 2:10)

Point to Ponder

Walk with God and you'll see Him accomplish His list.

Today's Journal

How can I better walk with God and allow Him to accomplish His to-do list for my life?

Prayer for the Day

Holy Spirit, Give me a stronger walk with You today. Amen.

DIVINE TO-DO LIST

MY WIFE LOVES to-do lists. If Heidi is waiting in an office waiting room or in a line she gets out her pen and paper makes a list. Personally, I do better with a day if I make a small list the night before. It brings order, even for someone like me who is not orderly by nature. In this chapter we see some important verses that are often referred to by Christians. *"For by grace you have been saved through faith. And this is not your own doing; it is the gift of God, not a result of works, so that no one may boast"* (Eph. 2:8-9. You are saved by grace, which is Divine kindness to you. Because of your sins you do not deserve to belong to God, and you can't do anything about it. Christ's death on the cross and rising to life again opens the door for you.

It is by grace, through your faith, that you are saved. Believing in what Jesus did by repenting of your sins and asking Jesus to live in you and work through you is how you are saved. But do not miss verse 10: *"For we are his workmanship, created in Christ Jesus for good works, which God prepared beforehand, that we should walk in them."* Now you have access to the Divine To- Do List.

Just like my wife and I make little lists of things we need to do, God has a to-do list for our lives as well. We probably never know all that is on the list. Once in a while God may tell you. If it is God's to-do list for me it must be important. Don't forget it is a list God is keeping. You accomplish it by walking with Him. Draw close to God through reading the Bible, prayer, and seeking Him in community with other believers. Try to understand how He is working in your life. The better we know Him, the better we cooperate with what He is trying to do in our lives. As God is molding us and shaping us, He is then accomplishing what is on His list. God has a plan for you and it is all-ready laid out, just walk in that plan today.

Ephesians 3

Scribe to the Heart

"Now to him who is able to do far more abundantly than all we ask or think..."

(Eph. 3:20)

Point to Ponder

God's amazing love for you is beyond what you can understand.

Today's Journal

God's amazing love for me makes me feel...

Prayer for the Day

Holy Spirit, Let me grasp more of how high, how deep, and how wide Your love is for me.

GOD'S AMAZING LOVE

SOME THINGS IN life must be experienced in order to have understanding of them. Before I knew my wife, people explained to me what it was like to be in love. I didn't quite understand because I had no reference point. Sure, there were girls that I liked when I was younger, but I didn't know what it was to truly love, be devoted to, or to care deeply about her spiritual, mental, and physical well-being. The same is true about being a father. I served in many positions where I pastored, coached, and mentored children and teenagers. I had nieces and nephews. But until I met my daughter, there was a type of love I still didn't know anything about.

Paul explains to the Ephesian church his prayer for them:

"That according to the riches of his glory he may grant you to be strengthened with power through his Spirit in your inner being, so that Christ may dwell in your hearts through faith—that you, being rooted and grounded in love, may have strength to comprehend with all the saints what is the breadth and length and height and depth, and to know the love of Christ that surpasses knowledge, that you may be filled with all the fullness of God." Ephesians 3:16-19

There are a few keys to our understanding. Paul wants them to know of the great love that can't be measured. He prays they will understand it. He also prays they will love each other and the world around them with that love. When a group of people experience God's love together, they love God back. They also love His people. Having an experiential knowledge of God's love is forever life-changing, and should also change the people around you.

Ephesians 4

Scribe to the Heart

"But grace was given to each one of us according to the measure of Christ's gift."

(Eph. 4:7)

Point to Ponder

We need each other to help us become more like Christ.

Today's Journal

In what way should I be helping another to become better?

Prayer for the Day

Holy Spirit, Reveal my role in the lives of others and give me wisdom to see how I can build up the body of Christ.

UNITY OF FAITH

WHEN YOU HEAR a sermon or read a book on what it means to be a Christian leader Ephesians 4:11-14 is often the starting point. It speaks to the different roles we all play in the body of Christ:

"And He gave the apostles, the prophets, the evangelists, the shepherds and teachers, to equip the saints for the work of ministry, for building up the body of Christ, until we all attain to the unity of the faith and of the knowledge of the Son of God, to mature manhood, to the measure of the stature of the fullness of Christ." Ephesians 4:11-14

We are made to make each other better. Some are gifted by God to lead. I have found I am a much better Christian when I am leading others because it is how I am made. I have also learned that I need people to lead me in the areas in which I am not strong. For example my wife is numbers-oriented and organized. She is thorough and skeptical of new things. This helps me because I am gifted in the area of being entrepreneural or starting things. For me to be successful I need her to help me bring sequence and order to my plans. She also helps me to assess the level of risk when trying something new. Without me she may have never tried many foods she likes today and her life would be very predictable. Without her I would always have my head in the clouds, starting new things before I finished other projects I started.

This is just one example, but in the context of Christ's church often times we judge each other by saying, "Why are they doing it that way?" "I would never do it like that." In truth, your way might be better. What seems obvious to you because of your strengths may not be obvious to someone else. Find a way to help bring another up in an area in which you are strong. More than likely, they'll help you, too. Our gifts and talents complete each other. The church is the hope of the world and is truly an unstoppable force when it is working right. We are to have unity in the faith and the knowledge of the Son of God. Learn about your Christian brothers and sisters and what makes them tick. Learn how God has uniquely created them.

Day 173

Ephesians 5

Scribe to the Heart

"For you may be sure of this, that everyone who is sexually immoral or impure, or who is covetous (that is an idolater), has no inheritance in the kingdom of Christ and God."

(Eph. 5:5)

Point to Ponder

Worship is monotheistic and marriage is monogamous.

Today's Journal

How important is it to understand the culture of the Ephesians in gaining understanding to God's will for marriage?

Prayer for the Day

Holy Spirit, Continue to purify me.

THE POINT

IT IS VERY easy in the day we live in to miss the point of this chapter entirely. Much can be said about the high calling of both the husband and the wife to Christian living. It is extremely unfair that we as Christians have allowed the feminist movement to take these verses out of context and use them against our faith as a declaration that the Bible is "behind the times."

For the sake of understanding God's Word, I want you to consider the context. There was social, economic, and religious pressure to worship Artemis (or Diana) of the Ephesians. The worship of this god was likely sexual and resulted in a promiscuous attitude in this city. It was a religion of female dominance over men. Paul addresses this small church of young believers to turn away from this type of thinking. The calling is to be in a monotheistic relationship with the one true God, along with a monogamous relationship with one spouse of the opposite sex.

Paul takes it one step further by describing reasons why men and women go together. We have different roles because we are different. He teaches we should cling to each other. One woman is to be with one man for life. It is not good to be a part of this sexually immoral and permissive world. It will hurt you. Therefore, a woman should submit to her husband's authority. A man should take his authority as seriously as Christ would. Love your wife and your family with a love beyond what you have known. Love her even to the point of death, just like Christ would.

If only men and women in our day would understand this better. What would our homes be like? What would our families be like? Paul knew these people needed a special understanding about sexuality and relationships to have Christian marriages in Ephesus. Shouldn't we consider the same warnings in the day and age in which we live?

Day 174

Ephesians 6

Scribe to the Heart

"Put on the whole armor of God, that you may be able to stand against the schemes of the devil."

(Eph. 6:11)

Point to Ponder

We do not fight against flesh and blood but authorities in heavenly places.

Today's Journal

If my fight is not against flesh and blood, then why is it I still get mad at other people?

Prayer for the Day

Open your Bible to Ephesians 6 and pray through the Armor of God (verses 10-20) one piece of armor at a time.

ARMOR ALL THE TIRES

BECAUSE WE ARE born into sin, we tend to focus on protecting the wrong things. Take a car for instance. We wax the paint to protect it. We ensure we put the right gas in the tank and quality oil in the engine. We'll even buy products like Armor All to rub into the sides of our tires to protect the rubber. There is nothing wrong with any of that. But today I want you to ask yourself: Are there important things that you should be protecting, but are not?

If you were going into a battle you would make sure you had your armor. You would have all of the items listed in verses 10-20 of this chapter. Guess what? You *are* born into a battle. When I read these verses, I see Paul sitting in a jail cell trying to dream up how to communicate this deep truth about the war we are in and how to wage it. How is Paul going to communicate that we fight against forces and powers we do not see? When he looks outside his cell, he sees a guard dressed in Roman garb.

The preacher Paul may have already had a good relationship with the guard as he talked to him about Christ. He probably would have asked him about being in hand to hand combat. Paul probably used the symbolism of the Roman garb to witness to the soldiers. We do know Paul had witnessed previously to at least one Roman jailer who became saved (Acts 16).

Let's not focus on protecting the wrong things. Put on the full armor of God. Truth is like a belt that keeps your pants up. It holds you together. Live it and know it. Have the breastplate of righteousness in place: Live a life of holiness and pray that way. Your battle shoes carry you with peace and the readiness to share. Have the shield of faith. Make sure you have the helmet of salvation. And have the only offensive weapon mentioned—the sword. It is the Word of God. Pray through all of these verses mentioned above. Realize you are in a battle and choose to fight the good fight today and every day. Remember Paul's instructions: "*Finally, be strong in the Lord and in the strength of his might. Put on the whole armor of God, that you may be able to stand against the schemes of the devil. For we do not wrestle against flesh and blood, but against the rulers, against the authorities, against the cosmic powers over this present darkness, against the spiritual forces of evil in the heavenly places*" (Eph. 6:10-12).

Day 175

Philippians 1

Scribe to the Heart

"For it has been granted to you that for the sake of Christ you should not only believe in him but also suffer for his sake,"

(Phil. 1:29)

Point to Ponder

How we walk with God in our beatings teaches others about our faith.

Today's Journal

Can I allow God to shine through my current situation?

Prayer for the Day

Holy Spirit, Shine through my life in each and every circumstance.

END OF LIFE BEATINGS

AS A YOUNG man, Saul of Tarsus assisted in beating and brutally murdering Christians. Remember from Acts 7 he held the coats of the men who stoned Stephen; who so graciously forgave the men as they were doing it and peacefully went to be with the Lord as he was struck down. Young Saul witnessed the confidence Christians had in death. They were not afraid to meet their Maker on the other side because they experienced Him on this side.

Paul essentially is on death row in Rome. People are preaching Christ falsely just so Paul will get beaten harder and more frequently. Paul longs for the tasty banquets of his youth when he used to sit in important seats at important social events. I am sure he didn't like being treated like a piece of garbage. I am sure he figured his execution would not be peaceful and would likely be humiliating. He continued to love God and wanted Him to be glorified. He wanted those he pastored to live worthy of Christ. He knew that when you suffered with joy you proved the gospel to be authentically true.

"Only let your manner of life be worthy of the gospel of Christ, so that whether I come and see you or am absent, I may hear of you that are standing firm in one spirit, with one mind striving side by side for the faith of the gospel, and not frightened in anything by your opponents. This is a clear sign to them of their destruction, but of your salvation, and that from God." Philippians 1:27-28

In these verses Paul calls it proof of their destruction. These are Paul's golden years. Where was God? Why was this happening? So many strong believers have asked these questions. The strongest of believers are able to put God and others in front of themselves, and they realize they need the hard times to know God better. Joyce Meyer (Christian speaker and author) declares she would go through her childhood all over again if the alternative were to *not* go through it but not have the sweet fellowship, she has with God now.

Paul's beatings didn't slow him down. Let your life be worthy of the gospel! Stay strong! Paul practiced what he preached.

Philippians 2

Scribe to the Heart

"Your attitude should be the same as that of Christ Jesus."

(Phil. 2:5)

Point to Ponder

We are called to have the humble attitude of Christ towards others.

Today's Journal

Do I need to humble myself for a difficult person in my life? Can I do it?

Prayer for the Day

Lord Jesus, Allow me to humble myself for others today so that Your name can be glorified.

THE HIGHEST CALLING

IF SOMEONE ASKS you, "What is the highest calling a person can receive from God?" what would you say? Most of us think of a position of authority or we may think of a particular person. In this chapter Paul tells his original audience and tells us today, *"Your attitude should be the same as that of Christ Jesus"* (Phil. 2:5). We then see what was probably a New Testament era hymn Paul was reciting.

The lyrics go on to tell us that he considered being the very nature of God not something to be grasped (v. 6). In other words, Jesus was equal with the Father, but He acted like He was subservient to Him. He was obedient even to death, and in a sense gave up His glory temporarily to fight the battle with us. Because of his ultimate humility, sinners like us have a shot at redemption.

Notice what did it. Jesus emptied Himself of all entitlement. He is the one person who is deserving of titles. If anyone should feel entitled it should be Him, but that is not the nature of God. God's nature is to serve and to be obedient to a cause, even to the point of death. That cause is the redemption of mankind. I wonder how many times in a day do I have the opportunity to be humble? How many times do I have the opportunity to consider others better than myself, to let them get their own way, or to let them feel more important than me? Is this the highest calling: To die to self and allow God to work through us, even when it hurts? I think Paul would say it is.

Day 177

Philippians 3

Scribe to the Heart

"But whatever was my profit I now consider loss for the sake of Christ."

(Phil. 3:7)

Point to Ponder

*We should have no confidence in the flesh.
Our confidence should be in Christ.*

Today's Journal

What part of my approach to God should be flushed?

Prayer for the Day

Lord Jesus, Give me eyes to see the difference between religion and relationship activities.

FLUSH YOUR RELIGION

THE FLOW OF this letter shifts in this third chapter. When we started out, Paul has a humble and strong attitude as he begins writing, while on death row, to this group of Christians. In the previous chapter he is talking about Christ who by very nature was equal with God, but humbled Himself even to the point of death. Now Paul talks about where his own confidence lies. As a youngster, his confidence was in the flesh. It was in his heritage, tradition, religion, etc. It was in his ability to keep the law and memorize scripture. It was entirely works-based. Keeping the rules was the basis for how he lived.

It is fascinating how close many people live to this today. Do not allow your mind to jump into how someone worships in another denomination or tradition. The religious mindset is present in your church on some level. It is also present to some degree in your life and mine. Something in our sinful nature mixes with our desire to please God, and we get religion. I am not talking of the good deeds such as taking care of widows and orphans and remaining unstained by the world (James 1:27). I am talking of the belief that certain practices, services, or activities are what make us right with God.

We must remember when Paul was young Saul of Tarsus, he was a Pharisee. He was raised in it. He probably had what we know as the Old Testament memorized in order without chapters and verses, but as narrative. He would only take so many steps on the Sabbath day, and was full of many other legal practices. In his later years, once he experienced Christ, Paul counted it (the religious activities) all as loss. It was waste.

He is expressing such a strong point it is almost as if he just put his hand in it. The point is that putting our hope in practices, ceremonies, and our ability to work our way into heaven is useless. It is the stuff that is to be thrown out. It has no good purpose. It smells, ruins our clothes, and gets under our fingernails.

Day 178

Philippians 4

Scribe to the Heart

"Do not be anxious about anything, but in everything by prayer and supplication with thanksgiving let your requests be made known to God. And the peace of God, which surpasses all understanding, will guard your hearts and your minds in Christ Jesus."

(Phil. 4:6-7)

Point to Ponder

Peace comes with thanksgiving.

Today's Journal

Write a letter to God, expressing your worries. Thank Him and allow Him to give you peace about your circumstances.

Prayer for the Day

Lord Jesus, I thank You for_____. I am also thankful for__. Please help me with_____.

SURVIVAL SKILLS FROM DEATH ROW

HERE IS A man who is on death row in Rome. Just by looking at how they treated Jesus we know it was not a nice place to die. Chances are you will suffer and often times in public. Yet, Paul continues to give good counsel. He continues to point towards Jesus in a profoundly positive way. How?

The answer: Prayer. Paul gives us a formula in our Scribe to the Heart verses today. Do not be anxious about anything (v. 6). Refuse to let anxiousness catch up with you. How do you do that? Take everything to God with prayer and petition (v. 6). Just in case you are tempted to start whining, do it all in the spirit of thanksgiving and give Him praise with everything (v. 6). This will lead to the peace of God which will transcend understanding (v. 7). This will guard your heart and your mind in Christ Jesus (v. 7).

In my life it has been the moments when I have felt the most helpless where I have experienced God the most. Believing we can help ourselves without God keeps us miserable. When we approach God like a little child, and give the problem over to Him, something mysterious happens. He takes care of His children, and we get to see Him do it.

Whatever your prayer is today, whatever your concern or problem, give it to God. Give Him thanks and praise. Give Him your trust and your faith and He will guard your heart and mind with a peace that passes all understanding.

Colossians 1

Scribe to the Heart

"He is the image of the invisible God, the firstborn of all creation."

(Col. 1:15)

Point to Ponder

Paul addresses gnosticism in the Bible. It isn't anything new.

Today's Journal

Does it surprise me that Paul addresses the same kinds of heresies which have resurfaced in recent years?

Prayer for the Day

Holy Spirit, Help me to know Your word and be able to show others where to find Your truth. Amen.

KNOWLEDGE

TEACHINGS THAT GO directly against Christian doctrine are called heresy. Unfortunately, from time to time heretical teachings actually surface within the church. A topic or twist on a doctrine will arise and too many ungrounded Christians jump on the bandwagon to believe the heretical teaching. If the heretical teaching gains enough popularity within the Christian community, people will flock to the bookstores and movies to find that "one new thing" they've been looking for.

Those who are openly against the church would love to put to bed the ideas of Jesus, the Bible, and Christianity. Opposers say the Bible is outdated, incorrect, and untrustworthy and because we live in a "modern" society we should know better. In truth, gnosticism that is regarded as newly discovered today is actually as old as Christianity itself. Paul addresses it here. To find out why it didn't survive then, take the gnostic arguments and put them against Paul's letter to this church in Colossae.

The gnostic teachings had found their way into the church. They believed they had "gnosis"—the Greek word for knowledge. It was a special knowledge from God. They believed all matter was evil and the cause of evil, so therefore they had a problem with Jesus being both God and man, and a problem with the crucifixion and resurrection. When you read the verses below you can begin to see the rub in doctrines:

"He is the image of the invisible God, the firstborn of all creation. For by him all things were created, in heaven and on earth, visible and invisible, whether thrones or dominions or rulers or authorities—all things were created through him and for him. And he is before all things, and in him all things hold together."

Colossians 1:15-17 Jesus was the image of the invisible God. He was the Word made flesh. He also created all things, both the angels and the angels gone rogue. He created the world. God allowed this letter to survive for us today. Heretical teachings are not new to the church. They are not new discoveries. They are merely distractions to our faith. Learn about these heresies. Dig deep! At the bottom of the filth you will still find the God of the Bible and the truth of Jesus Christ that will set you free.

Day 180

Colossians 2

Scribe to the Heart

"See to it that no one takes you captive by philosophy and empty deceit, according to human tradition, according to the elemental spirits of the world, and not according to Christ."

(Col. 2:8)

Point to Ponder

Sometimes you need to go back to the basics.

Today's Journal

Do I need to get back to the basics of my faith? How? Where has religion plagued me?

Prayer for the Day

Jesus, Teach me how to filter out religion and follow You.

CHURCH: THIS IS JESUS

HALL OF FAME coach Vince Lombardi is known to have begun each season by holding up a football and addressing his team by simply stating, "Gentlemen: This is a football." In other words, it was time to go back to the beginning. Let's get to the bottom of this and start with the basics. In this chapter, Paul does a similar thing by bringing it all back to Christ. He is saying, "Church: This is Jesus."

Paul appeals to them as spiritual thinkers by telling them that even though many have not seen him face to face, he is with them in spirit. Paul goes into great detail about the religious restrictions being put on them towards the end of the chapter. There were eating and drinking restrictions. There were Sabbath restrictions and new moon ideas.

The bottom line can be found in these verses:

"See to it that no one takes you captive by philosophy and empty deceit, according to human tradition, according to the elemental spirits of the world, and not according to Christ. For in him the whole fullness of deity dwells bodily, and you have been filled in him, who is the head of all rule and authority." Colossians 2:8-10

Don't let these kinds of people distract you. Do not let religious thinking take you captive. You are in Christ, who is the head of all rule and authority. There is no reason to get all wrapped up in that stuff because Jesus is all you need. Jesus gave you everything. Your life has been fulfilled in Christ. You can be at home with Him; at rest with Him. You can face this world and do anything you need to do. Religion always makes you fret and worry. It always makes you want to do more.

Jesus wants us to face this world as though we have been taken care of in Him. We belong to Him. Why would we worry about all of these other concerns? Sometimes we need to start over. Gentlemen: This is a football.

Colossians 3

Scribe to the Heart

"For you have died, and your life is hidden with Christ in God."

(Col. 3:3)

Point to Ponder

Our strength in Christ comes when we run and hide in Him.

Today's Journal

Do I run to Jesus or away from Jesus when I have a problem? What do I try and do in the flesh?

Prayer for the Day

Lord Jesus, Make me strong and mighty in You. Teach me to run and hide in You.

A LIFE HIDDEN IN GOD

PAUL NOW USES some of the gnostic influence to build his case to the Colossians. In this chapter, you see him saying, "Yes your flesh is bad. Stay away from sexual immorality, and evil desires." Paul wants us to know you don't do this by walking around thinking about it. Your life is hidden in Christ. You actually seek God and God walks with you through this life. Your fellow Christian brothers and sisters walk with you, in Christ.

Jesus paid a hefty price for us with His very life. Now we are called to hide. We are to run and hide in Him. We are to face this world with boldness, but that boldness comes from running and hiding in Him. Seeking Him in prayer, understanding His Word—these are the activities that help us to run and hide. Hiding is not weakness. As a Christian, it is where we get our strength.

The gnostics say you should just keep depriving yourself. They say all matter is evil, but in the power of your flesh overcome. This thinking makes no sense. In Christianity our flesh is evil. It is not mentioned in a positive light in the entire New Testament. But Christ came to us and gave us the power to run and hide in Him, not in our own evil flesh. Do you see the difference?

Colossians 4

Scribe to the Heart

"Epaphras, who is one of you, a servant of Christ Jesus, greets you, always struggling on your behalf in his prayers, that you may stand mature and fully assured in all the will of God."

(Col. 4:12)

Point to Ponder

Sometimes prayer is an intense fight, fought in places we do not see.

Today's Journal

Have I ever wrestled in prayer? What was it like?

Prayer for the Day

Holy Spirit, Awaken me to the battles I need to fight in the spiritual realm.

WRESTLING IN PRAYER

IT WAS JUST another day in the College Wrestling Room and our assistant coach Tony who was a world class wrestler and competitor himself, tells us to "partner up." I partner up with one of my normal workout partners, who was one of our better wrestlers.

Tony says, "OK, now go until the other guy quits."

When we did this drill, it was always my intention never to quit. I didn't care if I was winning or not. I am not someone who quits. So far, I was successful against my previous partners for this drill, but today I knew this was not going to be easy because Eric (an eventual four-time NCAA qualifier) never quit either.

We went hard. At times I would get the better of him and then it would turn and he'd better me. As time went on it became personal and very physical. I can only imagine how it would have gone if we weren't friends. We took swings at each other. We got very frustrated.

After 56 minutes of continuous wrestling Tony had us stop and let us leave practice early. It felt good. We battled and warred against each other and had moments we laughed about later. When I read Paul's words about Epaphras in the NIV version we see the words "wrestling in prayer."

This guy Epaphras was going to war in the spiritual realm. It was exhausting. It was challenging. There was something very intense about trying to minister to this culture. The cultic gnostic thinking had infiltrated the culture. There were spiritual strongholds in the heavenly realms.

Day 183

1 Thess. 1

Scribe to the Heart

"For we know, brothers loved by God, that he has chosen you, because our gospel came not only in word, but also in power and in the Holy Spirit and with full conviction. You know what kind of men we proved to be among you for your sake."

(1 Thess. 1:4-5)

Point to Ponder

Effective leaders prepare others for leadership.

Today's Journal

Would the apostles have been the same if Jesus had never left? Have I ever had to fill a void due to someone's absence?

Prayer for the Day

Holy Spirit, Help me to understand leadership in the way the apostles did.

TRUE FAITH

IF YOU LINE up the world's finest theologians and ask them this question: "How do you test the faith of a spiritual leader?" I don't know that many would come up with the answer I see here in our first chapter of 1 Thessalonians. What happens when you have to have faith that God will actually work in people without you? That answer, I believe, is the true test of the faith of a leader.

Paul, Timothy, and Silas are all credited in this chapter as sending a message to the church in Thessalonica. Paul worked closely with Timothy and Silas and close enough in Thessalonica that he put their names on the letter right with his. I am sure they preached, and they prayed. They cried out to their God. They watched God do amazing things.

At some point Paul, Timothy, and Silas had to release these people to God. Yes, the people began to imitate them. Yes, they became examples to all the people in Macedonia and Acadia. Could these men have said this to them had they stayed and been the apostolic experts?

Could the original apostles have been what they became in the book of Acts if Jesus never ascended? I am not looking for the proper theological answers like, "God can do what ever He wants." I am talking practically about how God does things. The most powerful and effective leaders lead so well that for someone to become like them, the leader must leave and get out of the way. That is why Paul planted so many churches. He wanted them to fly. When it was time, under the Lord's direction, Paul set them free.

1 Thess. 2

Scribe to the Heart

"For what is our hope or joy or crown of boasting before our Lord Jesus at his coming? Is it not you? For you are our glory and joy."

(1 Thess. 2:19-20)

Point to Ponder

Christians who are discipled correctly are the glory and joy of their teacher.

Today's Journal

How does God measure a successful ministry? How is God's measurement different from mine?

Prayer for the Day

Holy Spirit, Allow me to measure my influence according to how You see things.

GLORY AND JOY

ONE OF THE main internal shifts that happened for Paul from his former religious life was a genuine care for people. As a Pharisee, Saul (Paul) had Christians killed. His purpose was to get rid of the Christian movement and it seemed he didn't let anything stand in his way. He persecuted them with vengeance. For him to now say, "You are our glory and joy," signifies a great shift.

Paul went from having a killing mindset to a converting mindset. Now, he sees people as God sees them: As people who need help. He preaches to them and teaches to them, but most importantly, laboriously lives it out in front of them.

When he says, "you are our glory," he is saying they are something to be proud of to God. God is proud of their ministry and they are the proof. When he says, "You are *our* joy," he is letting them know that he and the others are proud of them. Saul didn't get it. Paul does. Paul knows the important thing is to love God with all your heart, and love your neighbor as yourself. He has seen these people meet Jesus and grow in the faith. As their leaders, these three men took great joy in that. Remember Timothy and Silas' name are also on the letter, although it seems to hint that Paul is doing most of the talking.

These Christians in Thessalonica faced persecution. Paul looked at them as the glory and joy of his ministry. Why? Because they were living out their faith. They loved God and each other. There was no church before Paul, Timothy, and Silas had arrived and now there were real Christians truly living for Jesus. As such, they were their glory and joy, and a glory and joy to Jesus.

Day 185

1 Thess. 3

Scribe to the Heart

"As we pray most earnestly night and day that we may see you face to face and supply what is lacking in your faith."

(1 Thess. 3:10)

Point to Ponder

A Christian leader takes joy in a disciple's fruit and never stops hoping for their continued development.

Today's Journal

Can I relate to this topic as either a teacher or a student?

Prayer for the Day

Holy Spirit, Guide me to excellence as a disciple-maker.

LIFELONG DISCIPLESHIP

FROM THE BEGINNING of my ministry experience, I always thought of myself as someone geared towards preaching and teaching the masses. I have always had a deep burden for people to grasp what the Bible is saying and then see them fully live it out. However, when I think of the times that I felt I was the most used by God, humbly, it is not those times of preaching sermons or teaching groups. I suspect the victories that are the biggest to God happened in times spent one-on-one with people.

Most pastors, when they run into a person, they used to lead in one fashion or another, will try to understand where that person currently is spiritually. Right or wrong, we want to know. We want to have some measurement about how things went back then. We like to know we made a difference.

In my early ministry to college students I promoted an incomplete theology. I saw it didn't work when life hit hard. I blamed myself a little when I saw people that I used to lead not respond in a Christian way to tragedy. Other times I was amazed at how God worked in people's lives. Over a period of years, eventually I truly got it. Heidi and I love talking to people we ministered to in the past who surprise us and show us what God has done in their lives. At the time we may not have felt they were with us at all, but God was working in mysterious ways and sometimes dealing with sins we didn't even know about. Today we now understand better.

Yet, like Paul, a true pastor always wants to help supply what is lacking. It is part of our calling, our DNA. Parents are the same way. Sometimes as parents we do this to a fault, but the desire to supply what is lacking is there. God calls people to lead and gives them a burden to get it right. While Paul took great joy in where they were, he never stopped hoping for more in the way of where they were going.

Day 186

1 Thess. 4

Scribe to the Heart

"For this is the will of God, your sanctification: that you abstain from sexual immorality; that each one of you know how to control his own body in holiness and honor."

(1 Thess. 4:3-4)

Point to Ponder

Sexual immorality keeps us from God's best. We need to be more aware of its trappings in our lives.

Today's Journal

How does sexual sin keep someone from God's best? How can I protect myself?

Prayer for the Day

Lord Jesus, I have been washed in Your blood. Keep my eyes and heart pure today and every day. Keep me from lust and sexual sin. It is by Your grace that You give me this ability.

A RECURRING CONCERN

IT SEEMS THAT whether Paul is talking to a young church or a church that is more established, sexual immorality is a big problem. Even here, as he writes to the Thessalonians, sexual immorality must be addressed.

My grandfather used to stand by the road when we would leave his house. He would always say, "Lock your doors." "Buckle your seatbelt." It was good advice. Similarly, Paul repeated his sound instruction to those he discipled. Like my grandfather, Paul had good reasons for repeating himself. If we didn't do those things, we could get severely injured or even die.

Paul brings up sexual immorality because it is something that will always keep us from God's best. You have to wonder do we spend enough time concerned with this today? Modern political correctness says we are being hateful if we call certain things wrong. The Bible teaches that premarital sex, living together before you are married, homosexuality, promiscuity, pornography, and lust are wrong behaviors.

We are bombarded with images every day that threaten our purity in this area. We have access to more garbage, and privately I might add, than ever before and it seems that the church doesn't want to give the proper attention to the matter. Paul gave proper attention to the dangers. He could be counted on to bring it up sooner or later for each church he mentored. We must not shy away from it, either.

Day 187

1 Thess. 5

Scribe to the Heart

"He who calls you is faithful; he will surely do it."

(1 Thess. 5:24)

Point to Ponder

Abiding in the presence of God helps us to do the will of the Father.

Today's Journal

What has God called me to? What is holding me back? How can I better connect with God today?

Prayer for the Day

Father, Give me a deeper connection with You. I know You love me and call me according to Your purposes for me. Help me to walk in holiness and with assurance of the things You have called me to do and be in this broken world.

HE WHO CALLS YOU

THE BIBLE IS cautious about calling man "faithful." Jesus knew what was inside man's heart. We read often of the deceitfulness of the heart and man's intentions. Paul ends this letter with a lot of encouragement for the church. It is slightly different from other letters, which could be because he is writing with Silas and Timothy.

I appreciate that at the end of this letter Paul reminds us that the God who calls us is faithful. When God calls us to do something, we will have the opportunity to do it. We will be given all of the right people, the right timing, and the right resources. He will do His part. Now the hotly debated question is does that mean our part always gets done? Some would say that "God is in control therefore it always gets done."

Personally, I don't believe everything God calls people to do gets done because He is entrusting people to do it. We are supposed to live and act a certain way that is in the will of the Father. We are supposed to be people of integrity. It doesn't always happen. God is actually so much in control that He gave us free will and He still remains in control. I don't understand it, all I know is my part is the part in question. That is why it is so important to pray and seek God. In our prayer we shouldn't want to move the hand of God as much as we should want to connect with God. When we stay in close connection with God, we can follow Him and do His will. Jesus lived this way (John 5:19-20). It is in Him that we live and move and have our being. When it comes down to it, that's what God is looking for in us: That we would connect with Him as sons and daughters.

Day 188

2 Thess. 1

Scribe to the Heart

"To this end we always pray for you, that our God may make you worthy of his calling and may fulfill every resolve for good and every work of faith by his power."

(2 Thess. 1:11)

Point to Ponder

Time is short.

Today's Journal

Time is short. So, what is my prayer? What should I be doing differently?

Prayer for the Day

Lord Jesus, Show me what I lack. Make me be all I can be for Your glory.

URGENCY

A COUPLE OF chapters ago it was purposely not addressed. Some of you know what I mean. 1 Thessalonians 4 is often used to teach end of days theology regarding the rapture of the church and we talked about sexual immorality instead. You need to know I purposely didn't address end of days at that point. By the end of *The New Testament Challenge* you will have some idea of where I stand on issues like the rapture of the church. But if you were disappointed, you must realize it is better for you to focus on matters that address the things you face every day (like temptations regarding sexual immorality).

There may not have been a huge amount of time between the writing of these two letters. We see some of the same themes in this letter as we saw in 1 Thessalonians. The themes of urgency and end things are found in both. When Paul wrote (with Timothy and Silas) 1 Thessalonians 4, the question of the day was, "What is going to happen to us if we die before Jesus comes?" They didn't understand what happened to their believing parents, aunts, uncles, etc. Paul lets them know that the dead go to Christ first, and then if you are alive when Jesus returns, you will go to meet Him as well (1 Thessalonians 4:13-18). These verses alone can't be used to teach about a rapture and timelines, though.

In 2 Thessalonians, again, not a lot of time has passed. Many of the concerns are the same. Paul is even still writing with Timothy and Silas to this church. We see in the cited verses below the urgency: *"To this end we always pray for you, that our God may make you worthy of his calling and may fulfill every resolve for good and every work of faith by his power, so that the name of our Lord Jesus may be glorified in you, and you in him, according to the grace of our God and the Lord Jesus Christ"* (2 Thess. 1:11-12).

The prayer for the believers is Thessalonica was that they would become worthy and be all they could be so that God would be glorified. This is all going to end one day. It is go-time right now. It doesn't matter who is persecuting you. It doesn't matter what the obstacle is. Jesus Christ is with you and we are praying for His grace on you to get it done.

Day 189

2 Thess. 2

Scribe to the Heart

"And then the lawless one will be revealed, whom the Lord Jesus will kill with the breath of his mouth and bring to nothing by the appearance of his coming."

(2 Thess. 2:8)

Point to Ponder

Be caught up in your worship. Jesus has won the battle.

Today's Journal

How can I be less caught up in my problems and more caught up in Jesus?

Prayer for the Day

Lord Jesus, Teach me to be caught up in worship with You. Help me to fight the good fight; leaning on You and knowing You already won. Amen.

STEP BACK

LET'S TAKE ANOTHER step back. Imagine yourself as a first century Christian. You have received a letter from Paul, Timothy, and Silas. You are given instructions in it, and it was read in front of the entire church. It, along with the first letter, was most likely revisited several times due to how rare distant parties communicated with each other in those days.

You learn that someone under Satan's direction is going to try to deceive many into believing he is God, and take a seat of authority in the temple. How would this make you feel? What would you do? Throughout history we can point to events that can be comparable to this. It is also theologically possible that Paul is pointing a future event. However, it is not the only option.

The main point of the message to these young, hard-working, devoted believers is that God is much bigger than whatever Satan puts in our way. The *man of lawlessness* in the cited verses is defeated with the righteous breath of Jesus Christ. God only has to blow on His enemies and it is over! He is that powerful. The message is: Stay in the game. Don't give up. Don't quit. Jesus is there for you, and He is beyond anything that will come your way. He will do way more than all you ask or could even think of (Ephesians 3:20).

So, what should you do? Don't get caught up in your trials. Be aware of them, but be caught up in your worship. Jesus has won your battle.

Day 190

2 Thess. 3

Scribe to the Heart

"Finally, brothers, pray for us, that the word of the Lord may speed ahead and be honored, as happened among you."

(2 Thess. 3:1)

Point to Ponder

Leading people to be dependent on Jesus Christ makes them strong.

Today's Journal

What do I need to depend on Jesus for today?

Prayer for the Day

Lord Jesus, By Your grace I am saved and in You I live and move and have my being. Help me with____today.

PRAY FOR US

IF YOU LOOK at the lives of some of the most famous and successful people you will see some commonalities in their stories. They have faced some kind of adversity. They overcame trouble or a setback. For example, Michael Jordan at one point wasn't good enough in high school to start for his high school basketball team. As a young person, Walt Disney was told he lacked creativity. Einstein struggled in school. Doesn't it seem weird? Yet, they succeeded hugely in their fields. And we love their stories.

What sets Christians apart from each other? Some Christians have really grasped understanding of where their success originates. They understand they always have to depend on God, even after they are successful. In the first verse of this chapter, we see that the writers of this letter know from where their help comes. Check out what Paul and the others pray for. They want prayer that God opens doors for them and their message carries forth like it did with the Thessalonians.

They didn't have the attitude that they had it figured out. They had the attitude that God and God alone reached people and we need prayer. We need to stay holy and united. We need to be dependent on Him. Their need for Jesus is what made them strong.

Day 191

1 Timothy 1

Scribe to the Heart

"To Timothy my true son in the faith: Grace, mercy and peace from God the Father and Christ Jesus our Lord."

(1 Tim. 1:2)

Point to Ponder

Paul showed love for Timothy by giving him instructions.

Today's Journal

Is there an aspect of God's instruction that I find hard to obey? Is it because I have a hard time believing He gave me this instruction out of love?

Prayer for the Day

Lord Jesus, I pray that I will receive Your instructions with the pure heart of a child, knowing You instruct me from a place of love.

MY TRUE SON

FIRST TIMOTHY WAS a letter written by the Apostle Paul to Timothy. It is the first letter of three known as the Pastoral Epistles; which includes 1 and 2 Timothy and the book of Titus. These are mentoring letters from the Apostle Paul to young Timothy and to Titus to guide them in the area of church leadership. These letters were also read aloud to the church.

Imagine being Timothy. Timothy hears he has a letter from Paul. He runs to the messenger and rips open the letter. He has so many things he wants to talk to Paul about. Timothy was a young pastor. We can be somewhat certain that he was under 30 years old. I believe it is a safe bet to say he was in his mid-20s or younger.

Paul refers to Timothy right away as "his true son in the faith." It must have been magnificent to hear those words. Timothy was leading a church in the trade city of Ephesus. Later in history this city housed a statue of an emperor that stood to be worshipped and was the cause of much Christian persecution. During the ministry of Paul, this city centered spiritually, economically, and recreationally around the goddess Artemis. If you remember from Acts 19, in many ways Christianity was not welcomed here. When Timothy read: "To my true son in the faith," I am sure it felt good and he focused on every word Paul had to say.

In this letter Paul instructs Timothy on church leadership. He encourages Him to keep going. I am sure it was the exact message Timothy needed for the many problems he was going through. In light of this, Timothy most likely clung to every promise. Timothy wanted to get it right, and he knew his heavenly father and his earthly spiritual father cared for him enough to give him specific instructions on how to do his best.

1 Timothy 2

Scribe to the Heart

"who desires all people to be saved and come to a knowledge of the truth."

(1 Tim. 2:4)

Point to Ponder

Arrive at biblical conclusions through much humility, study, and prayer.

Today's Journal

What is the role of women in the church?

Prayer for the Day

Holy Spirit, Guide me to come to biblical conclusions for the questions I face. Amen.

THE HEART OF GOD

WHEN THIS CHAPTER of the Bible comes up, often a very spirited discussion arises about the role of women in ministry. Some believe women have no place in pastoral or teaching positions. Others conclude that it is biblical that women can lead. Both camps are adamant about their point of view and what the Bible teaches about women in leadership or teaching roles in the church. There has been a divide on this issue for centuries and it will probably continue until the return of Christ. It is important that your theology is one that sets people free. We see Paul's missionary heart in verses 1-7. There is a need for order because God desires all people to be saved.

We should approach the issue of women in ministry with much humility as we search the scriptures. Never forget as you read through these letters to Timothy that you are reading someone else's mail. Ephesus was the center for Artemis. This important port city housed many travelers who could literally get off the boat and walk right to this massive cultic temple that was considered one of the seven wonders of the ancient world. Women priestesses (Amazons) were at the pagan temple and they had a cultic type of authority over men who traveled there. It was religious and possibly very sexual. Women got to be in charge.

The need for women to not have authoritative roles in this church was essential because much discipleship was needed. Remember, these are new converts who are not only dealing with gnosticism inside the church, but many who were saved came out of Artemis worship and all people of this region were influenced by Artemis in some way. It is probable that women were taking charge and not acting orderly. For the counter-cultural message of Christ to prevail, Paul needed to do something. When you search the scriptures to understand the role of women in the church, do the background work. Artemis has everything to do with this passage. God gives us order to build His kingdom in the best method available to the local people. I am not telling you which way to think, just to think clearly and thoroughly. Your conclusion is important.

1 Timothy 3

Scribe to the Heart

"Here is a trustworthy saying: If anyone sets his heart on being an overseer, he desires a noble task."

(1 Tim. 3:1)

Point to Ponder

God's leaders meet His moral qualifications.

Today's Journal

Do I feel I could serve as an elder or a deacon according to God's job description? Why or why not?

Prayer for the Day

Lord Jesus, Grow me into the servant You want me to be.

A GODLY JOB DESCRIPTION

WHEN A COMPANY writes a job description, they begin by identifying the tasks that the person doing the job must be able to perform. How many words can they type a minute? What is their level of education? In this chapter we see job descriptions for overseers (church elders) and deacons. If your church were picking a new pastor, board member, youth leader, etc., what type of qualifications would you look for? If you look online at postings for pastoral positions, you'll see that the job descriptions include things like preaching abilities, leadership development, visitation, strategic planning, carrying out tasks, and implementing programs.

When choosing a leader, it is important to evaluate essential skill sets. However, we see here that leadership in the church is primarily moral in nature. Before being named a deacon (which means servant), a servant should be tested against the qualifications listed here. These are essential for servanthood in the local church. Those selected as overseers (elders) must also hold to the standards listed here.

God's calling is not about skills, talents, or gifts. It is about fruit. I saw an interview with Christian artist Kirk Franklin on the *700 Club*. Although he was a church worship leader, he had an addiction he couldn't break. He didn't feel good about himself. Because of his talent, people either didn't see his addiction or they didn't want to. The gifts of the Spirit were confused with the fruit of the Spirit. A statement he made stuck with me: "The gifted in the church slide right by."

If someone can preach, lead worship, or administrate well, we have a habit of not examining his or her life. We are warned in this scripture to test servants (deacons) before plugging them into ministry. God cares about their personal devotion to Him. God cares about fruitfulness.

True fruitfulness is life-giving. Our connection to Christ produces spiritual fruit. Others can eat and be nourished from the energy and life we give. That fruitfulness is true and only stems from our connection to Jesus Christ.

Day 194

1 Timothy 4

Scribe to the Heart

"Until I come, devote yourself to the public reading of Scripture, to preaching and to teaching."

(1 Tim. 4:13)

Point to Ponder

Bible teaching is only passing along God's Word.

Today's Journal

Does 1 Timothy 4:13 give me comfort in regards to what I feel God calling me to do?

Prayer for the Day

Lord, Build in me the ability to teach and to live with my life centered on Your Holy Word.

COMFORT COMMAND

WE DON'T KNOW much about Timothy's personality, but he may have been tempted to be stressed. He pastored in a city that was not friendly to Christianity. He dealt with many new converts trying to live out their faith in a difficult environment. And let's not forget that Timothy is young and needs to pastor this church strategically and with great confidence and wisdom, as he leads people who may be twice his age. There may have been times when he looked out to sea and desperately wanted Paul to return to alleviate the enormous responsibility he felt while living out his calling to lead the people of this church.

Timothy is told in this chapter not to let people look down on his youth, but to set an example in speech, life, love, faith, and purity. He was also told not to neglect his spiritual gifts. He was to give himself completely to this. Finally, he is warned to watch both his life and his doctrine closely because that is what ensures salvation. No pressure, right? Only heaven and hell hang in the balance.

So, where is Timothy to find comfort? The comfort is in verse 13: *"Until I come, devote yourself to the public reading of Scripture, to preaching and to teaching."* It is important for Timothy to do the other things mentioned in verses 12-16, however this is the comfort command. Read Scripture and teach Scripture. He doesn't need to come up with anything new. He doesn't need to make up an answer to the problems of the people. He is to read Scripture and to teach it. When anyone teaches the Bible, all we are really doing is explaining an idea that God has recorded for us to know. I find comfort in that. Anyone who is feeling called to teach God's Word can also take comfort; it is *God's* Word. You don't have to make up a new word, just explain what His Word says.

Day 195

1 Timothy 5

Scribe to the Heart

"I charge you, in the sight of God and Christ Jesus and the elect angels, to keep those instructions without partiality, and do nothing out of favoritism."

(1 Tim. 5:21)

Point to Ponder

Treat all of God's people with respect.

Today's Journal

How have I shown favoritism to people in my life? How can I better follow God's command to not show favoritism?

Prayer for the Day

Lord Jesus, Help me to treat all people the same. Help me to treat them as You would treat them. Amen.

CAN'T GET NO RESPECT

AS WE ALREADY mentioned, Timothy was a young pastor. He was faced with many challenges pastoring new Christians, who were probably less mature than him spiritually, but many were probably much older than him physically. Timothy most likely was tempted to feel lonely and unappreciated.

Most of us would probably feel this way. God had burdened Timothy to lead God's people in this city. He was trained by the Apostle Paul himself. He was God's man, but from the way Paul encouraged him, we can surmise that the people he led may have seen him as too young to be in authority.

In this chapter, Paul explains to Timothy not to focus on the respect he is *not* getting. He explains in great detail the need to respect the station of life his people are in. Paul talks about several types of people. He tells him how to treat men older than him. He explains how to treat women, and especially widows. The message is: Open your eyes, Timothy. Forget about yourself. This is no time to focus on your insecurities, there is work to do. God's people have needs, and you are there to help them.

Verse 21 sums up how Timothy is to treat people. *"I charge you, in the sight of God and Christ Jesus and the elect angels, to keep those instructions without partiality, and do nothing out of favoritism."* Under the authority of God, His angels do not show favoritism. God's leader is out of the will of God when he or she decides to treat people differently based on how he or she feels about that person. It is a hard calling. Many church leaders take precautions so they can answer this hard calling. One example is when a pastor decides not to know the amount of money people contribute. Treat all of God's people fairly and with respect.

1 Timothy 6

Scribe to the Heart

"But godliness with contentment is great gain."

(1 Tim. 6:6)

Point to Ponder

Be thankful for what you do have.

Today's Journal

How can I better exercise contentment in my life?

Prayer for the Day

Lord Jesus, Empower me this day to live for You. Help me to be content and thankful for all the ways You take care of me.

SNAPSHOT

I HAVE A picture of my immediate family sitting in our living room. In this picture, I have one hand resting on my calm, cuddly dog, Munroe. I am leaning forward smiling happily. My other arm is around my wife, Heidi. She, too, is smiling ear to ear and is holding our daughter, Anna, who was only two months old at the time of the photo. Heidi's other hand is petting our other dog Gracie, who is sweetly looking up at Heidi and Anna. It is a great picture.

I call it a great picture because of who I see in the picture. This is my family. But let's go a little deeper as to what makes it great. I have other pictures of my family members in my home, but in this particular photo we are all together. And not only that, but for that moment in time everything looks just the way I want it to be—perfect.

After the photo was taken, Munroe went back to tracking in mud from outside and demanding attention from everyone who visits the house. Gracie went back to chewing on whatever she could get her jaws on, causing Heidi to more fully appreciate the phrase, "That is why we can't have nice things." Anna needed something, and Heidi and I stumbled through figuring out what she needed while she cried it out. But, for a second, everyone took their places. Everyone was content. Everyone paused as if to say, "Thank you God, what you have done here is good."

2 Timothy 1

Scribe to the Heart

"I am reminded of your sincere faith, a faith that dwelt first in your grandmother Lois and in your mother Eunice and now, I am sure, dwells in you as well. For this reason I remind you to fan into flame the gift of God, which is in you through the laying on of my hands."

(2 Tim. 1:5-6)

Point to Ponder

Look at your life through eyes of faith.

Today's Journal

Is there an area of my Christian walk that needs fresh wind and fresh fire?

Prayer for the Day

Lord Jesus, Give me fresh wind and a new flame to live for You today. Amen.

FAN INTO FLAME

I REMEMBER CAMPING in the woods when I was a young boy. I didn't know much about camping but I knew you needed wood if you wanted a fire to burn. I also knew you needed some paper or some kind of leaves to start the fire. Since we were not serious campers, we also needed matches. What really surprised me though was when the fire began to go out, an adult would get down beside the fire and blow on the hot coals. The fire would reignite. The flames caught on the leaves and the wood beside it and we were able to keep the fire going.

The first time I saw this, I found it strange. I had only ever seen air put *out* a fire before. One of the first things you learn about the small flame of your birthday candles is that wind will put it out. It was a new thing to learn that wind can transfer heat from a spark or hot coals to catch nearby debris on fire. Paul lays the groundwork for Timothy in this second letter by reminding him of the Jewish faith of his mother and grandmother. He is speaking to him as his spiritual father. He instructs: Fan into flame your spiritual gifts. We all believe in you.

Timothy may have been discouraged about his church. The letter seems to have been sent about five years after the first. Timothy may have been in another dry spell. Most likely the biggest form of discouragement for Timothy was that Paul was in prison and could be executed any day. Paul is the one on death row and he is sending Timothy a letter of encouragement. He explains to him in this first chapter that there is no reason not to keep going. You are called, you are gifted, and God loves you.

Paul doesn't really tell him how to fan into flame the gift given to him. Timothy probably already knew how. Timothy needed to change his mind from earthly to heavenly things. He also needed to focus on Jesus, the Author and Perfector of his faith. A fire was ready to be rekindled; the necessary debris was all there. All that was needed was fresh wind.

2 Timothy 2

Scribe to the Heart

"Share in suffering as a good soldier of Christ Jesus. No soldier gets entangled in civilian pursuits—since his aim is to please the one who enlisted him."

(2 Tim. 2:3-4)

Point to Ponder

Focus only on your commanding officer.

Today's Journal

What things am I involved in that distract me from God's mission for my life?

Prayer for the Day

Lord Jesus, Strengthen my ability to remain focused on You. Let me not get distracted on things that do not help me on my mission.

GOD'S SOLDIER

IN CHAPTER 2, Paul continues to give Timothy instruction on how to keep his faith on track. He uses a few examples of types of people who need strong focus to accomplish the task they set out to do. He speaks of an athlete and a farmer, which are both very disciplined types of people. Maybe the most fitting illustration he uses, however, is the soldier. He not only uses a soldier as the example of how we are supposed to be, but he also uses the position of commanding officer for how we are to view God.

We (Christians) are on a mission for Jesus. Timothy was pastoring the church of Ephesus. By the way Paul addresses Timothy it seems that people were gossiping about him and unhappy about something—possibly Timothy's leadership. Paul explains to Timothy that this kind of stuff (gossip, listening to false teaching, ignorant quarrels) steals your flame. It will put your fire out. Timothy must change his perspective. We must do the same. Make up your mind that you are a soldier on a mission. You will not concern yourself with anything outside of your mission. It is civilian matters to worry about the local gossip. You have strict orders from your commanding officer to stay on target. You are a soldier in a war with eternal consequences. Do not let the enemy distract you, because that is when you will go down, soldier.

Your assignment is to focus on the cross. Give Jesus your all. Jesus is your everything and you are to live for Him. You are to represent Him to the world. These are your orders, soldier.

2 Timothy 3

Scribe to the Heart

"But understand this, that in the last days there will come times of difficulty."

(2 Tim. 3:1)

Point to Ponder

Live for Jesus now and you will understand better later.

Today's Journal

What are some of the things going on around me that make it hard to focus on Jesus? What can I do about it?

Prayer for the Day

Lord Jesus, I commit to following You, even when I don't understand why. Amen.

THE LAST DAYS

I AM NOT a fan of any teaching that starts with newspaper clippings first and refers to scripture later. This is what often happens with many of those who preach that "the end is near." If you have something to say and you believe the end is near based on current events, allow God's Word to carry the weight of your argument.

Much needs to be straightened out about how we talk about the last days. In this instance Paul reminded Timothy of the days they were living in. 1.) The Messiah has already come. 2.) He died for your sins and mine. 3.) He defeated death and rose from the grave. 4.) He will come again to end things as we know them.

We live in the time between Jesus' ascension (following His resurrection) and when He will come back to judge the earth. Paul was referring to the "last days" as being current 2,000 years ago. These would be considered last days now, and possibly it could be another 2,000 years of last days. Then again, it might only be another day or two. We are not to know. So why does Paul bring it up here? Well, Paul wanted Timothy to know things are hard and they may get harder. People will look like church leaders or followers of Jesus, but in reality, they are not. There will always be a form of godliness, but it may be powerless because of sin and selfishness. The times you are living in are rough, but God sees you. God loves you. Live for Him and you will understand when you get to the other side.

Day 200

2 Timothy 4

Scribe to the Heart

"Do your best to come before winter. Eubulus sends greetings to you, as do Pudens and Linus and Claudia and all the brothers."

(2 Tim. 4:21)

Point to Ponder

Christians need each other.

Today's Journal

How have I neglected the relationships God has given me? What can I do better?

Prayer for the Day

Lord Jesus, I pray I will be a better steward with the relationships You have given me. Help me in this area.

RACE AGAINST THE CLOCK

IT IS IMPORTANT that we prioritize in our fast-paced lives. Paul's words to Timothy in this letter may have been the last words Timothy received from Paul. Paul knew it when he sent the letter, and Timothy knew it when he received it. At the very end we see what seems like a simple suggestion. *"Do your best to get here before winter."* Out of all that Paul had to say, why is this significant? Well, winter would have made travel hard and Paul probably figured that he would be executed before spring.

The entire way through this letter Paul encourages Timothy to stay in the fight. Continue to do right. Live for Jesus. Fight the good fight of faith. Fan into the flame the gift God has given you. But then, at the end, he asked the very busy, stressed-out young Timothy to take the time to make a trip to come see him in prison. Why does Paul do that? Timothy can't do anything about Paul's situation. Paul is waiting to die. What if Timothy got arrested too? He would be in the same situation. His life would be cut short and people would be left without a pastor. It would place Timothy in a dangerous situation. There are a million reasons why Timothy shouldn't go.

I don't believe either one of them saw it that way. Why? Because they knew they needed each other. They were fighting the good fight of faith together. They both loved Jesus. They both sought to live for Him. Timothy needed Paul, his spiritual father, to help him through the time he was going through, but Timothy also gets to minister to Paul. Paul needed prayers, encouragement, and a listening ear. This may have been the last thing Paul asked of Timothy.

We can't neglect the relationships God has given us. We must nurture them. We need our brothers and sisters in Christ to stay strong, and they need you, too.

Titus 1

Scribe to the Heart

"and at the proper time (God) manifested in his word through the preaching with which I have been entrusted by the command of God our Savior."

(Titus 1:3)

Point to Ponder

Being a Christian leader is a very serious responsibility.

Today's Journal

Am I ready to be a leader? What do I need to trust God with the most?

Prayer for the Day

Lord Jesus, Help me to be a Titus 1 Christian.

ANOTHER SON?

IN THE PREVIOUS two letters, Paul referred to Timothy as his "true son" in the faith. Paul uses this same phrase in this letter for Titus. Paul obviously had a special mentoring type of relationship with Titus. Paul explains who he is and establishes his apostolic authority in the first 3 verses:

"Paul, a servant of God and an apostle of Jesus Christ, for the faith of God's elect and their knowledge of the truth, which accords with godliness, in hope of eternal life, which God, who never lies, promised before the ages began, and at the proper time manifested in his word through the preaching with which I have been entrusted by the command of God our Savior." Titus 1:1-3

Then Paul goes into a similar explanation as to the one he gave Timothy as to what a church leader should look like. Paul left Titus in charge of appointing elders in every town in Crete. The qualifications laid out for Titus in Crete are the same as the qualifications explained for Timothy in Ephesus.

God wants church leaders to be a certain way, no matter where they are located or what period of time in which they live. They need to be able to teach, but aside from that, the rest of the qualifications are moral. They do not have anything to do with talent or ability. Paul built a close relationship with both Titus and Timothy. He referred to them as "sons" in the faith. He pursued them and desired for them to succeed. This topic of what a leader should look like was very important and central to the letters to both Timothy and Titus.

We are to take seriously the leadership roles we are given. We are not to take lightly the responsibility to recruit leaders with a strong walk. The church will suffer if its leaders do not walk strong, no matter how well they can teach, sing, or administrate.

Titus 2

Scribe to the Heart

"Declare these things; exhort and rebuke with all authority. Let no one disregard you."

(Titus 2:15)

Point to Ponder

To lead others you need to talk the talk.

Today's Journal

How can I be both a better student and a better teacher of God's Word?

Prayer for the Day

Lord Jesus, Empower me to know Your Word and to teach others to do the same. Amen.

TALK THE TALK

IN 1 TIMOTHY 3 we saw the need for an elder to be able to teach (1 Timothy 3:2). It is an important part of church leadership. We know there is much more to leadership than the teaching, however, what is taught in a church determines its direction. People in leadership need to walk the walk. But this requirement in Titus 2 means they need to know how to talk the talk as well.

For a church leader to instruct others, and ultimately develop people to be elders or church leaders themselves, they need to have strong theological reasoning. They need to be seasoned in the Scriptures. They need to be able to teach and instruct people in righteous living and give deep theological answers to life's toughest questions. Teaching God's Word is a high calling. James tells us that those who teach will be judged more strictly (James 3:1).

Paul wanted Titus to develop elders in every town. He wanted this movement to explode among the Cretans (where Titus was). To do that Titus needed to walk the walk, but he also needed to talk the talk. Those who do both can develop others to do the same. When this happens, there is no telling where a movement might go.

Titus 3

"Remind them to be submissive to rulers and authorities, to be obedient, to be ready for every good work, to speak evil of no one, to avoid quarreling, to be gentle, and to show perfect courtesy to all people."

(Titus 3:1-2)

Point to Ponder

We are called to submit to our leaders.

Today's Journal

How can I better trust that God will work through the people He has put in place to lead me?

Prayer for the Day

Lord Jesus, Give me a heart that trusts You to work through all people.

WHEN THE CHURCH IS WORKING RIGHT

THE FIRST TWO chapters of Titus dealt heavily with leadership and teaching. Paul found it important to explain to Titus the characteristics of teachers and leaders. In the last part of this letter, Paul devotes time to making sure people are submitting to the authorities they are under. We are not called to submit when it causes us to sin, however, we are called to submit if the disagreement is not a sin issue, but is just an opinion.

Having been in a spiritual leadership position and also being in the position where spiritual leaders are placed over me, I have learned that God works through imperfect people (Myself included). Sometimes I may have a better idea than the one being carried out, however if God has not given me the position to carry it out, it will not be blessed. There have also been times when I handled a situation wrongly, but God blessed it anyway. I am sure in those instances someone else was thinking they had a better idea than mine.

Leadership is tricky. God cares about our hearts. In regards to authority I always say, "Leadership is God-ordained but people- permissioned." God puts people in leadership positions, but for them to lead well they do need to win over the people whom they lead. They must exhibit characteristics such as those Paul explained to Titus in chapter 1. If God is calling you to a higher position of leadership, and you find yourself not wanting to follow the leadership you are under, you may find yourself stalled. God needs to show us how to be under authority before we are ready for more authority. God takes His time and works through imperfect people who make imperfect decisions. Ultimately when the church is working right God is carrying us. It is a great miracle that anything gets done at all.

Philemon

Scribe to the Heart

"and I pray that the sharing of your faith may become effective for the full knowledge of every good thing that is in us for the sake of Christ."

(Philem. 6)

Point to Ponder

God wants us to treat each other like brothers and sisters.

Today's Journal

How can I treat people more equally today?

Prayer for the Day

Lord Jesus, Give me spiritual eyes to see people in the way that You do.

USELESS HAS BECOME USEFUL

THIS IS A tiny little letter. It is only one chapter that is divided into 25 verses. It deals with a runaway slave named Onesimus. Onesimus belonged to Philemon. Paul most likely got to know both of them at the same time when he was in Colossae. Onesimus fled from Philemon and met up with Paul. In those days, slaves were treated better than how we might think. For some, selling themselves into slavery was the best option for financial stability. However, if a slave ran away, by law a slave could be killed or branded with a letter on his or her face so that everyone knew they were a criminal.

It seems that Paul played a part in the conversion of both Onesimus and Philemon. Onesimus' name means "useful." Paul makes a play on words when he says, *"Formerly he was useless to you, but now he has become useful both to you and to me"* (Philem. 11). He is saying that Onesimus was the opposite of his name, but now he was his name to both of them.

Paul convinced Onesimus to go back. He told him that he still belonged to his master by Roman law and needed to respect that. As for Philemon, Paul told him if anything is owed to him, Paul would pay for it. He also declares that Philemon owes Paul his very self. This probably means that Paul led him to faith.

Both men have a choice to do right. Philemon is called to treat his slave like a brother and not like a slave. This didn't mean that Onesimus wasn't going to still be his slave and work for him, but Paul reminds Philemon of his conversion and how much he owed Paul. Philemon must forgive, take him back, and treat him well. Paul leaves it up to him. He pushed but didn't force. He trusted God to work through the two people having the disagreement. Paul wanted two Christian men to treat each other as brothers and not just slave and master. This was a major cultural step. We have a choice to forgive people who wrong us and to treat people as brothers and sisters in Christ, regardless of who they are.

Hebrews 1

"Are they not all ministering spirits sent out to serve for the sake of those who are to inherit salvation?"

(Heb. 1:14)

Angels are sent to serve those who will inherit salvation.

Today's Journal

How valuable am I to God?

Prayer for the Day

Father, Show me how valuable I am to You. Thank You for thinking I am valuable.

ONLY MINISTERING SPIRITS

THE BOOK OF Hebrews is unique to the New Testament for many reasons. Hebrews is the first known New Testament sermon manuscript. We are not sure who authored this writing. I think we can safely say it wasn't Paul due to the writing style and because Paul always identified himself in his writings. The message of Hebrews is simple to understand. Jewish Christians were tempted to conform their Christian practices to their old ways. This way they could continue to worship Christ, but look like Jews who didn't. In other words, they tried to stay "safe" by keeping Jesus in the back unseen, and the Jewish traditions upfront and central.

It seems like a very practical idea. They could continue to worship without having the danger of persecution. After all, God doesn't want them to experience any hurt. He wants them to follow Him and live happily ever after. The message is prosperity, right? Wrong. God wants us to follow Him, but He tells us there is a cost. In this first chapter the author begins the discussion talking about Jesus and His superior nature. The author also talks about angels in these opening verses. Angels were very important to the ancient Jew. God showed up several times in the Old Testament in the form of an angel. Many traditions spoke of angel involvement as Moses received the commandments from God. Some people were even tempted to worship angels when they encountered one because they were so glorious (Revelation 22:8-9). Angels often declared, "Do not be afraid. Take courage!" They had a magnificent presence.

Yet the writer of Hebrews wants to declare who the Christian is in relation to Christ and the angels. Note the very last verse of the chapter. *"Are they not all ministering spirits sent out to serve for the sake of those who are to inherit salvation?"*

These magnificent creatures are sent to serve us, not because of anything we did, but because of the glorious price our Savior paid. In a sense, we outrank the angels. They are in the battle for us and sent to serve us. What does that say about how valuable we are to God?

Hebrews 2

Scribe to the Heart

"For because he himself has suffered when tempted, he is able to help those who are being tempted."

(Heb. 2:18)

Point to Ponder

Jesus has been there.

Today's Journal

What am I dealing with? How can Jesus relate to what I am going through?

Prayer for the Day

Lord Jesus, Walk with me through my pain. Thank You for understanding.

3 A.M.

I WAS SOUND asleep after a late, high-pressure night during a time when I was a candidate for a new church position, and the phone rang. We could hear that someone was leaving a message, so Heidi ran to the phone. A moment later, she screamed! I became fully awake. There was an accident and her brother B.J. was gone. He was a perfectly healthy 19 year-old who had his entire life ahead of him. Why did it happen?

As the family got together and the funeral plans began to unfold, I realized something; I had no answers. My seminary and on the job training, thus far had equipped me with theological reasons and explanations for why things happen the way they do. I still believe those reasons, however, none of them were adequate in explaining the situation. None of them brought true comfort. *I am the pastor in this family, why don't I have the answers everybody wants? Why don't I have the words?* Not only was I dealing with my own grief, and feeling pressure to help with the grief of everyone else, but I was having my own crisis of faith. To say the least, the pain I felt was devastating. *How could this happen?* My head and my heart couldn't reconcile their differences.

As time passes, B.J. is still sorely missed. We would do anything to have him back. He was carefree, sarcastic, funny, and a great person to be around. There is a hole in our family and our hearts. Why this happened the way it did, we are not sure. But, God used all of our pain. Now, when I talk to someone who has lost someone, I am slow to give answers. In fact, I don't give answers unless that is what they ask for. I don't get mad when they are mad at God. I let them swear at me if they need to, and I let them tell God they don't believe in Him. Why? Because I have been there.

The death and resurrection of Jesus is important. We can't be saved without it. However, something else is usually forgotten. Jesus has been where we are. We learn that through this chapter. He went through the entire human experience. He was tempted in every way and was given the same options of disobedience. Yet, He always chose the high road. Jesus understands you because He has been in your shoes. Give Him a chance.

Hebrews 3

Scribe to the Heart

"For Jesus has been counted worthy of more glory than Moses — as much more glory as the builder of a house has more honor than the house itself."

(Heb. 3:3)

Point to Ponder

God is our builder.

Today's Journal

Am I allowing God to build me how He wants to?

Prayer for the Day

Lord Jesus, Mold me, make me, shape me.

GOD THE BUILDER

MY THREE-YEAR-OLD NIECE knows the chant: "Bob the Builder, Can he fix it? Yes, he can!" She raises her hands into the air in victory. The chant doesn't work if said the other way around, "Can it fix Bob?" Why is it not that way? We know the answer to that question. The concept is ridiculous that a non-living object can do anything on its own for a living person. Buildings need their builders. Builders are greater than the buildings themselves.

Anyone who is not doing what's right seems to have an excuse as to why they choose to act the way they do. "I was born this way. I have just always done it this way. I don't believe I am doing anything wrong. It feels good." The list goes on. A popular excuse for these Jewish believers could have been, "We are following the traditions of Moses. We follow them because he is our great prophet. God interacted with him in a special way. God used him to take care of us in a special way. It is important that we listen to this great authority." It all sounds good. The hard truth is the Jewish believers were returning to their traditions to stay safe from persecution, not out of loyalty to Moses.

The speaker addresses this situation by letting the people know who was the builder, and who was the building. Moses couldn't save himself. He couldn't do the things he did on his own power. He didn't create the direction in which he was to lead. He was a follower. He was a work in progress like everyone else.

However, Jesus was different; Jesus was a man, who was tempted in every way, yet remained perfect. Jesus was the builder. Now the speaker has established why we need to listen to Jesus over Moses. He is the God the Builder. "Can He fix us? Yes, He can!"

Day 208

Hebrews 4

Scribe to the Heart

"For good news came to us just as to them, but the message they heard did not benefit them, because they were not united by faith with those who listened."

(Heb. 4:2)

Point to Ponder

Fear and faith are evil twins.

Today's Journal

What am I holding back from God? What do I need to give Him by faith?

Prayer for the Day

Lord Jesus, Teach me to live by faith, not by fear. Reveal the fears in my life and strengthen me as I rely on You to destroy them.

FEAR: FAITH'S EVIL TWIN

WHAT DRIVES HOW you relate to God? Is it fear or faith? Take a look at how our chapter begins today: *"Therefore, while the promise of entering his rest still stands, let us fear lest any of you should seem to have failed to reach it. For good news came to us just as to them, but the message they heard did not benefit them, because they were not united by faith with those who listened"* (Hebrews 4:1-2).

On the outside, fear and faith can look the same; almost like twins. It's only when you get up close you can see the beautiful face of faith, or the tiny, dirty blackheads on the face of fear. By both faith and fear, people do very similar things. Many people go to church and read their Bibles for no reason but because they are afraid of God. Faith, however, tells us there is something more to this life. Faith tells us we will be blessed by reading the Bible. We will experience emotional freedom and connect with God more intimately by going to a worship service.

These Jewish believers were returning to the worship of the past because of fear. Long ago, Moses and the people of Israel worshipped through sacrifices that pointed to a Messiah in the future. They worshipped by faith. Now, the Messiah has come, and by fear people are reverting to the old ways instead of worshipping the Messiah. Faith calls you to a new standard. It is risky. Fear keeps you in the past. It keeps you weighed down and frozen in place.

Today, as you read this message, combine it with faith. It is not about how much Bible you know, but rather how you apply faith to the Word of God. What are you holding back from God? What do you need to give Him by faith?

Hebrews 5

"Although he was a son, he learned obedience through what he suffered."

(Heb. 5:8)

Point to Ponder

Pain teaches obedience.

Today's Journal

Where is my pain? What does God want me to learn through my pain?

Prayer for the Day

Lord Jesus, Thank You that You walk with me in my pain. Use it to help me follow You better.

NO PAIN, NO GAIN

THIS SECTION OF the sermon is very weighty. Through verses 12-14 we see some verses often quoted by pastors to motivate us to spiritual maturity. We also see the priestly order of Melchizedek come up. We will revisit this again within the next couple of days.

Today, we are to ponder something else. *"In the days of his flesh, Jesus offered up prayers and supplications, with loud cries and tears, to him who was able to save him from death, and he was heard because of his reverence. Although he was a son, he learned obedience through what he suffered"* (Hebrews 5:7-8).

An important theme of Hebrews is that Jesus understands us. He has been here. When Jesus came to earth, He remained God, but in taking on human form, He emptied Himself. To become the sinless human, He needed to live like us. He had to learn how to walk and talk. Consider this: He even had to learn how to obey. His pain taught Him obedience. This doesn't mean He was ever disobedient, but His pain prepared Him for the cross, which ultimately prepared Him for glory.

In the life of a submitted follower of Christ, pain causes obedience. Sadly, often when Christians go through pain, we don't see obedience. Why doesn't a Christian always obey God in his or her pain? The answer is this; there was already an unsubmitted area of that person's life and the pain brought it to light.

When our pain causes us to sin, it is time to take a good hard look at ourselves. It is time to seek God, ask for answers, pray, and have Him deal with us. It is a growth moment. When you are strong in the Lord, pain will make you stronger. It will make you search your heart for the strength to follow His will. Like an Olympic athlete, when you feel the burn you will dig deeper and harder. You know that when you push through your pain there is a reward on the other side. You know the truth: No pain, No gain.

Hebrews 6

"So that you may not be sluggish, but imitators of those who through faith and patience inherit the promises."

(Heb. 6:12)

Your level of commitment never stays the same.

Today's Journal

Am I a better Christian than I was two weeks ago? Two months ago? Two years ago? Why or why not?

Prayer for the Day

Lord Jesus, Draw me into a deeper relationship with You every day of my life.

ARE YOU BETTER THAN YOU WERE YESTERDAY?

ONE DAY IN eighth grade, I sat on the mat dressed and ready for practice. We stretched out, but were waiting for a special guest. Coach Kevin, the head coach of the high school wrestling team, made his way across town to visit us, the junior high wrestling team. The high school team was doing very well. There was a lot of excitement in our town and no lack of talent on its way through the system.

I sat on the mat, listening to Coach Kevin tell us how we were progressing like we were supposed to. High school wrestling was a little more physical, but it was nothing we wouldn't be able to handle. This wasn't his main point, however. Coach Kevin was a good teacher, and he knew with jr. high students he needed to keep it simple. He did. His lesson stayed with me. He explained that two weeks ago we were not the same as we were that day. Either we had gotten better or we had gotten worse. Either we were cutting corners and becoming weaker or we were pushing harder and getting tougher. Either our single leg takedown was better or it had gotten slower and sloppier. You can't be the same as you were two weeks ago. You are always changing.

Hebrews 6:1-6 causes much controversy. Most of the time this passage is brought up regarding an individual's salvation. Can you lose it or not? But that is not what this passage is about. I can't settle it for you with a one-page entry, but I want to suggest to you that this was a sermon to group of believers. The point was: Do not shrink back. They must press forward in community. They must represent Christ well to the persecuting world around them. They must stand strong or their witness would be ruined. Even if they are asked to die, they must not hide their faith. Look at what comes next in verse 9: *"Though we speak in this way, yet in your case, beloved, we feel sure of better things— things that belong to salvation."* The preacher explains the expectation. A little further down we see a command to be disciplined: *"So that you may not be sluggish, but imitators of those who through faith and patience inherit the promises."* Today I ask you: Are you a better Christian than you were two weeks ago?

Hebrews 7

Scribe to the Heart

"The former priests were many in number, because they were prevented by death from continuing in office, but he holds his priesthood permanently, because he continues forever."

(Heb. 7:23-24)

Point to Ponder

Jesus is our great High Priest forever.

Today's Journal

What does it mean to me to have Jesus as my great High Priest?

Prayer for the Day

Lord Jesus, I trust You as my great High Priest, who took care of my sins forever. Thank You.

ONCE A PRIEST, ALWAYS A PRIEST

IN THE OLD Testament, the Levites (one of the twelve tribes of Israel) were the ones set aside by God appointed to the priestly offices. Aaron was the first High Priest. Once a year the High Priest would perform special sacrifices on behalf of all the people. First, there was sacrifice for the sins of the priest so that he may enter the Holy of Holies area. Once there, he would then perform the sacrifice for the sins of the nation. This was a foreshadowing of what was to come. The priest himself couldn't take away the sins of the people. He couldn't even take away his own sin. But it became very apparent that sin was costly and could only be atoned through a perfect blood sacrifice.

The author wants his/her audience to know that Jesus is the great High Priest. In fact, He is their priest forever. One of the excuses the Christian Jews were making for slipping back into their comfortable Old Testament practices was that Jesus did not come from the tribe of Levi. Our speaker then takes them back to Melchizedek, who is found in Genesis 14, in the story of Abraham. Melchizedek was a priest and his name meant "king of righteousness" (Hebrews 7:2). He was also the king of Salem, which meant "king of peace" (Hebrews 7:2). We don't know about his father or mother, his genealogy, or the beginning or ending of his days (Hebrews 7:3).

The author also reminds the reader that many hundreds of years later the psalmist wrote about the coming Messiah: "*You are a priest forever, after the order of Melchizedek*" (Psalm 110:4, Hebrews 7:17). The speaker builds the case further by explaining Jesus is of the order of Melchizedek. He lives forever. He only has to offer one sacrifice. He is perfect and blameless. He took care of our sins once and for all. He is our priest forever. He is both King and Priest, like Melchizedek. The speaker declares to the Jewish listeners: It is not your sacrifices God is after. It is the perfect sacrifice God is after, and that sacrifice was made once and for all. You no longer have to chase after God for His approval. He approves of you—just follow Him.

Hebrews 8

Scribe to the Heart

"They serve a copy and shadow of the heavenly things. For when Moses was about to erect the tent, he was instructed by God saying, 'See that you make everything according to the pattern shown you on the mountain.'"

(Heb. 8:5)

Point to Ponder

Religious exercises are a symbol of a heavenly reality.

Today's Journal

A heavenly reality that I celebrate using earthly symbols is...

Prayer for the Day

Lord Jesus, Use a religious symbol to teach me more about You today.

A SHADOW OF THINGS TO COME

IN THE DAYS of Moses, Ancient Israel was given very specific commands as to how they were to construct the tabernacle. There were specific instructions for the priest. There were specific instructions for how to do the animal sacrifices. God gave very specific directions for everything and if these directions were not followed the penalty could be death. One of these directions was for the High Priest. A cord was tied around his ankle before he entered the Holy of Holies so the people could pull him back out if he died in the presence of the Lord, due to not properly purifying himself before entering (Exodus 28:33-35). On one occasion Aaron's sons died because they made offerings that were not commanded, and tried to make worship into a showy affair (Leviticus 10:1-3). Imagine, the High Priest of Israel, Moses' own brother, lost two sons (who were priests) on the same day due to not following the commands of the Lord.

It is not hard to see how the Jews could slip back into some of their religious practices. Following the rules gives us comfort. They probably thought, "Our ancestors have always done this. It is important to keep doing these things. We want God to be happy with us, don't we?"

The reason this was so serious is that God wanted things to resemble a heavenly reality. Much of our modern day Christian practices are also done to resemble a heavenly reality. We take communion together to celebrate a heavenly reality. That heavenly reality is that Jesus took care of our sins, and as a community we can celebrate and fellowship with Him there. Jesus paid the ultimate price. The sacrificial system was merely a shadow of things to come.

Day 213

Hebrews 9

Scribe to the Heart

"So Christ, having been offered once to bear the sins of many, will appear a second time, not to deal with sin but to save those who are eagerly waiting for him."

(Heb. 9:28)

Point to Ponder

You have been entrusted with a holy inheritance.

Today's Journal

Am I a spoiled brat? Or am I the one in the family using my inheritance to make the world a better place?

Prayer for the Day

Lord Jesus, I pray that I will always use my inheritance well. I want my story to reflect Your story in this world. Amen.

HOLY TRUST FUND

"AND JUST AS *it is appointed for man to die once, and after that comes judgment, so Christ, having been offered once to bear the sins of many, will appear a second time, not to deal with sin but to save those who are eagerly waiting for him*" (Hebrews 9:27-28).

There are two common types of story outcomes related to receiving an inheritance that I want you to consider today.

The first one is the story of a couple who worked their entire lives. They worked hard, but could never get ahead. One day, out the blue, they find out they are related to royalty; they are long lost heirs to a fortune left to them by a family member who has departed. The family inherits the money, but they continue to work hard. The difference is now they do it out of love. They love God, they love people, and use their inheritance to make the world a better place. They live happily ever after.

There is also another story; one of a child who is a spoiled brat. He never learns any discipline. He never applies himself to anything useful. The child's parents work hard their entire lives and are well known and accomplished in their respective fields. In the end they die, and he is the only heir. The child has now reached adulthood and inherits all of their money. He spends the rest of a meaningless earthly existence living in excess. He is unhappy, lonely, and unfulfilled. He did not live happily ever after. Life to him never became about anything other than himself.

What is interesting about these two very different stories is that both of them are potentially your story. Jesus took away your sins. He paid your sin debt in full. As a Christian you have access to Him through the Spirit, prayer, His word, and the fellowship of other believers. What an amazing finding it was, the day you first realized Christ has taken care of you and you belong to Him for all of eternity. On that day, you became royalty. You inherited more than you could ever have imagined. Let me ask the defining question: From the moment of your salvation on, which type of story are you writing? Are you the spoiled brat, wasting your inheritance? Or, are you the family member who is using your inheritance to make this world a better place?

Hebrews 10

"But we are not of those who shrink back and are destroyed, but of those who have faith and preserve their souls."

(Heb. 10:39)

Through the blood of Jesus we can now draw close.

Today's Journal

How can I draw closer to God?

Prayer for the Day

Lord Jesus, Let me draw closer to You today. Thank You for shedding Your blood for me.

DRAW CLOSE

AT THE COMMAND of God, Moses went forward to the mountain. When he spent time in the presence of God his face began to glow. He had to veil his face before the Jews because it frightened them. They couldn't approach the mountain because they feared death, and rightfully so. Moses acted as an intermediary for the people in the Old Testament. He had a very special relationship with God. He brought the commandments from God to the people. He spent days talking with God face to face, as a friend would.

Up to this point in Hebrews we have been talking about how Jesus is both Perfect Priest and Perfect Sacrifice. Now, what is our response? We should feel a great deal of assurance. We are to live by faith and not shrink back. Before Jesus came there was a sense that most couldn't draw close to God. The New Testament Christian can draw close. We don't have to run away with fear.

In my home, we now have two dogs. We adopted a second dog that was about one year old at the time we got her. She was very timid. She didn't take to us right away. When we first got her, she slipped from her collar and ran away. We chased her, watching our new dog of 20 lbs. cross six lanes of traffic and run onto a service road to the local highway. She found a patch of woods and lived there for a day. She was spotted several times running around, until someone finally caught her. When she was returned to us, we named her Gracie. It was only by God's grace and the prayers of many that she was returned and we still have her today.

Gracie had bad owners before us. She didn't trust anyone. She trusted herself and her own ability to survive over those who could take care of her. Now that she has experienced us spoiling her, she is not going anywhere. She sometimes rolls around on the floor for no reason, other than to express her own contentment. When the door opens, she is less likely to run away than our other dog. She found that it is safe to draw close, and the experience of drawing close tells her she would never want to go back and try to make it on her own. Like Gracie, by grace you have been saved. Your Master now calls you to draw close.

Hebrews 11

Scribe to the Heart

"Now faith is the assurance of things hoped for, the conviction of things not seen."

(Heb. 11:1)

Point to Ponder

Your faith is tested through your pain.

Today's Journal

When my faith is tested, does it prove real?

Prayer for the Day

Lord Jesus, Teach me more about my faith today. I want to have a deep faith that is rooted in You alone.

IS MY FAITH REAL?

HEBREWS CHAPTER 11 is known as "The Faith Chapter." As the preacher continues on, building towards the end of the sermon, we now see faith being defined. Real faith can be touched, tasted, and felt. It is acted upon. We learn in this chapter that faith is how we please God. We read a list of names in this chapter of people who went through trial after trial by faith. They did strange things like hide babies (v. 23) or leave their home on God's command without knowing where they were going (v. 8).

Experience has taught me that you can only truly be confident in someone else's faith if you have observed it being tested. On day 206 of our study I spoke of the death of my younger brother-in-law, B.J. My wife was a committed Christian, dedicated to the campus ministry we were doing. We were candidates at the time for the next ministry we would tackle together.

Before B.J.'s death, I had seen my wife's faith in action. She was strong and she discipled many girls in the way they should go.

When her brother died, she went through the entire grieving process. She was angry. She was sad. She was worn out. She cried on her way to work and tried to pray, but some days could only say, "Help." I stood by and worried about her. Her faith was tested.

Now she is one of the strongest Christian people you will ever meet. She trusts for me when I doubt. She encourages me when I am down. She repeats words I have said to others when I need to hear them. Her faith has been strengthened three times over. We would do anything to have B.J. back. We would have rather seen this happen a different way, but it didn't. God used what was there to test Heidi. She passed because she leaned on Him. She learned that her faith was real. God met her in her pain.

Day 216

Hebrews 12

Scribe to the Heart

"Looking to Jesus, the founder and perfecter of our faith, who for the joy that was set before him endured the cross, despising the shame, and is seated at the right hand of the throne of God."

(Heb. 12:2)

Point to Ponder

Vision of a heavenly reality keeps us faithful in our earthly circumstances.

Today's Journal

Can I endure the cross of life's circumstances knowing that with Jesus, sooner or later we win?

Prayer for the Day

Lord Jesus, I pray that I will remain faithful by having heavenly vision during my earthly circumstances, both today and every day.

HEAVENLY VISION DURING EARTHLY REALITY

IT WAS A special moment. I was about to be baptized by fire. We don't like these moments, but God does. God uses difficult moments to change us, remake us, and ultimately restore us to what we were meant to be. I was called into the office. I sat down. I was told to sign a document, which had words on it that were not true. Insulted, I was told I was unqualified for what I do. That was also not true, my qualifications were solid for the job I had. All three of us in the room knew why I was there. I was then told it was my last day at that job.

That day was the beginning of the rest of my life. It changed my family's future. It shaped my destiny. That moment helped to inspire me to become an entrepreneur. It also helped me to finish this book. There were instances in the months that followed in which I made mistakes. I brought some pain and failures onto myself. It was trying on me and my family. But I look back and I am thankful. God put me through the fire to test me. It all started because of a decision that was about doing the right thing, and not playing a game Jesus didn't want me to play.

This is what Hebrews is about. This sermon manuscript was written to a group of people who were struggling to be faithful to God during an intense time of persecution. What keeps a believer faithful? The same thing that keeps Jesus faithful, it is the vision of a heavenly reality during our earthly circumstances. Sooner or later Jesus makes it all right and we win.

Day 217

Hebrews 13

Scribe to the Heart

"Jesus Christ is the same yesterday and today and forever."

(Heb. 13:8)

Point to Ponder

Jesus is the same every day.

Today's Journal

The fact that Jesus never changes gives me comfort because...

Prayer for the Day

Lord Jesus, Thank You that You never change. Show me more about what that means.

JESUS IS THE SAME EVERYDAY

AS THE SERMON we know as Hebrews comes to a close, we can reflect on what was said to this audience and apply it to our own lives. The Jewish believers are urged not to slip back into their Old Testament ways. Those ways were once the way of faith, but now are a way of fear. The covenant has been completed so there is no longer any sacrifice for sins. There is no reason to go back. Now we must stand for the Messiah who has come. We know that Messiah is Jesus of Nazareth.

It seems the Jews needed to know that Jesus Christ was always the plan and He never changes. That is why our writer says, *"Jesus Christ is the same yesterday and today and forever"* (Hebrews 13:8).

People are always changing. Sometimes we change for the good and sometimes we change for the bad. Only hours ago, I was in the car. I like to flip from station to station while I am in the car. Sometimes I stop on a song because I like it, and after a minute I change it again and think maybe I don't like that song anymore. Jesus is always the same. Something else I noticed as I was flipping through the stations: On one station a popular female artist was singing about the love of her life. She was singing about how she would have never guessed that it would be over in only three years. She speaks of holding him in her heart. One day they will meet again. On another station that same artist was singing about the love of her life, and here she was saying, "So long—I don't need you." It was angry. It was bitter. Possibly she is singing of the same person.

All people go up and down. Even people we respect. A person's moods can be extreme. They will be very happy, then they will be very sad. They go up and they go down. Sometimes when people are emotional, they will break promises or act in ways they wouldn't have acted only an hour before. You never have to worry about that with your King. Jesus Christ is the same yesterday, today, and forever.

James 1

"But be doers of the word, and not hearers only, deceiving yourselves."

(Jas. 1:22)

Point to Ponder

Focusing on common sense Christianity will help you live a godly life.

Today's Journal

In what areas of my daily life am I tempted? How can I prepare myself and be a doer of the Word?

Prayer for the Day

Lord Jesus, Teach me a simple action to help me be a better disciple today.

MIRROR

THE BOOK OF James was written by the half-brother of Jesus, early first century church leader, James. We see James in the book of Acts as an active leader of the church. However, during Jesus' earthly life, James didn't follow Him. This man grew up with Jesus. He ate dinner with Him. No doubt he tried to tempt Jesus by fighting with Him. Because Jesus truly was the Christ, James eventually came around.

James fascinates me because this book is considered wisdom literature. He takes on the role of a sage or an expert to communicate deep truths. Many of these deep truths are neglected in Christian teaching. Even though they are deep, they are also commonsense Christianity.

There are several little pieces of wisdom in the first chapter.

I would like you to focus on these verses:

"But be doers of the word, and not hearers only, deceiving yourselves. For if anyone is a hearer of the word and not a doer, he is like a man who looks intently at his natural face in a mirror. For he looks at himself and goes away and at once forgets what he was like. But the one looks into the perfect law, the law of liberty, and perseveres, being no hearer who forgets but a doer who acts, he will be blessed in his doing" (James 1:22-25).

I want you to focus on the mirror. Someone who hears God's Word and goes away not following what was heard is like someone who looks into the mirror and immediately forgets what he looks like. What we are looking at here is the law that gives liberty.

After you read your Bible it is not OK to gossip about someone. Someone who regularly spends time with God in prayer shouldn't look like the devil. The battle continues. We need God to truly change how we think and act. Our desires that lead us away tempt us to sin, but when sin grows up it brings death. James reminds us that the Christian life is hard, and we need to focus on the areas in which we are tempted. Spend time thinking about what tempts you. Preparation and time in God's Word will ready you for the moment of temptation. It's deep and it's common sense, all at the same time.

Day 219

James 2

Scribe to the Heart

"If you really fulfill the royal law according to the Scripture, 'You shall love your neighbor as yourself,' you are doing well. But if you show partiality, you are committing sin and are convicted by the law as transgressors."

(Jas. 2:8-9)

Point to Ponder

*Faith and works are married partners. We **do** because of our **who**.*

Today's Journal

How is not showing favoritism an act of faith?

Prayer for the Day

Holy Spirit, Help me to see people like You do. Amen.

FAITH AND WORKS

THE FAITH VS. works conversation goes all the way back to this letter written by James. "Faith without works is dead!" the Wesleyans and Arminians chant. The most neglected part of this chapter is the topic of favoritism. The focus of this chapter when quoted deals with the relationship between what we do and who we are, however there is also something very practical and useful.

Imagine James actually had to tell these early Christians not to treat people differently according to their social standing. I am so glad that we live in a day that the church has gotten past this. Obviously, that's a sarcastic comment; we prioritize and size up people all the time. It is a temptation that is always there, especially for pastors and church board members who count the money. When a person comes in who has more than most, it is very tempting to give them special attention. James would say give them special attention, but give everyone that same special attention.

Don't tell someone you will pray for them when you can meet their need yourself. If someone walks into your church naked would you say, "We will pray for you?" Absolutely not. But sometimes we hold on to what we have when we are the answer to the problem. Our works do not save us. The Bible is clear on that point. However, Jesus Christ working through us always shows up in our works. Do not do things to be noticed or seen. Do things out of holy reverence and security because He does notice and see you.

James 3

Scribe to the Heart

"Not many of you should become teachers, my brothers, for you know that we who teach will be judged with greater strictness."

(Jas. 3:1)

Point to Ponder

Those who lead and teach are especially accountable.

Today's Journal

What do I think it means that those who teach will be judged more strictly?

Prayer for the Day

Holy Spirit, Guide the words I say, particularly when I am seeking to instruct someone. Make me accountable and help me to be stable and responsible with what I say.

NOT MANY? REALLY?

THE CHRISTIAN EDUCATION Team must find James' statement in verse 1 very frustrating. It's a problem for those who need to fill classrooms with Sunday School teachers to read that James, the half-brother of Jesus Christ, is telling people that "not many" should teach because it is a high calling. Teachers will be judged with much greater strictness. How do those responsible for finding teachers reconcile this, when the normal method of operations is to have to work hard to find bodies to instruct classes in church?

James is saying if you are not ready, don't do it. Once you take on this role you put yourself out there. Your life will be looked at more closely. Think about it. If you see someone from a church acting worldly, you think about their involvement in that church. If they just go to church and really don't act out their faith, it is not the same thing as if it is someone in leadership.

Pastors will be evaluated the hardest. Pastors have been thrown out of churches for all kinds of reasons. Sometimes it is because they truly sinned in deep ways and justifiably something needed to happen. Other times it could be something very, very small. Anyone in leadership, but especially anyone who has teaching responsibilities, has a big responsibility in the kingdom. It is important to note when Paul gives Timothy the qualifications of church leaders, being able to teach is very important (1 Timothy 3:2). In other words, teaching and the fact that you will be judged more severely are all tied to leadership. So, a person can't be a board member, treasurer, worship leader, etc. and think they are exempt from this verse. This means all leaders should be able to teach at least a little as well. This doesn't mean you must be a theological expert or you must be particularly gifted at it, but if you have leadership responsibility, having the ability to present truths from God's Word is part of the package.

James 4

Scribe to the Heart

"What causes quarrels and what causes fights among you? Is it not this, that your passions are at war within you?"

(Jas. 4:1)

Point to Ponder

We are educated far beyond our level of obedience.

Today's Journal

Do I ever make judgments or get angry because of what is going on in my heart? What should I do about it?

Prayer for the Day

Holy Spirit, I pray that You will help me get rid of any jealousy that exists in my life.

THE HARD TRUTH ABOUT THE PRACTICAL

I FIND IT strange that a person can go to church his or her entire life, be deeply indoctrinated with solid biblical teaching, and still live like the devil. Others notice it plainly and quite frankly it is a strike against that person's witness. On the other hand, another person might hear one simple biblical truth and, by faith, apply it genuinely to his or her life. The first type of Christian is sitting in a renowned church beside PhDs and Doctorates and can hold their own in the Sunday school conversation. The second Christian is mentored by someone who also has a pure heart to follow God. They go to church with others who are hungry to live for Jesus and know Him.

Of the two, who is going to know Jesus more intimately? The person who heard simple truth, and applied it with faith? Or the deep thinker who applies none of what he/she knows?

We should strive to be a different kind of Christian. I want to know God deeply. I want deep theological teaching, and I want to apply that teaching to my life. I want to know how to discern when something coming from the pulpit is junk or not. But the trials and temptations in my life have taught me I need God. Understand what I am saying, simply and plainly, I need Jesus. I need Him in my life as much as anyone!

One day when my daughter was a toddler, she came running towards me screaming at the top of her lungs because she wanted me to read her a book. The book was about Jesus. She continued screaming, "Daddy I need Jesus! I need Jesus!" She obviously had no idea how true of a statement that was.

It is hard for us to hear what James writes in verse 1. We fight with each other because of the stuff going on inside of us. We can blame the devil. We can blame others or our circumstances. However, it's the selfishness within us is that holds us down. It is so easy to understand, but so hard to apply. It can only be done through the power of the Holy Spirit because of the shed blood on the cross for you. I heard Joyce Meyer (a Christian speaker and author) explain it this way, "We are educated far beyond our level of obedience." Continue to be educated, but it is really about obeying what you know.

James 5

Scribe to the Heart

"Elijah was a man with a nature like ours, and he prayed fervently that it might not rain, and for three years and six months it did not rain on the earth. Then he prayed again, and heaven gave rain, and the earth bore its fruit."

(Jas. 5:17-18)

Point to Ponder

Elijah, a man of prayer, was just like us.

Today's Journal

What holds me back from believing I am someone special, created for great things?

Prayer for the Day

Holy Spirit, Empower me to believe that You can and will work through me every day.

WHO, ME?

I HAVE AN NFL documentary recorded at home about Kurt Warner. Kurt Warner is a former NFL quarterback with quite a story. Kurt Warner was an "almost guy" for much of his football career. He didn't start as a quarterback in college until his senior year. He had a good season and tried out with the Green Bay Packers. He made the camp team but was cut early.

He bagged groceries before returning to professional play. He made the Rams team as a potential third string quarterback. After much trial and tribulation, he became the second-string quarterback. No other team wanted him and he was completely under the radar with the Rams.

In the preseason, the starting quarterback went down with an injury. Kurt Warner finally had his chance. Kurt Warner started in the quarterback position for the rest of the season and possibly played the best season any quarterback has ever played. They won the Super Bowl and will always be remembered as the Greatest Show on Turf.

One of the most fascinating things about this story can be heard in the interviews. Initially, people were not sure he was ready. People didn't know he could do it. I saw a clip with Dick Vermeil, the head coach of the Rams, explaining to the press that they were going with Kurt Warner and expressing his belief that Kurt could do the job. He explained that Kurt was able to play the position and lead this team. There would be no void.

The cited verses, James 5:17-18, are among my favorites. We all need someone to give us the nod. Just like the great coach endorsed Kurt Warner for him to have his chance, Jesus Christ endorses us. Elijah was just like us and he went to the greatest tyrant of his day and said, "It will not rain because I prayed. Stop sacrificing children to Baal. Stop all the madness." He went back years later, after prayer, and declared that it would rain. We're told here that he was a man just like us. So, when you are called to do something, anything at all, know that Jesus Christ Himself gives you the nod!

Day 223

1 Peter 1

Scribe to the Heart

"Blessed be the God and Father of our Lord Jesus Christ! According to his great mercy, he has caused us to be born again to a living hope through the resurrection of Jesus Christ from the dead."

(1 Pet. 1:3)

Point to Ponder

We have been born again to a living hope.

Today's Journal

Have I been born again to a living hope through the resurrection of Christ? What does this mean?

Prayer for the Day

Holy Spirit, Reveal to me what it means to be born again to a living hope through the resurrection of Christ. Let me set my hope fully on the grace of God.

WHAT WOULD YOU DO?

THERE IS A popular T.V. show called *What Would You Do?* The reason for having such a show is that it is much more interesting to see life played out on camera, than simply asking someone, "What would you do?" and hearing their verbal answer. I would like to think I would do this or that when under certain circumstances, but what actually happens under pressure or what I actually do when faced with a decision can be completely different. Action is where the rubber meets the road.

Peter is writing a letter to people who are greatly distressed. They are not doing well. The Roman government feels threatened by Christianity. Serious persecution is breaking out. The recipients of this letter do not understand why their loving, heavenly Father is allowing them to suffer. Peter is to encourage them in this intense time. They were in a "What would you do?" moment.

Us theological types often look at this first chapter and try to develop theologies of free will and grace. What gets lost is Peter was writing to real people under very real persecution. These people were scattered all over Asia. This was a bad situation.

Peter explains to them that they were born again to a hope that never fades. They get to start over. The future is wide open. Yes, you can lose your life, but what has been given to you can't be taken away. It is vital that you stay strong and live for Jesus. It is more important now than it has ever been before. Love Him. Follow Him, maybe even to a death like His, but don't forget Jesus already defeated death.

1 Peter 2

Scribe to the Heart

"Be subject for the Lord's sake to every human institution, whether it be to the emperor as supreme, or to the governors as sent by him to punish those who do evil and to praise those who do good."

(1 Pet. 2:13-14)

Point to Ponder

Submit to authorities.

Today's Journal

Do I find submitting to authorities hard? In what ways?

Prayer for the Day

Father God, Teach me about submission. Show me areas where I am not fully submitted to those You have put in authority over me.

HOLY SUBMISSION

AS A STUDENT of Jesus, Peter sought to follow Him. He sought to love Him, but he was bold and sometimes had his own ideas as to what Jesus should be doing. Even at the end of Jesus' earthly ministry Peter doesn't seem to get it. Peter cut off Malchus's ear, who was the servant of the high priest (John 18:10). He is clearly not the perfect example of submission in the gospels. After the death, resurrection, and ascension of Jesus something happened. Peter was empowered by the Spirit at Pentecost, but also he learned great lessons about submission. I am sure some of it took place as early as the cross. Other lessons took great pain and much time.

One of the most interesting accounts in the gospels is when Jesus shows up on the beach while Peter, James, and John are fishing. Peter swam to Him. He was excited to see Him. Jesus asked Peter three times on that beach if he loved Him, and told Peter to feed His sheep. Every time Peter says, "Yes." Peter was grieved because Jesus asked him three times. That was because Peter denied Him three times (John 21:15-19).

Even in that moment when Jesus gives Peter an opportunity for obedience Peter is resistant. Peter was told that when he became old he would not dress himself and he would be led somewhere where he doesn't want to go. Jesus then says, "Follow Me." Imagine. He saw the holes in His hands. Peter doesn't miss a beat and looks at John. "What about him?" Peter asked (John 21:21). Jesus explained to Peter that what happened to John was not Peter's concern. Peter was to follow Jesus (John 21:22).

Here, much later in his life, Peter is writing to persecuted Christians, telling them to submit to authorities and honor the emperor. The story of what happened on the beach may or may not have been common knowledge because the gospel of John wasn't written yet. When Peter's time came his last request was that since he knew he didn't deserve to die like Christ, he wanted to be crucified upside down. Throughout his life he learned to obey and that obedience prepared him to go down in history as a great martyr of the faith.

Day 225

1 Peter 3

Scribe to the Heart

"But in your hearts regard Christ the Lord as holy, always being prepared to make a defense to anyone who asks you for a reason for the hope that is in you."

(1 Pet. 3:15)

Point to Ponder

The best witness is allowing God to be seen through you when things are hard.

Today's Journal

What is my answer for the hope that is within me?

Prayer for the Day

Father, Empower me to showcase You and the hope that is within me.

THE PROBLEM WITH PROSPERITY

GOD WANTS TO give His kids good gifts. No matter what your age, you are His child. He is your heavenly Father. He loves you. He wants to bless you. I don't believe He is against us having things, as much as He is against things having us.

The problem with Prosperity Teaching typically is the one-sidedness of it. Sometimes we are called to suffer and it is for doing good. Sometimes non-believers need to see Jesus, and the only way it will happen is by watching you, the believer, go through something hard.

The thinking is: Man is not impressed by how much you praise God in times of success and riches. He wants to see you praise God when the sky falls in. He wants to know how deep the roots are when the trunk is completely severed. Does this faith live or is it fake? Is it an act? Is it self-deception? What does it look like when the bottom falls out? When the bottom falls out is Christ there? Do you lean on Him?

Peter was asking these believers to lean on Jesus in a time of great stress. He asked them to lean on Him when it was hard, and they were going through some of the hardest struggles of their lives.

In verse 15 of this chapter, Peter told these believers to be ready with an answer for why they were hopeful. We must be ready, too. People will see you continue to follow Jesus through the hardest times in your life. This will have the greatest impact on the people around you. It was true for Peter's audience. It is true for us today. God loves you and is using you, especially when your pain and sorrow are at their peak.

1 Peter 4

Scribe to the Heart

"With respect to this they are surprised when you do not join them in the same flood of debauchery, and they malign you; but they will give an account to him who is ready to judge the living and the dead."

(1 Pet. 4:4-5)

Point to Ponder

Break away from the pack to live a more holy life.

Today's Journal

How do I need to break away from the pack?

Prayer for the Day

Father God, Teach me where I need to break away from the pack. Help me live a more holy life. Show me how to do it.

SURPRISE NON-PARTY

I STOOD ON dry land and watched. The normal rituals to any race were present. Engines were revving. The racers would brace themselves before the first turn. This was the first Jet Ski race I had ever seen. After some quick fighting for position, one racer took the lead. He began to break away from the pack. They were making extra waves by being close to each other. There were a few wrecks. There were some stalled machines. But I saw the racer in first place continue to build on his lead the entire time. He dominated. He hit the turns with such grace and poise. He was focused and no one touched him the rest of the race.

When someone is extremely good at something, I mean really good, able to dominate their competition, it excites me. There were many hours of discipline I am sure went into that race. He was mentally and physically ready for it. However, it really came down to what he did at the very beginning.

I was a college student when I became a Christian. I had some good influences in my life and a found new fire for Jesus that helped me greatly. I remember telling my teammates in the offseason that the party scene was no longer my thing. It was lonely when I first withdrew from it because even some of my Christian friends were falling into that world. But I quickly found friends who were not interested in that world either.

One thing I noticed later, as a College Ministry Director, was the students that stumbled over and over again never seemed to break away from the pack. They would withdraw and go back, and go back and forth. The temptations kept coming because they would be invited and pressured to come back to the party. The only way to leave a sinful lifestyle is to leave. Hit the first corner and break away. Be prayed up. Don't stall the vehicle or get caught in someone else's wake. You must make a decision and keep going. My friends were still my friends, we just didn't do the same things at night. I gained their respect and found out who my true friends were. The pressure to be a part of that world was gone. By the grace of God, I hit the first corner and broke away from the pack.

1 Peter 5

Scribe to the Heart

"Humble yourselves, therefore, under the mighty hand of God so that at the proper time he may exalt you."

(1 Pet. 5:6)

Point to Ponder

Stay humbled under the mighty hand of God to live your best.

Today's Journal

Have I experienced blessing during humility? Have I been humbled following a time of pride?

Prayer for the Day

Father, My desire is to be humble. Keep Your mighty hand upon me and guide me. Amen.

DANGER: PRIDE ZONE!

WHEN I WAS newly married, I had a mentor much older than me. In some ways, I had a hard time understanding him. But one thing I will remember is that he loved his wife. He always said he would never say he would never cheat on her because he felt that was pride and it opened him up for temptation. He truly believed he would never cheat on his wife, but he didn't walk around saying it. There is something dangerous about us thinking we are above temptation in any area.

Verse 5 of this chapter tells us that God opposes the proud. He opposes us when we are proud, but gives grace to the humble. The devil also looks for the proud as someone to devour. In other words, the Bible teaches us that when we humble ourselves under the mighty hand of God, He exalts us and promotes us beyond our own capabilities. When we become prideful (often after God blessed us for being humble) He has to pull back and remove His hand of blessing.

This also gives the devil an opportunity, for he is like a roaring lion looking for the prideful so that he may devour them. What a concept, be humble! In other words, trust God as your ultimate source. Trust God. Humble yourself under His hand. When He blesses you for it, stay there and give him credit. You want to stay in His hand. When we begin to take credit for the good in our own lives, we become our own gods. The hand of Almighty God goes away. When we are on our own in the spiritual, so to speak, the enemy forces who want to destroy us may be able to do just that.

Be confident in God, not in your own flesh. Stay humbled by the mighty hand of God. Do not trust in yourself to solve your problems. Trust in your God. He will lift you up in due time.

2 Peter 1

"His divine power has granted to us all things that pertain to life and godliness, through the knowledge of him who called us to his own glory and excellence."

(2 Pet. 1:3)

Point to Ponder

We are empowered with all we need to live for God.

Today's Journal

What are my thoughts on verses 3 & 4 of this chapter?

Prayer for the Day

Father, Teach me to follow You empowered by the Holy Spirit and with the humility of Christ. Amen.

GRACE EMPOWERED OR JUST A SINNER?

THE TESTIMONY OF how someone became a Christ-follower is a powerful example of the grace of God. I was lost, but God found me. I was a sinner, but now I am saved. I was blind to the things of God, but now I see. It is true that we are only sinners saved by grace. We deserved to die and be separated from God for all eternity, but God saved us. People are sadly mistaken however if they think that moment of salvation is all Christ means them to have. Once you know Jesus you are empowered by the Holy Spirit to live a life of power. You are no longer just a sinner saved by grace, you are empowered and under the direction of God; you are a mighty vessel. You are a part of the church. The church is the only force on earth of which it is said that the very gates of hell can't stand against (Matthew 16:18). Since these words were spoken to Peter from Jesus Himself, no one understood it in the same way he did.

In the first letter, Peter wrote to these distressed believers, talking about being born again of a seed that can't perish (1 Peter 1:3-5). In this letter he wants them to know they are empowered over sin and evil. They are partakers of the very nature of God Himself. If you were raised in an environment that focused only on being a sinner, this stuff sounds blasphemous to you; even demonic. The truth is we started out as helpless sinners in need of God's grace, but we are much more than that now.

Don't let anyone tell you that you are not empowered by God to live a life of faith that will shake the very foundations of hell. You are now empowered to hear from God, to say no to sin, to live with power, love, and freedom. As I write this I almost feel like Peter. Did you notice when the apostles got real excited their sentences would run on? Peter does this at the beginning of both of his letters and Paul does so in Ephesians 1. Why? Because they knew what it meant to live in the flesh, and they knew what it meant to walk with God Almighty. They couldn't hold back their excitement. Neither should we.

2 Peter 2

Scribe to the Heart

"But these, like irrational animals, creatures of instinct, born to be caught and destroyed, blaspheming about matters of which they are ignorant, will also be destroyed in their destruction, suffering wrong as the wage for their wrongdoing."

(2 Pet. 2:12-13a)

Point to Ponder

Ignorance leads to destruction.

Today's Journal

The world says, "Ignorance is bliss." God says, "Ignorance leads to destruction." How are these two statements vastly different? What do I believe?

Prayer for the Day

Holy Spirit, Reveal more about Yourself to me. Show me more about this amazing world You created. Amen.

IGNORANCE IS NOT BLISS

ONE OF THE core teachings I gather from Jesus is found in Matthew during the Sermon on the Mount. *"Seek and you will find"* (Matthew 7:7b). We live in a day that people tailor the truth they believe to match their personal preferences and lifestyle choices. The New Age World says that things become true simply because someone decides it is true. This thinking elevates people to god-status. A tailor-made truth declares that it is OK for everyone to decide what is true for them. This is a dangerous, deadly game to play.

As I read about false prophets and false teachers in this chapter, I can't help but think about the reality of the world we live in. People have their own agendas. They spout off about things they don't understand. Atheists are on social media trying to disprove God. Honestly, an ant has a better chance of disproving my existence. People are pushed to do and focus on what feels good, while God's Word teaches us that the flesh is not a good guide. In fact, there is not a single verse in the New Testament that compliments, our flesh in anyway. The flesh is our downfall. It is our weakness.

God's Word is provable. It is active and living (Hebrews 4:12). It is different from anything else and God encounters people and convicts them in His own way, on His own terms, and in His own time. Some want to be God, and some want to worship the true and living God. Which are you?

In the cited verses to the left, Peter is talking to those false teachers, who in their ignorance will be destroyed. Pray for them. Love them. Show Jesus to them. If you are one who doubts or isn't sure yet, dig deep. Truth will set you free. Dig into God's Word. Dig into science. Learn philosophy. God's truth will always shine forth if you are truly seeking it. Don't become blinded with pride by your own ignorance.

2 Peter 3

Scribe to the Heart

"But the day of the Lord will come like a thief, and then the heavens will pass away with a roar, and the heavenly bodies will be burned up and dissolved, and the earth and the works that are done on it will be exposed."

(2 Pet. 3:10)

Point to Ponder

Our time is coming like a thief in the night.

Today's Journal

What does it mean that "God is patient, yet comes like a thief"?

Prayer for the Day

Lord Jesus, Teach me both about Your patience and your imminent judgment.

LIKE A THIEF

THESE VERSES ARE often neglected in the study of end things: *"The Lord is not slow to fulfill his promise as some count slowness, but is patient toward you, not wishing that any should perish, but that all should reach repentance. But the day of the Lord will come like a thief, and then the heavens will pass away with a roar, and the heavenly bodies will be burned up and dissolved, and the earth and the works that are done on it will be exposed"* (2 Peter 3:9-10).

I believe these verses are neglected because you can't put them into a chart or a graph. When Jesus comes, it seems that we will not be able to count the days from a Rapture of the church through seven years and a bunch of events which lead up to the Coming of Christ, like many have taught.

These verses suggest there will be scoffers. People will be getting married and be given in marriage. There will be normal life going on, and not necessarily horrible tribulation everywhere. There will be people going about their business focusing on the wrong things. Then WHACK! Like a thief, Jesus will come back.

Verse 9 teaches us that God is patient. He gives people a chance. He doesn't want anyone to perish, but we are given free will. He is patient and pursues us. One of the things that brings more people to repentance is verse 10. He will come quickly. We don't know when, so don't put it off. I came to repentance in part out of fear. I heard a message on the radio in my car that made me scared that I would wreck and not get a chance to get right. When I reached my college home, a book I had sent for about the grace of God titled *Power for Living* was waiting for me. I sent for it because my childhood hero, Philadelphia Eagle legend Reggie White, endorsed it. I learned of God's love as I read. I found what I was looking for and asked Jesus to lead my life. The reality of eternal separation from God got my attention. The message of who God is showed me to love and trust Him. In this passage God gives us a message of "hurry," yet He is patient, not wanting anyone to perish. Take your time and be sure, but be aware your time is anytime. God wants real repentance. He doesn't play games. If you know the truth, then you are accountable.

1 John 1

Scribe to the Heart

"This is the message we have heard from Him and declare to you: God is light; in Him there is no darkness at all."

(1 John 1:5)

Point to Ponder

In God there is no darkness.

Today's Journal

What does it mean to have darkness in my heart?

Prayer for the Day

Lord Jesus, Reveal to me where I have darkness in my life. Help me to extinguish the darkness. Amen!

IN HIM THERE IS NO DARKNESS

IMAGINE LOOKING INTO your own soul. What would you see? Many of us would have a mixture of sections of light and patches of darkness. The dark areas are the things we are trying to keep from others, God, or even ourselves. We lie to ourselves. We live with half-truths, prejudices, anger, guilt. We are a wall of emotions, feelings, and history.

As we enter into the book of 1 John, we are already familiar with the author, the Apostle John. We know about him from reading the gospel of John (the very first book we read in *The New Testament Challenge*) and he is credited for writing these next three epistles. John referred to himself as the "disciple whom Jesus loved" over and over again. John knew Jesus loved Him in spite of all of his shortcomings. Imagine this: In Jesus there is no darkness at all. He was full of hope and love. He is all that is good and lovely and righteous. We are full of garbage, but He loves us regardless.

When we truly experience Jesus, we realize a few things. One of the things we realize is God is holy. He is perfect. There is no darkness in Him. Nothing false, nothing ugly. Also, He doesn't weigh us down with guilt over our imperfections. He calls us quietly. When we come to Him, He begins to shine His light on our darkness. It is absolutely beautiful. This letter is weighty. There are some difficult verses in this letter. Keep in mind as you read them that you are reading the thoughts of a man who experienced being loved by God, a God of no darkness. Remember the author, John, and all you know about his first-hand experiences with His Savior.

1 John 2

Scribe to the Heart

"My little children, I am writing these things to you so that you may not sin. But if anyone does sin, we have an advocate with the Father, Jesus Christ the righteous."

(1 John 2:1)

Point to Ponder

A real Christian lives for Jesus.

Today's Journal

"A real Christian lives for Jesus." What does that mean?

Prayer for the Day

Lord Jesus, Let me live in grace and not in guilt. Let me remain accountable as I seek to walk how You walked. Thank You for being my advocate.

THE MARK OF A CHRISTIAN

"WE KNOW THAT we have come to know Him if we obey His commands. The man who says, 'I know Him,' but does not do what He commands is a liar, and the truth is not in Him. But if anyone obeys His word, God's love is truly made complete in Him. This is how we know we are in Him: Whoever claims to live in Him must walk as Jesus did" (1 John 2:3-6).

We see in the above verses that if we claim to know Jesus, but do not do what He says, we are liars and the truth is not in us. We also see from verse 1 that if we do sin, we have someone who speaks in our defense—Jesus Christ, the Righteous One. These two ideas seem to contradict each other. One idea tells us that if we are sinners, we are liars. The other idea reflects a forgiving God who speaks on our behalf when we fall short. How can both ideas be true?

John is speaking about the mark of a Christian. This chapter, like many others in the New Testament, is filled with more depth than we can elaborate on in one page. To bring it to a bottom line: We are supposed to live in this tension. Salvation is by grace. It can't be earned. We come to Christ broken and He fixes us. At the same time when someone lives in habitual sin and never changes, then their talk is cheap. A person can claim to know Jesus and not really know Him. If a life is not changed or is not in the process, we can't assume that someone knows Jesus. It isn't true because they say so. The devil is referred to as the great deceiver and the father of lies.

We need to walk as Jesus walked. Christianity goes against the grain of the culture. If it is easy for you to follow Jesus, you need to reevaluate because Jesus came to redeem you from this world's system. He came to save you from your fleshly desires, and He did it by grace. When you fall back to the ways of your old self, the Righteous One speaks to the Great Judge on your behalf. He speaks on behalf of those who truly know Him.

1 John 3

Scribe to the Heart

"How great is the love the Father has lavished on us, that we should be called children of God! And that is what we are! The reason the world does not know us is that it did not know Him."

(1 John 3:1)

Point to Ponder

Following Jesus is an alien concept.

Today's Journal

Who can I win over for Christ using a method he or she has never seen before? How can I reach them? What is my plan?

Prayer for the Day

Lord Jesus, Show me how to be an alien for You in this culture. I pray that I will not be known for conforming to the ways of the world.

CROSS-EYED

IN MY FIRST week of seminary I remember the new students sitting down with those in charge of the In-Ministry program I was in. It was a seminary program for students who were already engaged in full-time ministry. Seminary is a very exciting, interesting, yet odd place. Academia, whether in a great Christian institution like the one I attended or in the secular sense, creates an atmosphere where students are trying to impress the powers that be. What makes that odd in a seminary is students find ways to tell people how humble they are, or how inadequate they are, but God uses them anyway. It is almost the opposite of what people put forward in a secular situation, but the goal is still the same, drawing attention to one's self.

Following times in class when students were asked to pray, I looked around wondering if anyone understood what was said. I say this with the utmost respect and appreciation for my seminary experience. It was awesome, but even there, a touch of the world's system is present. There was a definite need to put on a show. I met one student who was different. He didn't care what people thought of him. As he talked with great joy about his expectations of seminary, he was very candid. He used words that were out of bounds. He spoke openly, and hid nothing.

I found it refreshing and so did most of the people in the room. Yet, everyone at some point looked at this student cross-eyed. Why? He didn't fit the mold. He refused to play the game. I had never seen someone like him before. When we look at this chapter, the words in the first verse stick out to me. The reason the world doesn't know God's children is it doesn't know Christ. When we truly follow Christ, it will be noticeable. We are strangers to this world when we follow Christ. When the love of God overflows from within our hearts, people take note because we look different. We no longer fit the world's mold. To truly follow after Jesus is to love Him, and love people. It is so easy to understand, but it is rarely done. If you do it right people will look at you cross-eyed.

1 John 4

"We love because he first loved us."

(1 John 4:19)

Point to Ponder

Understanding how unlovable you are helps you to forgive and love others.

Today's Journal

How can I allow God to make me more lovable? How can I allow God to use me to better love others?

Prayer for the Day

Lord Jesus, Thank You for loving me, even when I am unlovable. Let me love others, even those who are difficult for me to love.

LOVE

"WE LOVE BECAUSE he first loved us. If anyone says, 'I love God,' yet hates his brother he is a liar. For anyone who does not love his brother, whom he has seen, cannot love God, whom he has not seen, And He has given us this command: Whoever loves God must also love his brother" (1 John 4:19-21).

One of the major differences between Christianity and other religions is the fact that God reaches out to us in love first. All other religions include an attempt to get God's attention or approval. Christianity is about God reaching out to us, and making a way for us. It is about Him loving us. Our response is to love Him back. When we truly encounter Jesus, it changes us. We are faced with His love, and low and behold, we become burdened to love. As the verses above remind us, we fall short if we hate our brother. If we have been touched by the love of God, it should be a small thing to give that love back to God's creation. Yet we make it a big deal.

It is a requirement. Do you catch that? These verses say if you love God, you must love your brother also. That doesn't mean you are not saved if you don't do it, but it is stated as a standard. God gives you grace and love you don't deserve and you must give it back to others who also don't deserve it. You must love them, regardless of what they have done to you. What does that mean? It means you must be able to pray for them, see them without having feelings of wanting to hurt them, and you actually want what is best for them. This takes prayer and hard work.

Spending time with God and realizing how much you are loved, along with understanding how much you don't deserve it, helps a great deal. It is hard to grasp how unlovable we are. This understanding helps you to forgive and love others.

1 John 5

Scribe to the Heart

"And this is the confidence that we have toward him, that if we ask anything according to his will he hears us."

(1 John 5:14)

Point to Ponder

Approach God with confidence because He hears you.

Today's Journal

How can I pray according to God's will?

Prayer for the Day

Lord Jesus, My desire is to pray according to Your will. Teach me what that means today.

HE HEARS US

WHAT A FASCINATING letter this is. There is a call to Holy Christian living. We are told of the great love of God and how it should motivate us to love others. This letter is full of deep theological truth. Through our experience with God's love for us we should have confidence to approach our Holy God.

If we ask anything according to His will, He hears us. Sometimes we may ask something that is not according to His will and we hear no answer. One of the more powerful principles I have learned is there are certain prayers God always seems to answer. For example, it is God's will for you to know your sins. You are to know your problems. God wants to help you if you are willing to search your own heart. When you pray to become a better Christian, God hears you. When you pray that more people will be reached by your testimony, God hears you.

Understanding how much God loves you leads to loving others. You will find yourself extremely confident in approaching God. God also hears you when you pray according to His desires for your life. It is absolutely beautiful. It seems so easy, so why is prayer and holy living so hard? The reason is God leaves us with responsibility. We need to take the initiative. He died for you. He rose for you. He lives inside of you. The least you can do is try to follow after Him. If you take one step of faith, He will take the next one with you.

2 John 1

Scribe to the Heart

"I rejoiced greatly to find some of your children walking in the truth, just as we were commanded by the Father."

(2 John 1:4)

Point to Ponder

True Christian leadership cares about discipleship.

Today's Journal

How important is growth in the life of a Christian? Why did the Apostle John take such joy in seeing growth in others?

Prayer for the Day

Lord Jesus, Show me how to grow in my obedience to You and to help someone else to do the same today.

THE APOSTLE'S JOY

THE APOSTLE JOHN writes a short letter here. I am almost certain he probably never thought we would be reading this almost 2,000 years into the future. But God knew. The letter is very short, but we can learn a great deal from its content. First, we see a letter addressed to the chosen lady and her children. She is addressed as someone who is possibly leading a house church. It is also possible that John is talking about her biological children, and not just children of the faith.

I would like to draw your attention to one specific verse. The apostles were the original pioneers of our faith. It was taught to them directly from Jesus. Did you ever wonder what would make them happy? Here is an answer from John: *"I rejoiced greatly to find some of your children walking in the truth, just as we were commanded by the Father"* (2 John 1:4). Did you catch it? It gives Him great joy that some of them are catching the vision. Just a few of them are getting it. The apostle poured his heart out. He is talking with a leader he trusts to disciple others and it gives him great joy that just a few people are following the truth and doing what they are supposed to be doing.

It shines a whole new light on evangelism and discipleship, doesn't it? John understood that not many would follow the way of Christ, but those who did were called to follow the road less traveled. It would be hard, and it made John glad to know that a few people were doing it right.

Day 237

3 John 1

Scribe to the Heart

"I have no greater joy than to hear that my children are walking in the truth."

(3 John 1:4)

Point to Ponder

One of life's greatest joys is discipling people who then truly practice their faith.

Today's Journal

What do I find so great about the joy of which John is speaking?

Prayer for the Day

Lord Jesus, Help me take great joy in ministering to others. Give me a glimpse into the fruit of my labor so I may know the great joy that the Apostle John experienced.

FATHER JOHN

WHEN I SAY "Father John" I am not referring to the great apostle in a priestly sense, but in a parental role. In our previous entry we talked about the joy received by John when he saw his disciples doing what is right in the name of Christ. As you can see in our Scribe to the Heart verse today, it is a parental connection John feels in this letter. What does this parent care about most? What brings him the greatest joy? It is hearing His children are walking in the truth.

Obedience to the truth and an authentic pursuit of Christ are the greatest gifts a person can give back to their pastor or spiritual leader. My wife and I just received a letter from a former student of a college ministry we were in charge of several years ago. We saw her come to faith in Christ. We saw her come alive in Christ. We were invited to her wedding. Today we got a picture and letter and heard of many exciting things. As a leader, occasionally in the down times you look back and question: Did it all mean anything? This student told us of many exciting things, but what stands out to me is that she is newly married and she and her husband are trying to segue from their current jobs into the world of youth ministry. They have experienced Jesus Christ, and desire to give back. There is no greater joy than knowing God used you in the lives of people who will influence the lives of other people. The Apostle John knew this joy and this is why we see his comments in the short little letters here in 2 and 3 John.

Jude

Scribe to the Heart

"For certain men whose condemnation was written about long ago have secretly slipped in among you. They are godless men, who change the grace of God into a license for immorality and deny Jesus Christ our only Sovereign and Lord."

(Jude 1:4)

Point to Ponder

Don't be fooled by false disciples.

Today's Journal

Do all of the people I go to church with know Jesus?

Prayer for the Day

Lord Jesus, Teach me about loving Your children. Show me the people who are lost. Deepen my knowledge of You so that I will have a sincere and honest relationship with You. Amen.

DON'T BE FOOLED

THERE ARE SOME important questions that need answered. First of all, who is our author, Jude? Jude introduces Himself as, *"a servant of Jesus Christ and brother of James"* (Jude 1:1). Who is James? Remember, James introduced himself in his letter as, *"a servant of God and of the Lord Jesus Christ"* (James 1:1). Both of these men where the half-brothers of Jesus. Why didn't Jude say this? These men didn't follow Him while He walked the earth with them. Now they are leaders of the original Christian church.

Wouldn't it have given them more authority to cite the fact they were Jesus' brothers? Maybe they believed it was more powerful to be His disciple then to be related to Him. Maybe for Jude and James it was about being true, real, and honorable. Maybe they didn't want to claim status based on family heritage. Maybe they wanted status based on knowing Jesus and who Jesus is to them.

The main topic of this short letter is, some people with bad motives have worked their way into the church. They are deceivers who do not truly follow Jesus. They have their own motives for being there. There are people in our churches who are similar. Some people who talk the talk but do not walk the walk are there for social reasons. Maybe they think it will help them make job contacts by being there. That seems harmless enough. Some people are involved in church because churches are trusting and loving and are a target for people who desire to hurt families and children. Not so harmless.

However, *any* false disciples of Jesus hurt the kingdom. Unbelievers see all of us Christians the same. We are disciples of the sinless Son of God. We believe something and want to live for it with all of our hearts. Or do we? Do they see something else? Not everyone who claims to know Jesus is a good representative of Him or His grace. Many who claim Him do not even know Him at all. Don't be fooled. Jude tells us what we are to do about this in verses 20-23: Build your faith, pray in the Holy Spirit, keep yourself in the love of God, have mercy on those who doubt. A lot of wisdom is packed in this little letter.

Revelation 1

Scribe to the Heart

"The revelation of Jesus Christ, which God gave him to show his servants the things that must soon take place. He made it known by sending his angel to his servant John."

(Rev. 1:1)

Point to Ponder

Read Revelation as a message sent to first century Christians.

Today's Journal

Does it change my perspective on Revelation to consider the original audience of this book?

Prayer for the Day

Lord Jesus, Help me to play by the rules when reading to apply Your word to my life. Amen.

DO YOU SEE WHAT GOD SEES?

THE BOOK OF Revelation was the last book written in the New Testament. Revelation was written by the John the Apostle. Many believe in approximately 90 A.D. Christians were under intense persecution from the Roman Empire. Revelation is a special work of literature. Revelation is special to ancient literature buffs because it has characteristics of three ancient genres. Revelation is Prophecy and Apocalyptic literature. But first, Revelation is an Epistle. It is an ancient letter to seven specific churches mentioned, and possibly others not mentioned. This is possibly the most neglected aspect in most of today's teaching about Revelation. The people were given a message that was read aloud in each of these churches. It was intended primarily for them. If you hear a sermon or a teaching about Revelation what are the chances you will miss the meaning of a passage if the message starts with today's newspaper headlines? It is a dangerous game. We must play by the rules to get clean interpretations. This requires us to focus on the original audience and author.

What is fascinating about these seven churches is they were all groups of believers who had problems. They were just like us. The fact that we consider the original audience first and we are not the primary audience doesn't make it less relevant for us. It makes it more relevant. These people had the same problems we do today and they were trying to follow Jesus under persecution as well. Jesus has John address the letter to the churches. There is also the symbolism of an angel assigned to each church. I wonder, do we have angels assigned to our churches? Maybe there is one watching over the churches in your area. It is interesting to think about, but our focus must always be on Christ.

This book is a reminder that we are a part of a battle we do not completely understand. Our true enemy is hidden. There are ministering Spirits helping us on our behalf (Hebrews 1:14). Read the words to the churches in the next chapter and relate to them. The book of Revelation is sending a message. There is missing information from our perspective so God helps us to see through His eyes.

Revelation 2

Scribe to the Heart

"To the angel of the church in Ephesus write: These are the words of Him who holds the seven stars in His right hand and walks among the seven golden lampstands."

(Rev. 2:2)

Point to Ponder

God holds the angels in His hands and walks with us.

Today's Journal

How much does it mean to me to know that God is large enough to hold the angels in His right hand? What does it mean to me to know that He walks among us?

Prayer for the Day

Lord Jesus, Thank you for Your amazing power. Amen.

HE WHO WALKS AMONG THE LAMPSTANDS

THERE IT IS! I love when God shows me something new. You can study His word for years and when He decides it is time for you to see something that is when you will see it. In the last chapter we learned that the lampstands are the seven churches and the stars are the angels assigned to each church.

Originally, I thought it was the other way around. I was disappointed because I wanted to write about how God holds us in the palm of His hand and walks among the angels. Then I realized as Jesus Christ penned a specific letter for each of the seven churches. He found it especially pertinent to mention He holds the angel of each church in the palm of His hand and walks among us the lampstands.

The angel is watching over the church and doing battle with the evil one and all of the powers of darkness. How big does God have to be to hold the very angels in His hand? Yet He walks among us. He is detailed enough to walk amongst the church. What an amazing picture of the power and sovereignty of God. God is in complete authority holding our hands and helping us while guiding the angels. He is big enough to still be in complete authority and allow us to be free-willed beings. It is simply amazing.

As John penned the message to each of these first four churches notice the formula. With the exception of Smyrna, who is the only church who doesn't receive any form of discipline or call to repentance, God praises them for what they do first. Then there is a call to repentance. Finally, each church receives a reminder that God will bless them for living truly for Him. He will bless them even in spite of the persecution they were under. They may die here, but they will receive a heavenly blessing, and it all started with a reminder. He is big enough to hold the angels in His hands and gentle enough to walk amongst us.

Revelation 3

Scribe to the Heart

"He who has an ear, let him hear what the Spirit says to the churches."

(Rev. 3:22)

Point to Ponder

We desperately need to understand God's word to these early churches.

Today's Journal

Which of the churches mentioned do I most relate to? What did I learn from reading God's word to that church?

Prayer for the Day

Lord Jesus, I pray that I will properly interpret and understand Your word. I pray for spiritual growth. Let me hear You speak to me.

HE WHO HAS AN EAR

AT THE END of Jesus' instruction, affirmation, and discipline of the churches we see an interesting verse. *"He who has an ear, let him hear what the Spirit says to the churches"* (Rev. 3:22). Jesus actually says these words to each of the churches specifically. In the first century, writing was done generally in the male tense. Just because the masculine pronoun "he" is what is translated, women are not excluded from this warning. Jesus used this phrase in Matthew 11:15, 13:9, 13:43, Mark 4:23, 7:16, Luke 14:35. The prophet Isaiah used similar words in his book (Isaiah 42:20). With all of these references to look back on, the understanding for the audience would have been clear. This is a warning. It is saying: Don't be like the people in the past who heard the right words, but acted as if they had no ears.

Basically, the message is urgent and is meant for anyone who can hear. It is like telling your child to listen when you know they are not. He is speaking to anyone who is young, old, male, female, gentile, Jew. Everyone. You. Which message should you hear? The message the Spirit gave to the churches. This message was directly for seven specific churches who had assigned angels to them and who were people who struggled just like us. We must not forget to take into account the original audience that lived 2,000 years ago, halfway around the world, under the persecution of a vicious empire. However, if you have an ear, you desperately need the message Jesus had for these churches. God's word is living and active (Hebrews 4:12). It is so powerful and we desperately need it. By understanding the audience, author, and the message to these churches we can be wise beyond our years. If you have an ear, read on in the book of Revelation and understand what God's message is for you.

Revelation 4

Scribe to the Heart

"At once I was in the Spirit, and behold, a throne stood in heaven, with one seated on the throne. And he who sat there had the appearance of jasper and carnelian, and around the throne was a rainbow that had the appearance of an emerald."

(Rev. 4:2-3)

Point to Ponder

God's covenant gives security.

Today's Journal

What promises has God made to me, especially over the last several months as I have been taking The New Testament Challenge?

Prayer for the Day

Father, Teach me about Your covenant nature. I will rest in Your promises.

ENTER THE RAINBOW

I DECIDED TO avoid wrangling with the opinions of others over the 24 elders mentioned in this chapter. I will say it should be noted that there are 24 elders. There were twelve tribes of Israel and yes, there were twelve apostles, speaking possibly to Jesus completing that covenant in the New Testament. I am not entirely clear on how to put it together. These 24 elders have crowns. They are giving their crowns to God. We also read of elements of nature and it seems that a symbol of every representative of nature, whether in the air or on the ground, is worshipping and honoring our God.

There is something of note that I don't want you to miss. Around the throne is a rainbow. We know from Genesis that the rainbow is a symbol of God's covenant with man not to destroy the earth again in the way He brought judgment with the flood the first time (Genesis 6-8). There will be a final judgment but it will be different than the flood. This gives nature harmony as we await the coming of Jesus. The elders are also worshipping in harmony during this time of waiting.

The rainbow was to give the original readers security during this great tribulation. We know we belong to Jesus and God makes a long list of promises. He is not a politician running for office. There is no reason for him to lie. In fact, He can't lie, it is not in His nature. The rainbow promises there will not be another flood (Genesis 9:8-17). In contrast, judgment will come when He says it will come (2 Peter 3:10). God is in charge and many, like the elders, worship in heaven and on earth knowing this fact. The more we know it, the more we can be in harmony with His created order. Amen.

Day 243

Revelation 5

Scribe to the Heart

"And one of the elders said to me, 'Weep no more; behold, the Lion of the tribe of Judah, the Root of David, has conquered, so that he can open the scroll and its seven seals.'"

(Rev. 5:5)

Point to Ponder

Conquer through the ultimate sacrifice of Jesus Christ.

Today's Journal

"Conquer through sacrifice" is the ultimate message of Christianity. Elaborate or push back on this statement.

Prayer for the Day

Lord Jesus, Make me a conqueror. Teach me to conquer through sacrifice in this life.

CONQUER THROUGH SACRIFICE

THE MAIN MESSAGE of the book of Revelation is "conquer through sacrifice." This message is often neglected. At the time of great tribulation and scattering of Christians, the question is very easy to understand. *Why God are you allowing us to be beaten and killed and pursued by the pagans when we are faithful to you? When God, when will you deliver us? Why are the pagans and conformist being blessed?*

This was the bleeding heart of Christians; new and seasoned, young and old. Only when we see things from an apocalyptic perspective can we begin to understand. Apocalyptic literature takes us to God and we see through His eyes. That is the goal of Revelation. Its original audience was under such intense watch. It would have been easy to lose heart or deny the faith. But when we see John being asked to come up in the last chapter (Revelation 4:1), it is an invitation to stand next to God and see the apocalyptic, vital message tailored for a people who needed it. It hints that the reader is to make a perspective shift. We can apply this to our own lives by seeking God in our darkest moments knowing His perspective looks different.

Ultimately, it is not us who conquers through sacrifice. Yes, we need to lay down our lives and our own ambitions, but do not miss the key to understanding this book in this chapter. "No one is able to open the scroll," a strong angel proclaimed. Who is powerful enough but the Lion of the Tribe of Judah? He is the Root of David. He is a Lion and the seed of a great King. But when you look away and look back it is also a Lamb. The Lion and the Lamb are the same. The Lamb of God, Jesus Christ, laid down His life. He conquered through sacrifice. From God's perspective and now ours He is a conquering Lion and His death, resurrection, and ascension are the most heroic, lion-like actions we can ever imagine. This heroic Lion conquers not only as a Lion, but also the Lamb of the slaughter.

Revelation 6

Scribe to the Heart

"They cried out with a loud voice, 'O Sovereign Lord, holy and true, how long before you will judge and avenge our blood on those who dwell on the earth?'"

(Rev. 6:10)

Point to Ponder

God is fair.

Today's Journal

What if I saw the whole picture from God's perspective? What would that look like?

Prayer for the Day

Father, Help me see from Your perspective those things that currently I do not.

GOD IS MORE THAN FAIR

"WHEN HE OPENED *the fifth seal, I saw under the altar the souls of those who had been slain for the word of God and for the witness that had borne. They cried out with a loud voice, 'O Sovereign Lord, holy and true, how long before you will judge and avenge our blood on those who dwell on the earth?' Then they were each given a white robe and told to rest a little longer, until the number of their fellow servants and their brothers should be complete, who were to be killed as they themselves had been*" (Revelation 6:9-11).

Some of you have read the title and are ready to skip to the next page. Try to tell a mother who just lost her son God is fair. I know people who have been through all types of pain. Parents lose children. Young soldiers are killed defending our country while old politicians barter over oil. Cynical? Yes, I admit it. I love our country and our military, but let's at least agree that war is second best. It is necessary only because evil continues and will continue without the right resistance.

The Christians addressed in Revelation were going through a lot. God is saying here that it is going to get worse. There is going to be poverty, war, and death. There is going to be pain. There will be more martyrs. The picture is given of slain Christians under an altar asking how long until there is justice. There is actually a number God has in mind. Not just a number, but real people who are numbered to die before things change.

In our finite minds, we think this is not right. It is downright wrong! These people are being brutally persecuted. Yet God is winning converts through the willing sacrifice of the martyrs. From God's perspective He is winning the war. People observe and see something worth dying for, and they jump on board. They want to know this Jesus that changes people's lives and allows them to feel peace through the harshest of circumstances. Praise God we don't get what we deserve and that One conquered through sacrifice. He died and rose again. He sits at the right hand of God Almighty and seeks to bring us home. No matter how we get there, He will bring us home and we will be safe forever. Every tear will be wiped away. It will be awesome.

Revelation 7

Scribe to the Heart

"These are the ones coming out of the great tribulation. They have washed their robes and made them white in the blood of the Lamb."

(Rev. 7:14)

Point to Ponder

The fruit of our labor effects coming generations.

Today's Journal

What is God's dream for my legacy?

Prayer for the Day

Father, Help me to make decisions with a legacy mindset. Guide my thoughts and allow me to listen to the Holy Spirit.

SEEING RESULTS

WE WANT TO see results. Because we don't have God's apocalyptic view point, we don't see things as they are. It is stressful to toil over something for years and not see results. Yet people do it, and many do it by faith. There are missionaries who spend years in a country without seeing a single convert. This chapter of Revelation is foundational for understanding this book. We lose a lot in this chapter trying to understand the details. Entire doctrines have been built off of the 144,000 witnesses mentioned in this chapter. For now, we will leave them alone.

I want us to zero in on the white robes around the throne. First, we see there is a great multitude of the redeemed wearing white robes. They are worshipping the Lamb. They are from every nation, tribe, and tongue. Since it is mentioned with three different words, it is clear there are people who are reached from all nations, tribes (families) and tongues (languages).

You may hear someone quote verse 14 of this chapter and refer to the great tribulation mentioned in the verse as being about an end times period of seven years of tribulation immediately prior to the return of Christ. I do not agree with that viewpoint because only Christians converted during this time would be on earth. I don't see that found here. I don't think that is the tribulation referred to in verse 14.

The true meaning of the text is beautiful. These Christians have been persecuted. There has been great pain and loss. John sees a multitude of Jesus' followers redeemed in heaven. Remember Christianity was not what it is today. Jesus described it as a mustard seed, starting small and growing to be the largest tree in the forest (Matthew 13:31-32). The great tribulation is the persecution going on during this (John's) time period, approximately 90 A.D. The result is; through the years their pain is our gain. People will come to know Jesus from all nations, people groups and languages. These believers were called to conquer and they faithfully conquered by sacrifice. The result of their willingness to follow Jesus during persecution and even martyrdom is that we are reached. Beautiful!

Revelation 8

Scribe to the Heart

"Then I saw the seven angels who stand before God, and seven trumpets were given to them."

(Rev. 8:2)

Point to Ponder

God's team is the only team to be on because He will always complete His purposes.

Today's Journal

Could angels be assigned to churches, regions, nations, or families? How does the Bible help me understand this?

Prayer for the Day

Father, Teach me what Your word says regarding angels. Give me biblical understanding.

THE NUMBER SEVEN

THIS CHAPTER OF Revelation shows us the beginning of great pain and judgment on the earth. We have seen the number seven come up often as we go through Revelation. Here we read that there are seven angels with seven trumpets. They are in charge of blowing the trumpets and initiating God's judgment on the earth. Let's remember the angels from earlier in the story (Revelation 1:9-20). Each of the seven churches mentioned had an angel assigned to it.

It is very important to see that the churches had adequate representation before God Almighty. Someone was fighting for them in the spiritual realm. Angels were taking on the forces of evil to set things right for them. In the context of this story, we see that God uses seven angels to be a part of the initiation of judgment on the earth. This is for God's benefit, and the church can feel assured during this time. We are to look at this apocalyptically and trust God. From His perspective more people will be drawn to Him. He is bringing judgment and discipline to the earth. The church may feel some of the pain of it too, but we are on the side of the one who overcame. The Lamb who was able to open the scroll is our Savior (Revelation 5). These believers were in so much torment, knowing judgment was coming to their persecutors would have brought a great amount of relief in their spirit as they endured suffering.

An angel was assigned to each of the bodies of believers and it is the angels who are a part of the judgment. That means we are on the right team. It is vital for the Christian to be in right relationship to God—this unlocks the power and the forces of heaven. God's team is the only team to be on because He will complete His purposes.

Revelation 9

Scribe to the Heart

"They were told not to harm the grass of the earth or any green plant or any tree, but only those people who do not have the seal of God on the foreheads."

(Rev. 9:4)

Point to Ponder

God sets things right. We need to reach out to others instead of judging them.

Today's Journal

How can I avoid the temptation to take joy in the pain of someone who has hurt me?

Prayer for the Day

Holy Spirit, Guide me into a life of deeper prayer, always seeking You, forgiving others, reflecting Your goodness here on earth.

TO TAKE JOY OR NOT?

WE SEE SOME dark things happening as each of the trumpets are sounded. When the fifth sounds, an army of locusts rise up from a bottomless pit. They have faces like men, hair like women, and teeth like lions. Their king is the angel of the bottomless pit. It is demonic. They can only hurt those who do not belong to God, since those who have the sign of God on their forehead can't be touched. The sign of God is probably not something literal. At the time the Christians of John's time would have felt like they had a sign on their head because of the intense persecution under Roman rule.

Now here is the thought to play with. What is a Christian to do when others are in pain? The goal of Christianity is to reflect Christ. God gives these believers this imagery for comfort. It must have been tempting for them to say, "Yeah, finally these pagans who killed my family and hurt me are getting what they deserve! Praise God!" So, what is the proper response to this? One of the main concepts is: Do not take joy over the pain of the unbelievers. Pray for them. But don't take joy. A believer can be comforted knowing he or she will not go through this pain because God protects us.

Taking joy in others' pain is a real temptation. Part of trusting God is that we love others while not needing to get revenge or teach people a lesson when we are wronged. When we respond with prayer when someone else is in pain, we show Christ and we become better. Don't be bitter. Pray for those who hurt you, that they would repent when they are getting what they deserve. Be in the world but not of it. Reach out to your neighbor in sincere love and concern.

Revelation 10

Scribe to the Heart

"So I went to the angel and told him to give me the little scroll. And he said to me, 'Take and eat it; it will make your stomach bitter but in your mouth it will be sweet as honey.'"

(Rev. 10:9)

Point to Ponder

Whether bitter or sweet, you have been entrusted with a message.

Today's Journal

Why is it important for me to deliver the message God puts in my mouth? Why would a first century reader of Revelation see it as important that John was like Ezekiel?

Prayer for the Day

Father, Give me the wisdom and strength to take in the bitter and the sweet. Write Your word on my heart.

EATING PASTE

THERE IS ALWAYS one kid in the elementary school classroom who eats paste. Chances are, you remember who that kid was at your school. (If it was you, I am sorry.) Whether they did it for attention or they sincerely liked it for taste or texture, I don't know. But, they did it.

Eating paste is a little odd. We remember that kid because he or she stands out to us. You know what, though? God's people are a little odd, too. In John's vision, he is given a message much like the prophet Ezekiel was given a message on a scroll. He did the same thing with it that Ezekiel did. He ate it. It is said that it was sweet in his mouth, and bitter in his stomach.

Eating the scroll is symbolic of accepting the message. The taste is sweet because the message is of salvation. It is bitter in the stomach because it also pronounces judgments. Ezekiel was also proclaiming a message that people were not going to listen to. There are a lot of parallels.

One of the principles of the book of Revelation is that we are to understand its Old Testament parallels. Because God used an angel to give John a message, and having him eat the scroll like Ezekiel did (Ezekiel 3:3), John was then put on the same level as the Old Testament prophets. He is most likely going to have a similar experience pronouncing salvation and judgment to hard-hearted people.

Once he ate the scroll the message became a part of him. He will proclaim it to these people, no matter what their response. He will carry out this purpose with conviction. He will also not be popular with the audience. Like John, you must deliver God's message to the world around you.

Day 249

Revelation 11

Scribe to the Heart

"But after the three and a half days a breath of life from God entered them, and they stood up on their feet, and great fear fell on those who saw them."

(Rev. 11:11)

Point to Ponder

Jesus continues to call us to conquer through sacrifice.

Today's Journal

"Conquer through sacrifice." Does this mean something different to me now that we are halfway through the book of Revelation?

Prayer for the Day

Lord Jesus, Help me to conquer evil through my own sacrifice. Teach me to be more like You.

THE TWO WITNESSES

THESE TWO MEN are very intriguing. As I've said previously, the most important thing about interpreting scripture is your starting place. There is much that can be said and speculated about the two witnesses, however who and what they are will not be settled in one page. Let's just focus on the main point. Remember I said that the main message of the book is: "God conquers through sacrifice." Let's take a look at these two witnesses through that perspective. They are given powers that are attributed to things Moses and Elijah did in the Old Testament. They can withhold rain and dry up the rivers by turning them to blood. They are powerful witnesses. On the flip side of their efforts, the devil is dazzling the world with miracles and wonders.

These two witnesses are actually killed and not given proper burial, but are laid in the street for all to see. After 3 days they come alive again. At this, many scoff. But many believe! Now, whether we are talking about literal people or not isn't important, but the message of conquering through sacrifice prevails.

Imagine the devil wowing people with a big show. These powerful witnesses of Jesus Christ were willing to die for what they believed. Some people looked on and said, "Yes, the world's way of thinking is better." Others looked on and said, "They believed in something that was worth dying for."

The main question when considering the witnesses comes back to, "How would the Christians of the first century have read this?" The answer is still: Conquer through sacrifice. Live for Jesus and even if you die for Jesus, we still win. Jesus already won.

It is also important to note the Old Testament relationship. It is not to be focused upon so much that Moses and Elijah are the witnesses as much as it is important to understand the power of God's leaders. It carries over into the New Testament just like the Old. This would have been important to someone living in that time, just like the parallel in the last chapter with John and Ezekiel. The message here is that living completely for Jesus, even to the point of physical death, is worth it. Others will see it.

Revelation 12

Scribe to the Heart

"Then the dragon became furious with the woman and went off to make war on the rest of her offspring, on those who keep the command- ments of God and hold to the testimony of Jesus. And he stood on the sand of the sea."

(Rev. 12:17)

Point to Ponder

The devil is at war with our witness.

Today's Journal

If I was the devil, how would I try to wreck my testimony? How can I protect my testimony?

Prayer for the Day

Lord Jesus, My desire is to have a strong testimony. I want to represent You and keep your commandments. Help me to do this.

THE WAR ON YOUR WITNESS

THE PRACTICAL APPLICATION of this chapter is often neglected. In this portion of John's vision, he sees a woman who is pregnant. A dragon tries to hurt her and the baby. She is protected and given wings to fly. She is able to have her baby and the baby is not to be harmed. The dragon, when deciding to wage war, waves its tail and 1/3 of the stars fall from the sky. This most likely symbolic of angels turning from God to be a part of Satan's rebellion.

When you read commentaries and do online searches you will find most people are more concerned with what this means for their particular end of days theology than they are with what can be applied to us today. There will be a focus on the dragon or his heads or horns. But the main point is at the end of the chapter. The dragon is coming to wage war on the witness of the offspring of the woman. Who is her offspring? Is it the nation of Israel? No, it is the people who believe and follow the commandments of God and keep a good testimony of Jesus.

The accuser, the dragon, is still trying to make us look bad. Think about the most popular T.V. shows. Think about the Christian characters on them. Think of what makes them interesting. Usually it is the witness of the character. It is typically a very bad one. Why is it so? The depiction rings true. So, few truly walk with integrity. Many talk the talk, but so few walk the walk. The war against us is not so that we don't talk the talk. Everyone around us has heard it before. I am not saying we don't tell them again, but be different and show them too. The devil himself is at war with us so that we will not walk the walk. Be in prayer and go to war. Conquer through sacrifice by dying to self. Take up your own cross and follow Him.

Revelation 13

Scribe to the Heart

"This calls for wisdom: let the one who has understanding calculate the number of the beast, for it is the number of a man, and his number is 666."

(Rev. 13:18)

Point to Ponder

The devil's time to hurt you is short. The grace of God will last forever.

Today's Journal

What is the message of hope I read in these verses?

Prayer for the Day

Father, Reveal to me the hope in Your word.

THE NUMBER OF THE MAN

IF YOU WERE assigning numbers to names in Greek or Hebrew it is often said that the name Nero Caesar almost works. You do have to add an N to the end of the name to equal it out making it Neron Caesar. He was a vicious persecutor of Christians. He blamed them for burning the city of Rome. He brutally killed many. Using numbers to transliterate a name was common enough for the original audience to understand what was being said in this chapter.

Nero probably killed himself prior to the writing of Revelation, and the reference to him dying, but being resurrected with an even more cruel and brutal nature is significant to the original audience now that they were under the beginning of the persecution of Domitian. He was also a tyrant towards Christians. First century believers would have equated Nero with 666. They would have remembered Nero's persecution and took this to mean that Domitian's would be worse. It may have been already. The overall message to them was that God is greater.

If our beginning point, for examining Revelation is our current culture and our current situation we will end up with all kinds of interpretations to this book. Let's instead use some common sense. These were real people who received a real message, during a real time of need. This message was for them before it was for us. If we allow those who preach the gospel to start with newspaper headlines and current events, we rob the church of becoming fully equipped. Bad theology hinders the advancement of the gospel and the current walk of believers.

Christians would have heard this writing read aloud in their worship and understood exactly what it meant. Nero is 666. The reference deals with Caesar. In this case now it was Domitian. Ultimately, God is greater. Persecution will not last forever. John told these believers that the time of the antichrist was upon them, but it would be short (Revelation 12:12). He was conveying that, "Just like Nero is no more, the same will be true of Domitian who is persecuting you today."

Revelation 14

Scribe to the Heart

"Here is a call for endurance of the saints, those who keep the commandments of God and their faith in Jesus."

(Rev. 14:12)

Point to Ponder

Trust Jesus, even when evil seems to have its way.

Today's Journal

When evil prevails, what do I normally do? How can I better trust Jesus?

Prayer for the Day

Father, Lead me and let me follow You with all of my heart. Teach me to be true to You, regardless of what is going on around me.

BABYLON THE GREAT

IN THE LAST 500 years of scholarship there has been a lot of time spent in this text, trying to understand Babylon as a city. Is Babylon to be rebuilt before a time at the end? Is it referring to the injustice of a city in the first century? Is it referring to Rome during this time? The plain and simple message of this text aside from the specifics is that a day of reckoning is coming. We don't know when. Will it be in my lifetime or will it be 3,000 years from today? We don't know. But, know this, evil will not prevail.

I believe Babylon is used in this text because it was once a great empire. They were similar to the Romans. They took the Jews into exile. They ruled over them with evil. The question remember is; why is evil prospering while we are God's children? The great city that is resembled by a whorish woman is coming to an end. There will be a day when God sets it all straight. Even though we are called to love and reach out to other Christians who were being killed and imprisoned for their faith, we would have taken great encouragement from knowing that one day God is going to make it all right. Not only would they be in heaven reconciled with their loved ones who were separated from them, but they will be with God. Things will be OK. Endure. Press on. Notice Babylon the great is an adulterer causing others to do the same. The 144,000 witnesses are virgins. They are sexually pure. It is a very distinct contrast.

To be clear, Babylon was an empire in the past. First century believers would have received this message remembering Jews suffered under Babylon, which is no more. Now they are suffering under Rome, which currently is, but one day will also be no more.

Revelation 15

Scribe to the Heart

"Then I saw another sign in heaven, great and amazing, seven angels with seven plagues, which are the last, for with them the wrath of God is finished."

(Rev. 15:1)

Point to Ponder

Stick with Christ, even when it looks like the world is being blessed for evil.

Today's Journal

Can I follow Christ even when it hurts?

Prayer for the Day

Father, Help me to obey You, regardless of what behavior the world rewards.

BE TIED TO MOSES

"AND THEY SING the song of Moses, the servant of God, and the song of the Lamb, saying, "'Great and amazing are your deeds, O Lord God the Almighty! Just and true are your ways, O King of nations! Who will not fear, O Lord and glorify your name? For you alone are holy. All Nations will come and worship you, for your righteous acts have been revealed.'" Revelation 15:3-4

When you think of victory, think of Moses. He left Egypt in shame, but returned many years later to redeem the Jews from the tyranny of Egyptian rule. God used Moses to bring them out. Without a doubt the Egyptian Pharaoh (although a relative of Moses due to his adoption and upbringing) was the most powerful person in the world at that time. He was considered to be a god. God's choice to use Moses for the Exodus was a great and powerful event in the history of God's people. As first century Christians reading and/or hearing this vision, the parallel to Moses would be noticed: Those who didn't follow the beast are sitting on the shore playing a song of Moses. They have been redeemed, while angels are going to bring about wrath on the enemies of God. Namely we are talking about the pagan Romans who are persecuting the Christians. Most likely we are talking about people who branded themselves nationalist Romans. They wouldn't stand up to the empire for Christ.

Things were bad. It would have been terrible to be running for your life. It would have been awful to see your spouse or children killed or taken from you. Persecution is terrible. The cry of their hearts was *Why?* and *When is this going to end?* God shows His people they are on the right team. A day of reckoning is coming.

It is important to note this philosophy doesn't make people exempt from hard-times or the end-times. Be leery of theology that says Christians will not be around during a time of persecution because that is what shows Jesus to the non-Christians. It is how we respond to hard times, not prosperity, that wins the world. People need an answer when their lives fall apart. Christians have the answer.

Revelation 16

Scribe to the Heart

"('Behold, I am coming like a thief! Blessed is the one who stays awake, keeping his garments on, that he may not go about naked and be seen exposed!')"

(Rev. 16:15)

Point to Ponder

God sees the big picture.
We must trust Jesus.

Today's Journal

What situations cause me to be disheartened and tempted to slip in my trust in Jesus?

Prayer for the Day

Lord Jesus, I desire to love You and trust You with my whole heart. Strengthen me in my daily life and deepen my trust in You.

THE SEVEN BOWLS OF GOD'S WRATH

CHECK OUT THE subheading to this chapter: The Seven Bowls of God's Wrath. If this doesn't make you want to get saved, nothing will. In all seriousness, this is an intense chapter of the Bible. God is pouring out His wrath in the form of seven bowls on the earth. It seems to be something that affects people who are not followers of Jesus. It is extremely serious. The judgments are severe. It is very important that the original audience understood not to follow after the ways of the world. The believer was not to deny his or her faith. Believers were not to worship pagan gods. They were not to jump on board with the world's system. They were to stay the course.

In contrast we see people who don't know God becoming victims of all kinds of disasters, including a hailstorm that hurls one hundred pound stones from heaven. It is so bad that the people curse God. God really wants His people to know that following Him is the only way to navigate this life. Emperors and kingdoms rise and fall. We can't focus on people. We must trust Jesus, even when it doesn't look like we can.

Revelation 17

Scribe to the Heart

"They will make war on the Lamb, and the Lamb will conquer them, for he is Lord of lords and King of kings, and those with him are called and chosen and faithful."

(Rev. 17:14)

Point to Ponder

Christians belong to Christ. He will and does take care of us.

Today's Journal

How does the knowledge that Jesus takes care of me change my approach to life?

Prayer for the Day

Lord Jesus, Help me to understand You as a conqueror and one who does this by sacrifice.

THINGS ARE BAD

THE WOMAN SITTING atop the beast in this chapter is identified as Babylon and the great city. There are seven kings mentioned in verse 10. Five are has-beens, one is current, and one is yet to be. Under the duress of the situation, God still informs His people that there will be one more evil king and believers should be prepared for the evil kingdoms of the world to be united in evil together. Is Domitian not in power yet? Is he the final king? Is someone else the final evil king? It is not as cut and dry as some would have you believe.

The point is Christianity will always go against the grain of the culture and government. To truly live for Jesus, you will be different than the people around you. That is what being a Christian is. Soren Kierkegaard (a Danish philosopher who lived in the 1800s) pushed the issue that in a society where *everyone* is a Christian, in fact, no one is. We are to evangelize the world. It would be great if everyone truly started to follow Jesus, but it is the pushback we receive and having to stand in community with Christ and each other that truly makes us disciples. It's the times of persecution and the heartache of living against the grain of the culture that makes us strong in the faith.

In this chapter we can be encouraged that the King of Kings will return and rule. He will take care of this problem of unity in evil. He will take care of the problem of persecution. He will eliminate satanic leadership and government, like the one they were dealing with. He will take care of us. The bottom line, we belong to Jesus Christ. This conquering Lamb (see verse 14) keeps us with the theme of conquering through sacrifice.

Revelation 18

Scribe to the Heart

"For all nations have drunk the wine of the passion of her sexual immorality, and the kings of the earth have committed immorality with her, and the merchants of the earth have grown rich from the power of her luxurious living."

(Rev. 18:3)

Point to Ponder

God honors honesty and integrity.

Today's Journal

How important is honesty and integrity to my witness to the world?

Prayer for the Day

Father God, Show me where I need to take check of my honesty or integrity. Guide me to make Your decisions in my dealings with other people.

MERCHANTS BEWARE!

I FIND IT fascinating that from afar merchants are witnessing the fall of this great city and they dread her torment. We also see that the merchants have grown rich from her luxurious living. One of the ways evil prevails is it becomes part of the economy. The merchants, or those selling, make money off of the evil. We have seen this over and over again throughout the ages. We see it in Acts when Paul interacts with the Ephesians. There are blacksmiths and people who sell Artemis idols. This was central to the local economy (Acts 19). Paul's declaration that they need to worship the True God was a threat on their financial security.

Christians offering a product have to be prayerful about their business. We truly have to make sure that we are truthful and what we do is beneficial to others. We need to make sure that we are not wrapped up in corruption, that the companies and products we represent are respectable. It can be easy to become one of these merchants. There are many products and companies that are not glorifying to God.

So, Christian, how do you conduct your business? Do you always tell the truth? If you have employees, do you treat them with respect? Do you find ways for them to excel? Do you see them as subjects or do you practice servant leadership, wanting to do everything you can for them to be successful? Running a business in a godly way is more than just declaring you are a Christian company or salesperson. We need to be lovingly committed to our customers, employers, and employees. It seems the merchants were in trouble because they bought into Babylon; the world's system. Babylon is going down and what are the merchants to do?

Revelation 19

Scribe to the Heart

"And the angel said to me, 'Write this: Blessed are those who are invited to the marriage supper of the Lamb.' And he said to me, 'These are the true words of God.'"

(Rev. 19:9)

Point to Ponder

God rewards those who seek Him in the end.

Today's Journal

Does knowing God will make things right in the end change my perspective about what happens to me now?

Prayer for the Day

Father, Help me to trust that You will make things right in the end. Help me to stay true to You.

WHAT A PARTY

THERE IS GREAT excitement in heaven. The roar of the crowd, the worship of the Lamb, what a victory we see! Jesus Christ is King of Kings and Lord of Lords. The Beast is judged. Babylon is defeated, and we are invited to the marriage supper. We are His bride. We are to be in heaven together and with God forever. The smoke from the bottomless pit ascends forever, there is the picture of eternal judgment. Life is hard while we are on the way to where we are going. We are to keep moving forward. Sometimes it seems like doing the right thing isn't rewarded well. At the end of the battle you want to be on the side of righteousness.

These first century believers would have taken great comfort in this scene. It is hard for a battered wife or an abused child to find comfort. It is hard for people who are being mistreated in their jobs or bullied in school. When our hearts are hurt, we must fast forward our vision. Fast forward to know that Jesus is the answer. His victory can bring us comfort when it is hard. God will bring His people together in a great party where people will truly know each other and Him.

It seems as though you need to be corrupt to get ahead. It can be so hard to be a Christ-follower sometimes. But, fast forward into the future. There will be judgment and rectification. There will be a sudden turn of events. There will be a twist in the plot. It looks like evil is rewarded, but it was never so all along. God just needed to find out who was true. Is it you?

Revelation 20

Scribe to the Heart

"Then I saw an angel coming down from heaven, holding in his hand the key to the bottomless pit and a great chain."

(Rev. 20:1)

Point to Ponder

Stay faithful; we are called to reign with Christ.

Today's Journal

What does it mean to someone who has been mistreated to know that Christ is promising more and He will deliver?

Prayer for the Day

Lord Jesus, Show me the amazing plan You have for my life and for me to reign with You. Amen.

TO REIGN WITH CHRIST

IMAGINE THE VARIOUS churches who heard this letter read reaching this point of the writing and hearing these promises! "We are going to reign with Christ. Could that be right?" Someone nudges someone else, "Could we *really* be priests and kings? That must mean something else. It simply can't be right." It would have been such a shock to the system. It would have been such a weird idea that those who are weak in this world, and discarded, could ever be at the top of the food chain.

Try to explain this to someone who considers himself to be self-made. Try to explain it to an atheist who has had worldly success. They don't get it.

Now try and explain it to the homeless, the broken, and the hurting. They get it. Why? Because they have been mistreated. They have felt the world throwing them out. They have felt embarrassment and shame. They have experienced the injustice and intuitively know it is not fair. Life doesn't seem to be fair, but God is. God evens it out.

Regardless of the circumstances we must not lose heart. We must stay faithful. We mustn't allow ourselves to be victims. We must be victorious. We are victorious in Christ. Jesus Christ gives us the victory. He wins it for us. He wins! We reign with Christ. We are given authority under the leadership of Christ. It is and always will be amazing. We don't deserve it, no matter how we have been mistreated.

Revelation 21

Scribe to the Heart

"Then I saw a new heaven, and a new earth, for the first heaven and the first earth had passed away, and the sea was no more."

(Rev. 21:1)

Point to Ponder

The world's system will pass away and God's kingdom will reign.

Today's Journal

The world will pass away. God's kingdom will triumph. How should that affect how I live?

Prayer for the Day

Father God, Give me wisdom as I await Your kingdom.

NEW CITY

AT THIS POINT, we see Babylon and Jerusalem contrasted. The early church hearers of this letter would have recognized the sharp contrast between the religious center of Christianity and Judaism and the city of an empire that held them captive. The Roman Empire was headed this way.

God is promising to let His people go. He is intending to make them free. The most fascinating thing about setting them free is Jesus Christ doesn't want them to suffer forever. Not only is Babylon going to be judged just like we saw in the last chapter, but there will be a new Jerusalem. It is seen coming out of the sky with very specific measurements. This city is new and the capital of a new kingdom. Is it symbolic of Christianity completing the Jewish covenant? Maybe. It is important to note that Jerusalem, being the religious center, has a new temple. It is Jesus Christ Himself. He actually lights the city.

The imagery of this section is often overshadowed by people using these texts to push their own end of days theology. But, there is definitely an idea that the old worldly system will be judged and cast down, while a new kingdom is formed. Jerusalem is the city. It is the city of the great king (David). It was also the city that crucified the King of Kings and witnessed His resurrection. It is a new Jerusalem.

Revelation 22

Scribe to the Heart

"And behold, I am coming soon. Blessed is the one who keeps the words of the prophecy of this book."

(Rev. 22:7)

Point to Ponder

God restores His children in the end.

Today's Journal

How does God's promise to restore us in the end help me to live today, and every day of my life?

Prayer for the Day

Father, Thank You for sending Your Son Jesus the Christ to restore us in the end. No matter what I go through, help me to keep this focus. Amen.

THE PERFECT ENDING

WE HAVE FINALLY arrived at the perfect ending. The early listeners to this letter would have received it as absolutely perfect. So should we. The first century Jewish Christian, who knew the Old Testament books of Moses, knew where it all began. It began at the Tree of Life in the middle of the Garden of Eden.

Now in the middle of the city we find Jesus and the Tree of Life. In the garden remember there were two trees. Man could keep eating from the Tree of Life or they could eat from the Tree of the Knowledge of Good and Evil. Now things have been restored. Jesus is here and we can live forever. There is no need for the Tree of Sin and Rebellion anymore, for we have overcome through the blood of the Lamb that was slain. We have defeated the devil and he has gone to his destruction. The Ending is perfect. It is a promise. God has already been there. He knows the end of the story.

Knowing the end of the story, we need to move forward. We know we will be rewarded. We know we will reign with Jesus in heaven. We know it. So, why would we be anything but hopeful today? Don't fret. Don't worry about tomorrow. God has seen us and we are just fine.

It reminds me of a Disney movie called *The Kid*. Bruce Willis's character Russell meets himself as a child. He remembers what makes him the way he is. At the end he meets himself and understands where he is going. He discovers everything is going to be OK. With Jesus we are more than just OK, we have been restored to reign and be with Christ and His church.

CONGRATULATIONS!

You have completed the New Testament Challenge! When we choose to spend time with God in study and reflection on His word, we open our hearts to hear from His Holy Spirit. My prayer for you as you finish these pages is that although you may put this book on your shelf, I pray you will not quit reading God's Word.

Aaron Mitchell

Connect with us at: www.chaplapreneur.com

www.ingramcontent.com/pod-product-compliance
Lightning Source LLC
Chambersburg PA
CBHW071113080526
44587CB00013B/1331